MEDIEVAL LAYS AND LEGENDS
OF
MARIE DE FRANCE

MEDIEVAL LAYS AND LEGENDS OF MARIE DE FRANCE

Translated with an Introduction by
Eugene Mason

DOVER PUBLICATIONS, INC.
Mineola, New York

Bibliographical Note

This Dover edition, first published in 2003, is an unabridged republication of the Eugene Mason translation, originally published by J. M.
Dent & Sons, Ltd., London, in 1911 under the title *Lays of Marie de France
and Other French Legends.*

Library of Congress Cataloging-in-Publication Data

Marie de France, 12th cent.
    [Lais. English]
    Medieval lays and legends of Marie de France / Marie de France ;
translated with an introduction by Eugene Mason.
        p. cm.
    Originally published: Lays of Marie de France and other French
legends. London : J.M. Dent, 1911.
    ISBN 0-486-43137-1 (pbk.)
    1. Marie de France, 12th cent.–Translations into English. 2. Lays–
Translations into English. I. Mason, Eugene. II. Title.

PQ1494.L3E5 2003

2003060008

Manufactured in the United States of America
Dover Publications, Inc., 31 East 2nd Street, Mineola, N.Y. 11501

INTRODUCTION

THE tales included in this little book of translations are derived mainly from the " Lays " of Marie de France. I do not profess them to be a complete collection of her stories in verse. The ascription varies. Poems which were included in her work but yesterday are withdrawn to-day, and new matter suggested by scholars to take the place of the old. I believe it to be, however, a far fuller version of Marie's " Lays " than has yet appeared, to my knowledge, in English. Marie's poems are concerned chiefly with love. To complete my book I have added two famous mediæval stories on the same excellent theme. This, then, may be regarded as a volume of French romances, dealing, generally, with one aspect of mediæval life.

An age so feminist in its sympathies as ours should be attracted the more easily to Marie de France, because she was both an artist and a woman. To deliver oneself through any medium is always difficult. For a woman of the Middle Ages to express herself publicly by any means whatever was almost impossible. A great lady, a great Saint or churchwoman, might do so very occasionally. But the individuality of the ordinary wife was merged in that of her husband, and for one Abbess of Shrewsbury or Whitby, for one St. Clare or St. Hilda, there were how many thousand obscure sisters, who were buried in the daily routine of a life hidden with Christ in God ! Doubtless the artistic temperament burst out now and again in woman, and would take no denial. It blew where it listed, appearing in the most unexpected places. A young nun in a Saxon convent, for instance, would write little dramas in Latin for the amusement and edification of the noble maidens under her charge. These comedies, written in the days of the Emperor Otho, can be read with pleasure in the reign of King George, by those who find fragrant the perfumes of the past. They deal with the pious legends of the Saints, and are regarded with wistful admiration by the most modern of Parisian playwrights. In their combination of audacity and simplicity they could only be performed by Saxon religious in the times of Otho, or by marionettes in the more self-conscious life of to-day. Or, again, an Abbess, the protagonist of one of the great love stories of the world, by sheer force of personality, would compose letters to one—how immeasurably her moral inferior, in spite of his genius—expressing with an unexampled poignancy the most passionate emotions of the heart. Or, to take my third illustration, here are a woman's poems written in an age when literature was almost entirely in the hands of men. Consider the strength of character which alone induced these three ladies to stray from the beaten paths of their sex. To the average woman it was enough to be an object of art herself, or to be the inspiration of masterpieces by man. But these three women of the Middle Ages—and such as they—shunned the easier way, and, in their several spheres, were by deliberate effort, self-conscious artists.

The place and date of birth of Marie de France are unknown—indeed the very century in which she lived has been a matter of dispute. Her poems are written in the French of northern France; but that does not prove her necessarily to be a Frenchwoman. French was the tongue of the English Court, and many Englishmen have written in the same language. Indeed, it is a very excellent vehicle for expression. Occasionally, Marie would insert English words in her French text, the better to convey her meaning; but it does not follow therefrom that the romances were composed in England. It seems strange that so few positive indications of her race and home are given in her poems—nothing is contained beyond her Christian name and the bare statement that she was of

France. She took great pride in her work, which she wrought to the best of her ability, and was extremely jealous of that bubble-reputation. Yet whilst this work was an excellent piece of self-portraiture, it reveals not one single fact or date on which to go. A consensus of critical opinion presumes that Marie was a subject of the English Crown, born in an ancient town called Pitre, some three miles above Rouen, in the Duchy of Normandy. This speculation is based largely on the unwonted topographical accuracy of her description of Pitre, given in " The Lay of the Two Lovers." Such evidence, perhaps, is insufficient to obtain a judgment in a Court of Law. The date when Marie lived was long a matter of dispute. The Prologue to her " Lays " contains a dedication to some unnamed King; whilst her " Fables " is dedicated to a certain Count William. These facts prove her to have been a person of position and repute. The King was long supposed to be Henry the Third of England, and this would suggest that she lived in the thirteenth century. An early scholar, the Abbé de La Rue, in fact, said that this was " undoubtedly " the case, giving cogent reasons in support of his contention. But modern scholarship, in the person of Gaston Paris, has decided that the King was Henry the Second, of pious memory; the Count, William Longsword, Earl of Salisbury, his natural son by Fair Rosamund; and that Marie must be placed in the second half of the twelfth century. This shows that scholarship is not an exact science, and that such words as " doubtless " should not be employed more than necessary. A certain Eastern philosopher, when engaged in instructing the youth of his country, used always to conclude his lectures with the unvarying formula, " But, gentlemen, all that I have told you is probably wrong." This sage was a wise man (not always the same thing), and his example should be had in remembrance. It seems possible (and one hesitates to use a stronger word) that the " Lays " of Marie were actually written at the Court of Henry of England. From political ambition the King was married to Eleanor of Aquitaine, a lady of literary tastes,

who came from a family in which the patronage of singers
was a tradition. Her husband, too, had a pronounced liking
for literature. He was fond of books, and once paid a visit
to Glastonbury to visit King Arthur's tomb. These, perhaps,
are limited virtues, but Henry the Second had need of every
rag. It is somewhat difficult to recognise in that King of
the Prologue, " in whose heart all gracious things are
rooted," the actual King who murdered Becket; who turned
over picture-books at Mass, and never confessed or com-
municated. It is yet more difficult to perceive " joy as his
handmaid " who, because of the loss of a favourite city,
threatened to revenge himself on God, by robbing Him of that
thing—*i.e.*, the soul—He desired most in him; and whose
very last words were an echo of Job's curse upon the day
that he was born. Marie's phrases may be regarded, perhaps, as a courtly flourish, rather than as conveying truth
with mathematical precision. If not, we should be driven to
suggest an alternative to the favourite simile of lying like an
epitaph. But I think it unlikely that Marie suffered with a
morbidly sensitive conscience. There is little enough real
devotion to be met with in her " Lays "; and if her last
book—a translation from the Latin of the Purgatory of St.
Patrick—is on a subject she avoids in her earlier work, it
was written under the influence of some high prelate, and
may be regarded as a sign that she watched the shadows
cast by the western sun lengthening on the grass.

Gaston Paris suggests 1175 as an approximate date for
the composition of the " Lays " of Marie de France. Their
success was immediate and unequivocal, as indeed was to be
expected in the case of a lady situated so fortunately at
Court. We have proof of this in the testimony of Denis
Pyramus, the author who wrote a Life of St. Edmund the
King, early in the following century. He says, in that poem,
" And also Dame Marie, who turned into rhyme and made
verses of ' Lays ' which are not in the least true. For these
she is much praised, and her rhyme is loved everywhere; for
counts, barons, and knights greatly admire it, and hold it

dear. And they love her writing so much, and take such pleasure in it, that they have it read, and often copied. These Lays are wont to please ladies, who listen to them with delight, for they are after their own hearts." It is no wonder that the lords and ladies of her century were so enthralled by Marie's romances, for her success was thoroughly well deserved. Even after seven hundred years her colours remain surprisingly vivid, and if the tapestry is now a little worn and faded in places, we still follow with interest the movements of the figures wrought so graciously upon the arras. Of course her stories are not original; but was any plot original at any period of the earth's history? This is not only an old, but an iterative world. The source of Marie's inspiration is perfectly clear, for she states it emphatically in quite a number of her Lays. This adventure chanced in Brittany, and in remembrance thereof the Bretons made a Lay, which I heard sung by the minstrel to the music of his rote. Marie's part consisted in reshaping this ancient material in her own rhythmic and coloured words. Scholars tell us that the essence of her stories is of Celtic rather than of Breton origin. It may be so; though to the lay mind this is not a matter of great importance one way or the other; but it seems better to accept a person's definite statement until it is proved to be false. The Breton or Celtic imagination had peculiar qualities of dreaminess, and magic and mystery. Marie's mind was not cast in a precisely similar mould. Occasionally she is successful enough; but generally she gives the effect of building with a substance the significance of which she does not completely realise. She may be likened to a child playing with symbols which, in the hand of the enchanter, would be of tremendous import. Her treatment of Isoude, for example, in "The Lay of the Honeysuckle," is quite perfect in tone, and, indeed, is a little masterpiece in its own fashion. But her sketch of Guenevere in "The Lay of Sir Launfal" is of a character that one does not recall with pleasure. To see how Arthur's Queen might be treated, we have but to turn to the pages of a contemporary, and learn from Chrestien de Troyes' " Knight of the Cart," how an even more considerable poet than Marie could deal with a Celtic legend. The fact is that Marie's romances derive farther back than any Breton or Celtic dream. They were so old that they had blown like thistledown about the four quarters of the world. Her princesses came really neither from Wales nor Brittany. They were of that stuff from which romance is shaped. " Her face was bright as the day of union; her hair dark as the night of separation; and her mouth was magical as Solomon's seal." You can parallel her " Lays " from folklore, from classical story and antiquity. Father and son fight together unwittingly in " The Lay of Milon "; but Rustum had striven with Sohrab long before in far Persia, and Cuchulain with his child in Ireland. Such stories are common property. The writer takes his own where he finds it. Marie is none the less admirable because her stories were narrated by the first man in Eden; neither are Boccaccio and the Countess D'Aulnoy blameworthy since they told again what she already had related so well. Marie, indeed, was an admirable narrator. That was one of her shining virtues. As a piece of artful tale telling, a specimen of the craft of keeping a situation in suspense, the arrival of the lady before Arthur's Court, in " The Lay of Sir Launfal," requires a deal of beating. The justness and fineness of her sentiment in all that concerns the delicacies of the human heart are also remarkable. But her true business was that of the storyteller. In that trade she was almost unapproachable in her day. There may have been—indeed, there was—a more considerable poet living; but a more excellent writer of romances, than the author of " Eliduc," it would have been difficult to find.

The ladies who found the " Lays " of Marie after their own hearts were not only admirers of beautiful stories; they had the delicate privilege also of admiring themselves in their habit as they lived—perhaps even lovelier than in reality —amidst their accustomed surroundings. The pleasure of a modern reader in such tales as these is enhanced by the light they throw on the household arrangements and customs of the gentlefolk of the twelfth and thirteenth centuries. It may be of interest to consider some of these domestic arrangements, as illustrated by stories included in the present volume.

The corporate life of a mediæval household centered in the hall. It was office and dining and billiard room, and was common to gentle and simple alike. The hall was by far the largest room in the house. It was lighted by windows, and warmed by an open fire of logs. The smoke drifted about the roof, escaping finally by the simple means of a lantern placed immediately above the hearth. A beaten floor was covered by rushes and fresh hay, or with rugs in that part affected by the more important members of the household. The lord himself and his wife sat in chairs upon a raised daïs. The retainers were seated on benches around the wall, and before them was spread the dining table—a mere board upon trestles—which was removed when once the meal was done. After supper, chess and draughts were played, or (as we may see in " The Lay of the Thorn ") minstrels sang ballads and the guest contributed to the general entertainment by the recital of such jests and adventures as commended themselves to his taste. If the hall may be considered as the dining room of the mediæval home, the garden might almost be looked upon as the drawing room. You would probably get more real privacy in the garden than in any other part of the crowded castle, including the lady's chamber. It is no wonder that we read of Guenevere taking Launfal aside for a little private conversation in her pleasaunce. It was not only the most private, but also the most delightful room in the house— ceiled with blue and carpeted with green. The garden was laid out elaborately with a perron and many raised seats. Trees stood about the lawn in tubs, and there was generally a fountain playing in the centre, or possibly a pond, stocked with fish. Fruit trees and flower beds grew thickly about the garden, and a pleasanter place of perfume and colour and shade it would be difficult to imagine in the summer heat. The third room of which we hear continually in these romances is the lady's chamber. It served the purpose of a boudoir as well as that of a sleeping room, and consequently had little real privacy. It contained the marriage chest with its store of linen, and also the bed. This bed recurs eternally in mediæval tales. It was used as a seat during the day, and as a resting-place of nights. It was a magnificent erection, carved and gilded, and inlaid with ivory. Upon it was placed a mattress of feathers, and a soft pillow. The sheets were of linen or silk, and over all was spread a coverlet of some precious material. An excellent description of such a couch is given in " The Lay of Gugemar." This chamber served also as a bath room, and there the bath was taken, piping hot, in the strange vessel, fashioned somewhat like a churn, that we see in pictures of the Middle Ages.

Of the dress of the ladies who moved about the castle, seeing themselves reflected from Marie's pages as in a polished mirror, I am not competent to speak. The type of beauty preferred by the old romancers was that of a child's princess of fairy tale—blue-eyed, golden-haired, and ruddy of cheek. The lady would wear a shift of linen, " white as meadow flower." Over this was worn a garment of fur or silk, according to the season; and, above all, a vividly coloured gown, all in one line from neck to feet, shapen closely to the figure, or else the more loosely fitting bliaut. Her girdle clipped her closely about the waist, falling to the hem of her skirt, and her feet were shod in soundless shoes, without heels. The hair was arranged in two long braids, brought forward over her shoulders; as worn by those smiling Queens wrought upon the western porch of Chartres Cathedral. Out of doors, and, indeed, frequently within, as may be proved by a reference to " The Lay of the Ash Tree," the lady was clad in a mantle and a hood. It must have taken a great deal of time and travail to appear so dainty a production. But to become poetry for others, it is necessary for a woman first to be prose to herself.

I am afraid the raw material of this radiant divinity had much to endure before she suffered her sea change. In mediæval illustrations we see the maiden sitting demurely in company, with downcast eyes, and hands folded modestly in her lap. This unnatural restraint was induced by the lavish compulsion of the rod. If there was one text, above all others, approved and acted upon by fathers and mothers of the Middle Ages, it was that exhorting parents not to cocker their child, neither to wink at his follies, but to beat him on the sides with a stick. Turn to " The Lay of the Thorn," and mark the gusto with which a mother disciplines her maid. Parents trained their children with blows. Husbands (ah, the audacity of the mediæval husband) scattered the like seeds of kindness on their wives. In a book written for the edification of his unmarried daughters, Chaucer's contemporary, the Knight of La Tour Landry, tells the following interesting anecdote. A man had a scolding wife, who railed ungovernably upon him before strangers, " and he that was angry of her governance smote her with his first down to the earth; and then with his foot he struck her on the visage, and broke her nose; and all her life after that she had her nose crooked, the which shent and disfigured her visage after, that she might not for shame show her visage, it was so foul blemished. And this she had for her evil and great language that she was wont to say to her husband. And therefore the wife ought to suffer, and let the husband have the words, and to be master." May I give yet another illustration before we pass from the subject. This time it is taken not from a French knight, but from a sermon of the great Italian preacher, St. Bernardino of Siena. " There are men who can bear more patiently with a hen that lays a fresh egg every day than with their own wives; and sometimes when the hen breaks a pipkin or a cup he will spare it a beating, simply for love of the fresh egg which he is unwilling to lose. Oh, raving madmen! who cannot bear a word from their own wives, though they bear them such fair fruit; but when the woman speaks a word more than they like, then they catch up a stick, and begin to cudgel her; while the hen that cackles all day, and gives you no rest, you take patience with her for the sake of her miserable egg—and sometimes she will break more in your house than she herself is worth, yet you bear it in patience for the egg's sake. Many fidgetty fellows, who sometimes see their wives turn out less neat and dainty than they would like, smite them forthwith; and meanwhile the hen may make a mess on the table, and you suffer her. Have patience; it is not right to beat your wife for every cause, no! "

At the commencement of this Introduction I stated that Marie's romances are concerned mainly with love. Her talent was not very wide nor rich, and I have no doubt that there were facets of her personality which she was unable to get upon paper. The prettiest girl in the world can only give what she has to give. By the time any reader reaches the end of this volume he will be assured that the stories are stories of love. Probably he will have noticed also that, in many cases, the lady who inspires the most delicate of sentiments is, incidentally, a married woman. He may ask why this was so; and in answer I propose to conclude my paper with a few observations upon the subject of mediæval love.

I doubt in my own mind whether romance writers do not exaggerate what was certainly a characteristic of the Middle Ages. To be ordinary is to be uninteresting; and it is obvious that the stranger the experience, the more likely is it to attract the interest and attention of the hearer. Blessed is the person—as well as the country—who has no history. But it was really very difficult for the twelfth century poet to write a love story, with a maiden as the central figure. The noble maiden seldom had a love story. It is true enough that she was sometimes referred to in the choice of her husband : two young ladies in " A Story of Beyond the Sea " are both consulted in the matter. As a rule, however, her inclination was not permitted to stand in the way of the interests of her parents or guardians. She was betrothed in childhood, and married very young, for mercenary or political reasons, to a husband much older than herself. We read of a girl of twelve being married to a man of fifty. There was no great opportunity for a love story here; and the strange entreaty, on the part of the nameless French poet, to love the maidens for the sake of Christ's love, passed over the heads of the romance writers. Not that the mediæval maidens showed any shrinking from matrimony. " Fair daughter, I have given you a husband." " Blessed be God," said the damsel. There spoke a contented spirit. Things have changed, and we can but sigh after the good old times.

But the maiden inevitably became the wife, and the whirligig of Time brought in his revenges. The lady now found herself the most important member of her sex, in a dwelling filled with men. She had few women about her person, and the confidant of a great dame in old romance is, frequently enough, her chamberlain. These young men had no chance of marriage, and naturally strove to gain the attention of a lady, whose favour was to them so important a matter. A mediæval knight was the sworn champion of God and the ladies—but more especially the latter. The chatelaine, herself, found time hang heavily on her hands. Amusements were few; books limited in number; a husband not of absorbing interest; so she turned to such distractions as presented themselves. The prettier a lady, the sweeter the incense and flattery swung beneath her nose; for this was one of the disadvantages of marrying an attractive woman. " It is hard to keep a wife whom everyone admires; and if no one admires her it is hard to have to live with her yourself." One of these distractions took the shape of Courts of Love, where the bored but literary chatelaine discussed delicate problems of conduct pertaining to the heart. The minstrel about the lady's castle, for his part, sought her favourable notice not only by his songs but also by giving an object lesson of his melancholy condition. One would imagine that his proceedings were not always calculated to further their purpose. A famous singer, for instance, in honour of a lady who was named Lupa, caused himself to be sewn in a wolf's skin, and ran before the hounds till he was pulled down, half dead. Another great minstrel and lover bought a leper's gown and bowl and clapper from some afflicted wretch. He mutilated his forefinger, and sat before his lady's door, in the company of a piteous crowd of sick and maimed, to await her alms. No doubt he trusted that his devotion would procure him a different kind of charity. From such discussions as these, and from conduct such as this, a type of love came into being which was peculiar to the period. Since the lovers were not bound in the sweet and common union of children and home, since on the side of the lady all was of grace and nought of debt, they searched out other bands to unite them together. These they found in a system of devotion, silence and faithfulness, which added a dignity to their relations. These virtues they took so seriously that we find the Chatelaine of Vergi dying because she believed her lover to have betrayed her trust. The mediæval romancer contemplated such unions with joy and pity; but for all their virtues we must not deceive ourselves with words. Such honour was rooted in dishonour, and the measure of their guilt was that they debased the moral currency. Presently the greatest of all the poets of the Middle Ages would arise, to teach a different fashion of devotion. His was a love that sought no communion with its object, neither speech nor embrace. It was sufficient for Dante to contemplate Beatrice from afar, as one might kneel before the picture of a saint. I do not say that a love like this—so spiritual and so aloof—will ever be possible to men. It did not suffice even to Dante, for all his tremendous moral muscle. Human love must always and inevitably be founded on a physical basis. But the burning drop of idealism that Dante contributed to the passion of the Middle Ages has made possible the love of which we now and again catch a glimpse in the union of

Introduction

select natures.   And that the seed of such flowering may be
carried about the world is one of the fairest hopes and
possibilities of the human race.

EUGENE MASON.

The originals of these narratives are to be found in
Roquefort's edition of the "Poésies de Marie de France"; in
a volume of the Nouvelles Françoises en Prose, edited by
Moland and D'Héricault; and in M. Gaston Raynaud's text
of "La Chatelaine de Vergi."

NOTE

In the opening paragraph of his Introduction the trans-
lator implies that all fourteen of the "Lays" printed in this
volume are by Marie de France.   To-day, however, the
weight of opinion favours the attribution of "The Lay of
the Dolorous Knight," "The Lay of the Nightingale," and
"The Lay of the Thorn" to an anonymous author.   See
the edition of Marie de France by A. Ewert, 1944.

J. W.

1953.

CONTENTS

I

PROLOGUE

THOSE to whom God has given the gift of comely speech, should not hide their light beneath a bushel, but should willingly show it abroad. If a great truth is proclaimed in the ears of men, it brings forth fruit a hundred-fold ; but when the sweetness of the telling is praised of many, flowers mingle with the fruit upon the branch.

According to the witness of Priscian, it was the custom of ancient writers to express obscurely some portions of their books, so that those who came after might study with greater diligence to find the thought within their words. The philosophers knew this well, and were the more unwearied in labour, the more subtle in distinctions, so that the truth might make them free. They were persuaded that he who would keep himself unspotted from the world should search for knowledge, that he might understand. To set evil from me, and to put away my grief, I purposed to commence a book. I considered within myself what fair story in the Latin or Romance I could turn into the common tongue. But I found that all the stories had been written, and scarcely it seemed the worth my doing, what so many had already done. Then I called to mind those Lays I had so often heard. I doubted nothing—for well I know—that our fathers fashioned them, that men

1

should bear in remembrance the deeds of those who have gone before. Many a one, on many a day, the minstrel has chanted to my ear. I would not that they should perish, forgotten, by the roadside. In my turn, therefore, I have made of them a song, rhymed as well as I am able, and often has their shaping kept me sleepless in my bed.

In your honour, most noble and courteous King, to whom joy is a handmaid, and in whose heart all gracious things are rooted, I have brought together these Lays, and told my tales in seemly rhyme. Ere they speak for me, let me speak with my own mouth, and say,

" Sire, I offer you these verses. If you are pleased to receive them, the fairer happiness will be mine, and the more lightly I shall go all the days of my life. Do not deem that I think more highly of myself than I ought to think, since I presume to proffer this, my gift." Hearken now to the commencement of the matter.

II

THE LAY OF GUGEMAR

HEARKEN, oh gentles, to the words of Marie. When the minstrel tells his tale, let the folk about the fire heed him willingly. For his part the singer must be wary not to spoil good music with unseemly words. Listen, oh lordlings, to the words of Marie, for she pains herself grievously not to forget this thing. The craft is hard— then approve the more sweetly him who carols the tune. But this is the way of the world, that when a man or woman sings more tunably than his fellows, those about the fire fall upon him, pell-mell, for reason of their envy. They rehearse diligently the faults of his song, and steal away his praise with evil words. I will brand these folk as they deserve. They, and such as they, are like mad dogs—cowardly and felon—who traitorously bring to death men better than themselves. Now let the japer, and the smiler with his knife, do me what harm they may. Verily they are in their right to speak ill of me.

Hearken, oh gentles, to the tale I set before you, for thereof the Bretons already have made a Lay. I will not do it harm by many words, and here is the commencement of the matter. According to text and scripture, now I relate a certain adventure, which bechanced in the realm of Brittany, in days long gone before.

In that time when Arthur maintained his realm, the now in peace, the now in war, the King counted amongst his vassals a certain baron, named Oridial. This knight was lord of Leon, and was very near to his prince's heart, both in council chamber and in field. From his wife he had gotten two children, the one a son and the other a fair daughter. Nogent, he had called the damsel at the font, and the dansellon was named Gugemar—no goodlier might be found in any realm. His mother had set all her love upon the lad, and his father shewed him every good that he was able. When the varlet was no more a child, Oridial sent him to the King, to be trained as a page in the courtesies of the Court. Right serviceable was he in his station, and meetly praised of all. The term of his service having come, and he being found of fitting years and knowledge, the King made him knight with his own hand, and armed him in rich harness, according to his wish. So Gugemar gave gifts to all those about his person, and bidding farewell, took leave, and departed from the Court. Gugemar went his way to Flanders, being desirous of advancement, for in that kingdom ever they have strife and war. Neither in Loraine nor Burgundy, Anjou nor Gascony, might be found in that day a better knight than he, no, nor one his peer. He had but one fault, since of love he took no care. There was neither dame nor maiden beneath the sky, however dainty and kind, to whom he gave thought or heed, though had he required her love of any damsel, very willingly would she have granted his desire. Many there were who prayed him for his love, but might have no kiss in return. So seeing that he refrained his heart in this fashion, men deemed him a strange man, and one fallen into a perilous case.

In the flower of his deeds the good knight returned to his own land, that he might see again his father

and lord, his mother and his sister, even as he very
tenderly desired. He lodged with them for the space
of a long month, and at the end of that time had envy
to hunt within the wood. The night being come,
Gugemar summoned his prickers and his squires, and
early in the morning rode within the forest. Great
pleasure had Gugemar in the woodland, and much he
delighted in the chase. A tall stag was presently started,
and the hounds being uncoupled, all hastened in pursuit
—the huntsmen before, and the good knight following
after, winding upon his horn. Gugemar rode at a great
pace after the quarry, a varlet riding beside, bearing his
bow, his arrows and his spear. He followed so hotly
that he over-passed the chace. Gazing about him
he marked, within a thicket, a doe hiding with her
fawn. Very white and wonderful was this beast, for she
was without spot, and bore antlers upon her head. The
hounds bayed about her, but might not pull her down.
Gugemar bent his bow, and loosed a shaft at the quarry.
He wounded the deer a little above the hoof, so that
presently she fell upon her side. But the arrow glanced
away, and returning upon itself, struck Gugemar
in the thigh, so grievously, that straightway he fell from
his horse upon the ground. Gugemar lay upon the grass,
beside the deer which he had wounded to his hurt.
He heard her sighs and groans, and perceived the
bitterness of her pity. Then with mortal speech the doe
spake to the wounded man in such fashion as this,

" Alas, my sorrow, for now am I slain. But thou,
Vassal, who hast done me this great wrong, do not think
to hide from the vengeance of thy destiny Never may
surgeon and his medicine heal your hurt. Neither herb
nor root nor potion can ever cure the wound within your
flesh : For that there is no healing. The only balm to
close that sore must be brought by a woman, who for her

love will suffer such pain and sorrow as no woman in the world has endured before. And to the dolorous lady, dolorous knight. For your part you shall do and suffer so great things for her, that not a lover beneath the sun, or lovers who are dead, or lovers who yet shall have their day, but shall marvel at the tale. Now, go from hence, and let me die in peace."

Gugemar was wounded twice over—by the arrow, and by the words he was dismayed to hear. He considered within himself to what land he must go to find this healing for his hurt, for he was yet too young to die. He saw clearly, and told it to his heart, that there was no lady in his life to whom he could run for pity, and be made whole of his wound. He called his varlet before him,

" Friend," said he, " go forthwith, and bring my comrades to this place, for I have to speak with them."

The varlet went upon his errand, leaving his master sick with the heat and fever of his hurt. When he was gone, Gugemar tore the hem from his shirt, and bound it straitly about his wound. He climbed painfully upon the saddle, and departed without more ado, for he was with child to be gone before any could come to stay him from his purpose. A green path led through the deep forest to the plain, and his way across the plain brought him to a cliff, exceeding high, and to the sea. Gugemar looked upon the water, which was very still, for this fair harbourage was land-locked from the main. Upon this harbour lay one only vessel, bearing a rich pavilion of silk, daintily furnished both without and within, and well it seemed to Gugemar that he had seen this ship before. Beneath the sky was no ship so rich or precious, for there was not a sail but was spun of silk, and not a plank, from keel to mast, but showed of ebony Too fair was the nave for mortal man, and Gugemar held it in sore displeasure. He marvelled greatly from what country it had come, and wondered long concerning this harbour, and the ship that lay therein. Gugemar got him down from his horse upon the shore, and with mighty pain and labour climbed within the ship. He trusted to find merchantmen and sailors therein, but there was none to guard, and none he saw. Now within the pavilion was a very rich bed, carved by cunning workmen in the days of King Solomon. This fair bed was wrought of cypress wood and white ivory, adorned with gold and gems most precious. Right sweet were the linen cloths upon the bed, and so soft the pillow, that he who lay thereon would sleep, were he sadder than any other in the world. The counterpane was of purple from the vats of Alexandria, and over all was set a right fair coverlet of cloth of gold. The pavilion was litten by two great waxen torches, placed in candlesticks of fine gold, decked with jewels worth a lord's ransom. So the wounded knight looked on ship and pavilion, bed and candle, and marvelled greatly. Gugemar sat him down upon the bed for a little, because of the anguish of his wound. After he had rested a space he got upon his feet, that he might quit the vessel, but he found that for him there was no return. A gentle wind had filled the sails, and already he was in the open sea. When Gugemar saw that he was far from land, he was very heavy and sorrowful. He knew not what to do, by reason of the mightiness of his hurt. But he must endure the adventure as best he was able; so he prayed to God to take him in His keeping, and in His good pleasure to bring him safe to port, and deliver him from the peril of death. Then climbing upon the couch, he laid his head upon the pillow, and slept as one dead, until, with vespers, the ship drew to that haven where he might find the healing for his hurt.

Gugemar had come to an ancient city, where the King of that realm held his court and state. This King was full of years, and was wedded to a dame of high degree. The lady was of tender age, passing fresh and fair, and sweet of speech to all. Therefore was the King jealous of his wife beyond all measure. Such is the wont of age, for much it fears that old and young cannot mate together, and that youth will turn to youth. This is the death in life of the old.

The castle of this ancient lord had a mighty keep. Beneath this tower was a right fair orchard, together with a close, shut in by a wall of green marble, very strong and high. This wall had one only gate, and the door was watched of warders, both night and day. On the other side of this garden was the sea, so that none might do his errand in the castle therefrom, save in a boat. To hold his dame in the greater surety, the King had built a bower within the wall; there was no fairer chamber beneath the sun. The first room was the Queen's chapel. Beyond this was the lady's bed-chamber, painted all over with shapes and colours most wonderful to behold. On one wall might be seen Dame Venus, the goddess of Love, sweetly flushed as when she walked the water, lovely as life, teaching men how they should bear them in loyal service to their lady. On another wall, the goddess threw Ovid's book within a fire of coals. A scroll issuing from her lips proclaimed that those who read therein, and strove to ease them of their pains, would find from her neither service nor favour. In this chamber the lady was put in ward, and with her a certain maiden to hold her company. This damsel was her niece, since she was her sister's child, and there was great love betwixt the twain. When the Queen walked within the garden, or went abroad, this maiden was ever by her side, and came

again with her to the house. Save this damsel, neither
man nor woman entered in the bower, nor issued forth
from out the wall. One only man possessed the key of
the postern, an agèd priest, very white and frail. This
priest recited the service of God within the chapel, and
served the Queen's plate and cup when she ate meat
at table.

Now, on a day, the Queen had fallen asleep after meat,
and on her awaking would walk a little in the garden.
She called her companion to her, and the two went
forth to be glad amongst the flowers. As they looked
across the sea they marked a ship drawing near the land,
rising and falling upon the waves. Very fearful was the
Queen thereat, for the vessel came to anchorage, though
there was no helmsman to direct her course. The dame's
face became sanguine for dread, and she turned her
about to flee, because of her exceeding fear. Her maiden,
who was of more courage than she, stayed her mistress
with many comforting words. For her part she was very
desirous to know what this thing meant. She hastened
to the shore, and laying aside her mantle, climbed
within this wondrous vessel. Thereon she found no
living soul, save only the knight sleeping fast within
the pavilion. The damsel looked long upon the knight,
for pale he was as wax, and well she deemed him dead.
She returned forthwith to the Queen, and told her of
this marvel, and of the good knight who was slain.

" Let us go together on the ship," replied the lady.
" If he be dead we may give him fitting burial, and the
priest shall pray meetly for his soul. Should he be yet
alive perchance he will speak, and tell us of his case."

Without more tarrying the two damsels mounted
on the ship, the lady before, and her maiden following
after. When the Queen entered in the pavilion she
stayed her feet before the bed, for joy and grief of what

she saw. She might not refrain her eyes from gazing on the knight, for her heart was ravished with his beauty, and she sorrowed beyond measure, because of his grievous hurt. To herself she said, " In a bad hour cometh the goodly youth." She drew near the bed, and placing her hand upon his breast, found that the flesh was warm, and that the heart beat strongly in his side. Gugemar awoke at the touch, and saluted the dame as sweetly as he was able, for well he knew that he had come to a Christian land. The lady, full of thought, returned him his salutation right courteously, though the tears were yet in her eyes. Straightway she asked of him from what realm he came, and of what people, and in what war he had taken his hurt.

" Lady," answered Gugemar, " in no battle I received this wound. If it pleases you to hear my tale I will tell you the truth, and in nothing will I lie. I am a knight of Little Brittany. Yesterday I chased a wonderful white deer within the forest. The shaft with which I struck her to my hurt, returned again on me, and caused this wound upon my thigh, which may never be searched, nor made whole. For this wondrous Beast raised her plaint in a mortal tongue. She cursed me loudly, with many evil words, swearing that never might this sore be healed, save by one only damsel in the world, and her I know not where to find. When I heard my luckless fate I left the wood with what speed I might, and coming to a harbour, not far from thence, I lighted on this ship. For my sins I climbed therein. Then without oars or helm this boat ravished me from shore ; so that I know not where I have come, nor what is the name of this city. Fair lady, for God's love, counsel me of your good grace, for I know not where to turn, nor how to govern the ship."

The lady made answer,

" Fair sir, willingly shall I give you such good counsel as I may. This realm and city are the appanage of my husband. He is a right rich lord, of high lineage, but old and very full of years. Also he is jealous beyond all measure ; therefore it is that I see you now. By reason of his jealousy he has shut me fast between high walls, entered by one narrow door, with an ancient priest to keep the key. May God requite him for his deed. Night and day I am guarded in this prison, from whence I may never go forth, without the knowledge of my lord. Here are my chamber and my chapel, and here I live, with this, my maiden, to bear me company. If it pleases you to dwell here for a little, till you may pass upon your way, right gladly we shall receive you, and with a good heart we will tend your wound, till you are healed."

When Gugemar heard this speech he rejoiced greatly. He thanked the lady with many sweet words, and consented to sojourn in her hall awhile. He raised himself upon his couch, and by the courtesy of the damsels left the ship. Leaning heavily upon the lady, at the end he won to her maiden's chamber, where there was a fair bed covered with a rich dossal of broidered silk, edged with fur. When he was entered in this bed, the damsels came bearing clear water in basins of gold, for the cleansing of his hurt. They stanched the blood with a towel of fine linen, and bound the wound strictly, to his exceeding comfort. So after the vesper meal was eaten, the lady departed to her own chamber, leaving the knight in much ease and content.

Now Gugemar set his love so fondly upon the lady that he forgot his father's house. He thought no more of the anguish of his hurt, because of another wound that was beneath his breast. He tossed and sighed in his unrest, and prayed the maiden of his service to depart, so that he might sleep a little. When the maid was gone, Gugemar considered within himself whether he might seek the dame, to know whether her heart was warmed by any ember of the flame that burned in his. He turned it this way and that, and knew not what to do. This only was clear, that if the lady refused to search his wound, death, for him, was sure and speedy.

"Alas," said he, "what shall I do! Shall I go to my lady, and pray her pity on the wretch who has none to give him counsel? If she refuse my prayer, because of her hardness and pride, I shall know there is nought for me but to die in my sorrow, or, at least, to go heavily all the days of my life."

Then he sighed, and in his sighing lighted on a better purpose; for he said within himself that doubtless he was born to suffer, and that the best of him was tears. All the long night he spent in vigil and groanings and watchfulness. To himself he told over her words and her semblance. He remembered the eyes and the fair mouth of his lady, and all the grace and the sweetness, which had struck like a knife at his heart. Between his teeth he cried on her for pity, and for a little more would have called her to his side. Ah, had he but known the fever of the lady, and how terrible a lord to her was Love, how great had been his joy and solace. His visage would have been the more sanguine, which was now so pale of colour, because of the dolour that was his. But if the knight was sick by reason of his love, the dame had small cause to boast herself of health. The lady rose early from her bed, since she might not sleep. She complained of her unrest, and of Love who rode her so hardly. The maiden, who was of her company, saw clearly enough that all her lady's thoughts were set upon the knight, who, for his healing, sojourned in the chamber. She did not know whether his thoughts were given again to the dame. When, therefore, the lady had entered in the chapel, the damsel went straightway to the knight. He welcomed her gladly, and bade her be seated near the bed. Then he inquired,

"Friend, where now is my lady, and why did she rise so early from her bed?"

Having spoken so far, he became silent, and sighed.

"Sir," replied the maiden softly, "you love, and are discreet, but be not too discreet therein. In such a love as yours there is nothing to be ashamed. He who may win my lady's favour has every reason to be proud of his fortune. Altogether seemly would be your friendship, for you are young, and she is fair."

The knight made answer to the maiden,

"I am so fast in the snare, that I pray the fowler to slay me, if she may not free me from the net. Counsel me, fair sweet friend, if I may hope of kindness at her hand."

Then the maiden of her sweetness comforted the knight, and assured him of all the good that she was able. So courteous and debonair was the maid.

When the lady had heard Mass, she hastened back to the chamber. She had not forgotten her friend, and greatly she desired to know whether he was awake or asleep, of whom her heart was fain. She bade her maiden to summon him to her chamber, for she had a certain thing in her heart to show him at leisure, were it for the joy or the sorrow of their days.

Gugemar saluted the lady, and the dame returned the knight his courtesy, but their hearts were too fearful for speech. The knight dared ask nothing of his lady, for reason that he was a stranger in a strange land, and was adread to show her his love. But—as says the proverb—he who will not tell of his sore, may not hope for balm to his hurt. Love is a privy wound within the heart, and none knoweth of that bitterness but the heart alone. Love is an evil which may last for a whole life long, because of man and his constant heart. Many there be who make of Love a gibe and a jest, and with specious words defame him by boastful tales. But theirs is not love. Rather it is folly and lightness, and the tune of a merry song. But let him who has found a constant lover prize her above rubies, and serve her with loyal service, being altogether at her will. Gugemar loved in this fashion, and therefore Love came swiftly to his aid. Love put words in his mouth, and courage in his heart, so that his hope might be made plain.

"Lady," said he, " I die for your love. I am in fever because of my wound, and if you care not to heal my hurt I would rather die. Fair friend, I pray you for grace. Do not gainsay me with evil words."

The lady hearkened with a smile to Gugemar's speech. Right daintily and sweetly she replied,

" Friend, yea is not a word of two letters. I do not grant such a prayer every day of the week, and must you have your gift so quickly ? "

" Lady," cried he, " for God's sake pity me, and take it not amiss. She, who loves lightly, may make her lover pray for long, so that she may hide how often her feet have trodden the pathway with another friend. But the honest dame, when she has once given her heart to a friend, will not deny his wish because of pride. The rather she will find her pride in humbleness, and love him again with the same love he has set on her. So they will be glad together, and since none will have knowledge or hearing of the matter, they will rejoice in their youth. Fair, sweet lady, be this thy pleasure ?"

When the lady heard these words well she found them honest and true. Therefore without further prayings and ado she granted Gugemar her love and her kiss. Henceforward Gugemar lived greatly at his ease, for he had sight and speech of his friend, and many a time she granted him her embrace and tenderness, as is the wont of lovers when alone.

For a year and a half Gugemar dwelt with his lady, in solace and great delight. Then Fortune turned her wheel, and in a trice cast those down, whose seat had been so high. Thus it chanced to them, for they were spied upon and seen.

On a morning in summer time the Queen and the damoiseau sat fondly together. The knight embraced her, eyes and face, but the lady stayed him, saying,

" Fair sweet friend, my heart tells me that I shall lose you soon, for this hidden thing will quickly be made clear. If you are slain, may the same sword kill me. But if you win forth, well I know that you will find another love, and that I shall be left alone with my thoughts. Were I parted from you, may God give me neither joy, nor rest, nor peace, if I would seek another friend. Of that you need have no fear. Friend, for surety and comfort of my heart deliver me now some sark of thine. Therein I will set a knot, and make this covenant with you, that never will you put your love on dame or maiden, save only on her who shall first unfasten this knot. Then you will ever keep faith with me, for so cunning shall be my craft, that no woman may hope to unravel that coil, either by force or guile, or even with her knife."

So the knight rendered the sark to his lady, and made such bargain as she wished, for the peace and assurance of her mind.

For his part the knight took a fair girdle, and girt it closely about the lady's middle. Right secret was the clasp and buckle of this girdle. Therefore he required of the dame that she would never grant her love, save to him only, who might free her from the strictness of this bond, without injury to band or clasp. Then they kissed together, and entered into such covenant as you have heard.

That very day their hidden love was made plain to men. A certain chamberlain was sent by that ancient lord with a message to the Queen. This unlucky wretch, finding that in no wise could he enter within the chamber, looked through the window, and saw. Forthwith he hastened to the King, and told him that which he had seen. When the agèd lord understood these words, never was there a sadder man than he. He called together the most trusty sergeants of his guard, and coming with them to the Queen's chamber, bade them to thrust in the door. When Gugemar was found therein, the King commanded that he should be slain with the sword, by reason of the anguish that was his. Gugemar was in no whit dismayed by the threat. He started to his feet, and gazing round, marked a stout rod of fir, on which it is the use for linen to be hung. This he took in hand, and faced his foes, bidding them have a care, for he would do a mischief to them all. The King looked earnestly upon the fearless knight, inquiring of him who he was, and where he was born, and in what manner he came to dwell within his house. So Gugemar told over to him this story of his fate. He showed him of the Beast that he had wounded to his hurt; of the nave, and of his bitter wound; of how he came within the realm, and of the lady's surgery. He told all to the ancient lord, to the last moment when he stood within his power. The King replied that he gave no credence to his word, nor believed that the story ran as he had said. If, however, the vessel might be found, he would commit the knight again to the waves. He would go the more heavily for the knight's saining, and a glad day would it be if he made shipwreck at sea. When they had entered into this covenant together, they went forth to the harbour, and there discovered the barge, even as Gugemar had said. So they set him thereon, and prayed him to return unto his own realm.

Without sail or oar the ship parted from that coast, with no further tarrying. The knight wept and wrung his hands, complaining of his lady's loss, and of her cherishing. He prayed the mighty God to grant him speedy death, and never to bring him home, save to meet again with her who was more desirable than life. Whilst he was yet at his orisons, the ship drew again to that port, from whence she had first come. Gugemar made haste to get him from the vessel, so that he might the more swiftly return to his own land. He had gone but a little way when he was aware of a squire of his household, riding in the company of a certain knight. This squire held the bridle of a destrier in his hand, though no man rode thereon. Gugemar called to him by name, so that the varlet looking upon him, knew again his lord. He got him to his feet, and bringing the destrier to his master, set the knight thereon. Great was the joy, and merry was the feast, when Gugemar returned to his own realm. But though his friends did all that they were able, neither song nor game could cheer the knight, nor turn him from dwelling in his unhappy thoughts. For peace of mind they urged that he took to himself a wife, but Gugemar would have none of their counsel. Never would he wed a wife, on any day, either for love or for wealth, save only that she might first unloose the knot within his shirt. When this news was noised about the country, there was neither dame nor damsel in the realm of Brittany, but essayed to unfasten the knot. But there was no lady who could gain to her wish, whether by force or guile.

Now will I show of that lady, whom Gugemar so fondly loved. By the counsel of a certain baron the ancient King set his wife in prison. She was shut fast in a tower of grey marble, where her days were bad, and her nights worse. No man could make clear to you the great pain, the anguish and the dolour, that she suffered in this tower, wherein, I protest, she died daily. Two years and more she lay bound in prison, where warders came, but never joy or delight. Often she thought upon her friend.

"Gugemar, dear lord, in an evil hour I saw you with my eyes. Better for me that I die quickly, than endure longer my evil lot. Fair friend, if I could but win to that coast whence you sailed, very swiftly would I fling myself in the sea, and end my wretched life." When she had said these words she rose to her feet, and coming to the door was amazed to find therein neither bolt nor key. She issued forth, without challenge from sergeant or warder, and hastening to the harbour, found there her lover's ship, made fast to that very rock, from which she would cast her down. When she saw the barge she climbed thereon, but presently bethought her that on this nave her friend had gone to perish in the sea. At this thought she would have fled again to the shore, but her bones were as water, and she fell upon the deck. So in sore travail and sorrow, the vessel carried her across the waves, to a port of Brittany, guarded by a castle, strong and very fair. Now the lord of this castle was named Meriadus. He was a right warlike prince, and had made him ready to fight with the prince of a country near by. He had risen very early in the morning, to send forth a great company of spears, the more easily to ravage this neighbour's realm. Meriadus looked forth from his window, and marked the ship which came to port. He hastened down the steps of the perron, and calling to his chamberlain, came with what speed he might to the nave. Then mounting the ladder he stood upon the deck. When Meriadus found within the ship a dame, who for beauty seemed rather a fay than a mere earthly woman, he seized her by her mantle, and brought her swiftly to his keep. Right joyous was he because of his good fortune, for lovely was the lady beyond mortal measure. He made no question as to who had set her on the barge. He knew only that she was fair, and of high lineage, and that his heart turned towards her with so hot a love as never before had he put on dame or damsel. Now there dwelt within the castle a sister of this lord, who was yet unwed. Meriadus bestowed the lady in his sister's chamber, because it was the fairest in the tower. Moreover he commanded that she should be meetly served, and held in all reverence. But though the dame was so richly clothed and cherished, ever was she sad and deep in thought. Meriadus came often to cheer her with mirth and speech, by reason that he wished to gain her love as a free gift, and not by force. It was in vain that he prayed her for grace, since she had no balm for his wound. For answer she showed him the girdle about her body, saying that never would she give her love to man, save only to him who might unloose the buckle of that girdle, without harm to belt or clasp. When Meriadus heard these words, he spoke in haste and said,

"Lady, there dwells in this country a very worthy knight, who will take no woman as wife, except she first untie a certain crafty knot in the hem of a shirt, and that without force or knife. For a little I would wager that it was you who tied this knot."

When the lady heard thereof her breath went from her, and near she came to falling on the ground. Meriadus caught her in his arms, and cut the laces of her bodice, that she might have the more air. He strove to unfasten her girdle, but might not dissever the clasp. Yea, though every knight in the realm essayed to unfasten that cincture, it would not yield, except to one alone.

Now Meriadus made the lists ready for a great jousting, and called to that tournament all the knights who would aid him in his war. Many a lord came at his bidding, and with them Gugemar, amongst the first. Meriadus had sent letters to the knight, beseeching him, as friend and companion, not to fail him in this business. So Gugemar hastened to the need of his lord, and at his back more than one hundred spears. All these Meriadus welcomed very gladly, and gave them lodging within his tower. In honour of his guest, the prince sent two gentlemen to his sister, praying her to attire herself richly, and come to hall, together with the dame whom he loved so dearly well. These did as they were bidden, and arrayed in their sweetest vesture, presently entered in the hall, holding each other by the hand. Very pale and pensive was the lady, but when she heard her lover's name her feet failed beneath her, and had not the maiden held her fast, she would have fallen on the floor. Gugemar rose from his seat at the sight of the dame, her fashion and her semblance, and stood staring upon her. He went a little apart, and said within himself,

"Can this be my sweet friend, my hope, my heart, my life, the fair lady who gave me the grace of her love? From whence comes she; who might have brought her to this far land? But I speak in my folly, for well I know that this is not my dear. A little red, a little white, and all women are thus shapen. My thoughts are troubled, by reason that the sweetness of this lady resembles the sweetness of that other, for whom my heart sighs and trembles. Yet needs must that I have speech of the lady."

Gugemar drew near to the dame. He kissed her courteously, and found no word to utter, save to pray that he might be seated at her side. Meriadus spied upon them closely, and was the more heavy because of their trouble. Therefore he feigned mirth.

" Gugemar, dear lord, if it pleases you, let this damsel essay to untie the knot of your sark, if so be she may loosen the coil."

Gugemar made answer that very willingly he would do this thing. He called to him a squire who had the shirt in keeping, and bade him seek his charge, and deliver it to the dame. The lady took the sark in hand. Well she knew the knot that she had tied so cunningly, and was so willing to unloose; but for reason of the trouble at her heart, she did not dare essay. Meriadus marked the distress of the damsel, and was more sorrowful than ever was lover before.

" Lady," said he, " do all that you are able to unfasten this coil."

So at his commandment she took again to her the hem of the shirt, and lightly and easily unravelled the tie.

Gugemar marvelled greatly when he saw this thing. His heart told him that of a truth this was his lady, but he could not give faith to his eyes.

" Friend, are you indeed the sweet comrade I have known ? Tell me truly now, is there about your body the girdle with which I girt you in your own realm ? "

He set his hands to her waist, and found that the secret belt was yet about her sides.

" Fair sweet friend, tell me now by what adventure I find you here, and who has brought you to this tower ? "

So the lady told over to her friend the pain and the anguish and the dolour of the prison in which she was held ; of how it chanced that she fled from her dungeon, and lighting upon a ship, entered therein, and came to this fair haven ; of how Meriadus took her from the barge, but kept her in all honour, save only that ever he sought for her love ; " but now, fair friend, all is well, for you hold your lady in your arms."

Gugemar stood upon his feet, and beckoned with his hand.

" Lords," he cried, " hearken now to me. I have found my friend, whom I have lost for a great while. Before you all I pray and require of Meriadus to yield me my own. For this grace I give him open thanks. Moreover I will kneel down, and become his liege man. For two years, or three, if he will, I will bargain to serve in his quarrels, and with me, of riders, a hundred or more at my back."

Then answered Meriadus,

" Gugemar, fair friend, I am not yet so shaken or overborne in war, that I must do as you wish, right humbly. This woman is my captive. I found her : I hold her : and I will defend my right against you and all your power."

When Gugemar heard these proud words he got to horse speedily, him and all his company. He threw down his glove, and parted in anger from the tower. But he went right heavily, since he must leave behind his friend. In his train rode all those knights who had drawn together to that town for the great tournament. Not a knight of them all but plighted faith to follow where he led, and to hold himself recreant and shamed if he failed his oath.

That same night the band came to the castle of the prince with whom Meriadus was at war. He welcomed them very gladly, and gave them lodging in his tower. By their aid he had good hope to bring this quarrel to an end. Very early in the morning the host came together to set the battle in array. With clash of mail and noise of horns they issued from the city gate, Gugemar riding at their head. They drew before the castle where Meriadus lay in strength, and sought to take it by storm. But the keep was very strong, and Meriadus bore himself as a stout and valiant knight. So Gugemar, like a wary captain, sat himself down before the town, till all the folk of that place were deemed by friend and sergeant to be weak with hunger. Then they took that high keep with the sword, and burnt it with fire. The lord thereof they slew in his own hall; but Gugemar came forth, after such labours as you have heard, bearing his lady with him, to return in peace to his own land.

From this adventure that I have told you, has come the Lay that minstrels chant to harp and viol—fair is that song and sweet the tune.

III

THE LAY OF THE DOLOROUS KNIGHT

Hearken now to the Lay that once I heard a minstrel chanting to his harp. In surety of its truth I will name the city where this story passed. The Lay of the Dolorous Knight, my harper called his song, but of those who hearkened, some named it rather, The Lay of the Four Sorrows.

In Nantes, of Brittany, there dwelt a dame who was dearly held of all, for reason of the much good that was found in her. This lady was passing fair of body, apt in book as any clerk, and meetly schooled in every grace that it becometh dame to have. So gracious of person was this damsel, that throughout the realm there was no knight could refrain from setting his heart upon her, though he saw her but one only time. Although the demoiselle might not return the love of so many, certainly she had no wish to slay them all. Better by far that a man pray and require in love all the dames of his country, than run mad in woods for the bright eyes of one. Therefore this dame gave courtesy and good will to each alike. Even when she might not hear a lover's words, so sweetly she denied his wish that the more he held her dear and was the more her servant for that fond denial. So because of her great riches of body and of heart, this lady of whom I tell, was prayed and required in love by the lords of her country, both by night and by day.

Now in Brittany lived four young barons, but their
names I cannot tell. It is enough that they were desirable in the eyes of maidens for reason of their beauty, and
that men esteemed them because they were courteous of
manner and open of hand. Moreover they were stout and
hardy knights amongst the spears, and rich and worthy
gentlemen of those very parts. Each of these four knights
had set his heart upon the lady, and for love of her
pained himself mightily, and did all that he was able, so
that by any means he might gain her favour. Each
prayed her privily for her love, and strove all that he
could to make him worthy of the gift, above his fellows.
For her part the lady was sore perplexed, and considered
in her mind very earnestly, which of these four knights
she should take as friend. But since they all were
loyal and worthy gentlemen, she durst not choose
amongst them ; for she would not slay three lovers
with her hand so that one might have content. Therefore to each and all, the dame made herself fair and
sweet of semblance. Gifts she gave to all alike. Tender
messages she sent to each. Every knight deemed himself
esteemed and favoured above his fellows, and by soft
words and fair service diligently strove to please. When
the knights gathered together for the games, each of
these lords contended earnestly for the prize, so that he
might be first, and draw on him the favour of his dame.
Each held her for his friend. Each bore upon him her
gift—pennon, or sleeve, or ring. Each cried her name
within the lists.

Now when Eastertide was come, a great tournament
was proclaimed to be held beyond the walls of Nantes,
that rich city. The four lovers were the appellants in
this tourney, and from every realm knights rode to
break a lance in honour of their dame. Frenchman
and Norman and Fleming ; the hardiest knights of

Brabant, Boulogne and Anjou; each came to do his devoir in the field. Nor was the chivalry of Nantes backward in this quarrel, but till the vespers of the tournament was come, they stayed themselves within the lists, and struck stoutly for their lord. After the four lovers had laced their harness upon them, they issued forth from the city, followed by the knights who were of their company in this adventure. But upon the four fell the burden of the day, for they were known of all by the embroidered arms upon their surcoat, and the device fashioned on the shield. Now against the four lovers arrayed themselves four other knights, armed altogether in coats of mail, and helmets and gauntlets of steel. Of these stranger knights two were of Hainault, and the two others were Flemings. When the four lovers saw their adversaries prepare themselves for the combat, they had little desire to flee, but hastened to join them in battle. Each lowered his spear, and choosing his enemy, met him so eagerly that all men wondered, for horse and man fell to the earth. The four lovers recked little of their destriers, but freeing their feet from the stirrups bent over the fallen foe, and called on him to yield. When the friends of the vanquished knights saw their case, they hastened to their succour; so for their rescue there was a great press, and many a mighty stroke with the sword.

The damsel stood upon a tower to watch these feats of arms. By their blazoned coats and shields she knew her knights; she saw their marvellous deeds, yet might not say who did best, nor give to one the praise. But the tournament was no longer a seemly and ordered battle. The ranks of the two companies were confused together, so that every man fought against his fellow, and none might tell whether he struck his comrade or his foe. The four lovers did well and worshipfully, so that all men deemed them worthy of the prize. But when evening was come, and the sport drew to its close, their courage led them to folly. Having ventured too far from their companions, they were set upon by their adversaries, and assailed so fiercely that three were slain outright. As to the fourth he yet lived, but altogether mauled and shaken, for his thigh was broken, and a spear head remained in his side. The four bodies were fallen on the field, and lay with those who had perished in that day. But because of the great mischief these four lovers had done their adversaries, their shields were cast despitefully without the lists ; but in this their foemen did wrongfully, and all men held them in sore displeasure.

Great were the lamentation and the cry when the news of this mischance was noised about the city. Such a tumult of mourning was never before heard, for the whole city was moved. All men hastened forth to the place where the lists were set. Meetly to mourn the dead there rode nigh upon two thousand knights, with hauberks unlaced, and uncovered heads, plucking upon their beards. So the four lovers were placed each upon his shield, and being brought back in honour to Nantes, were carried to the house of that dame, whom so greatly they had loved. When the lady knew this distressful adventure, straightway she fell to the ground. Being returned from her swoon, she made her complaint, calling upon her lovers each by his name.

" Alas," said she, " what shall I do, for never shall I know happiness again. These four knights had set their hearts upon me, and despite their great treasure, esteemed my love as richer than all their wealth. Alas, for the fair and valiant knight ! Alas, for the loyal and generous man ! By gifts such as these they sought to gain my favour, but how might lady bereave three of life, so as to cherish one. Even now I cannot tell for whom I have most pity, or who was closest to my mind. But three are dead, and one is sore stricken ; neither is there anything in the world which can bring me comfort. Only this is there to do—to give the slain men seemly burial, and, if it may be, to heal their comrade of his wounds."

So, because of her great love and nobleness, the lady caused these three distressful knights to be buried well and worshipfully in a rich abbey. In that place she offered their Mass penny, and gave rich offerings of silver and of lights besides. May God have mercy on them in that day. As for the wounded knight she commanded him to be carried to her own chamber. She sent for surgeons, and gave him into their hands. These searched his wounds so skilfully, and tended him with so great care, that presently his hurt commenced to heal. Very often was the lady in the chamber, and very tenderly she cherished the stricken man. Yet ever she felt pity for the three Knights of the Sorrows, and ever she went heavily by reason of their deaths.

Now on a summer's day, the lady and the knight sat together after meat. She called to mind the sorrow that was hers ; so that, in a space, her head fell upon her breast, and she gave herself altogether to her grief. The knight looked earnestly upon his dame. Well he might see that she was far away, and clearly he perceived the cause.

"Lady," said he, "you are in sorrow. Open now your grief to me. If you tell me what is in your heart perchance I may find you comfort."

"Fair friend," replied she, "I think of what is gone, and remember your companions, who are dead. Never was lady of my peerage, however fair and good and gracious, ever loved by four such valiant gentlemen, nor ever lost them in one single day. Save you—who were so maimed and in such peril—all are gone. Therefore I call to mind those who loved me so dearly, and am the saddest lady beneath the sun. To remember these things, of you four I shall make a Lay, and will call it the Lay of the Four Sorrows."

When the knight heard these words he made answer very swiftly,

" Lady, name it not the Lay of the Four Sorrows, but, rather, the Lay of the Dolorous Knight. Would you hear the reason why it should bear this name ? My three comrades have finished their course ; they have nothing more to hope of their life. They are gone, and with them the pang of their great sorrow, and the knowledge of their enduring love for you. I alone have come, all amazed and fearful, from the net wherein they were taken, but I find my life more bitter than my comrades found the grave. I see you on your goings and comings about the house. I may speak with you both matins and vespers. But no other joy do I get— neither clasp nor kiss, nothing but a few empty, courteous words. Since all these evils are come upon me because of you, I choose death rather than life. For this reason your Lay should bear my name, and be called the Lay of the Dolorous Knight. He who would name it the Lay of the Four Sorrows would name it wrongly, and not according to the truth."

" By my faith," replied the lady, " this is a fair saying. So shall the song be known as the Lay of the Dolorous Knight."

Thus was the Lay conceived, made perfect, and brought to a fair birth. For this reason it came by its name ; though to this day some call it the Lay of the

Four Sorrows. Either name befits it well, for the story tells of both these matters, but it is the use and wont in this land to call it the Lay of the Dolorous Knight. Here it ends; no more is there to say. I heard no more, and nothing more I know. Perforce I bring my story to a close.

IV

THE LAY OF ELIDUC

Now will I rehearse before you a very ancient Breton
Lay. As the tale was told to me, so, in turn, will I tell
it over again, to the best of my art and knowledge.
Hearken now to my story, its why and its reason.

In Brittany there lived a knight, so courteous and so
brave, that in all the realm there was no worthier lord than
he. This knight was named Eliduc. He had wedded in
his youth a noble lady of proud race and name. They
had long dwelt together in peace and content, for their
hearts were fixed on one another in faith and loyalty.
Now it chanced that Eliduc sought his fortune in a
far land, where there was a great war. There he loved
a Princess, the daughter of the King and Queen of those
parts. Guillardun was the maiden's name, and in all
the realm was none more fair. The wife of Eliduc had to
name, Guildeluec, in her own country. By reason of
these two ladies their story is known as the Lay of Guildeluec and Guillardun, but at first it was rightly called
the Lay of Eliduc. The name is a little matter; but
if you hearken to me you shall learn the story of these
three lovers, in its pity and its truth.

Eliduc had as lord and suzerain, the King of Brittany
over Sea. The knight was greatly loved and cherished
of his prince, by reason of his long and loyal service.
When the King's business took him from his realm,
Eliduc was his master's Justice and Seneschal. He

governed the country well and wisely, and held it from the foe with a strong hand. Nevertheless, in spite of all, much evil was appointed unto him. Eliduc was a mighty hunter, and by the King's grace, he would chase the stag within the woods. He was cunning and fair as Tristan, and so wise in venery, that the oldest forester might not gainsay him in aught concerning the shaw. But by reason of malice and envy, certain men accused him to the King that he had meddled with the royal pleasaunce. The King bade Eliduc to avoid his Court. He gave no reason for his commandment, and the knight might learn nothing of the cause. Often he prayed the King that he might know whereof he was accused. Often he begged his lord not to heed the specious and crafty words of his foes. He called to mind the wounds he had gained in his master's wars, but was answered never a word. When Eliduc found that he might get no speech with his lord, it became his honour to depart. He returned to his house, and calling his friends around him, opened out to them this business of the King's wrath, in recompense for his faithful service.

"I did not reckon on a King's gratitude; but as the proverb says, it is useless for a farmer to dispute with the horse in his plough. The wise and virtuous man keeps faith to his lord, and bears goodwill to his neighbour, not for what he may receive in return."

Then the knight told his friends that since he might no longer stay in his own country, he should cross the sea to the realm of Logres, and sojourn there awhile, for his solace. His fief he placed in the hands of his wife, and he required of his men, and of all who held him dear, that they would serve her loyally. Having given good counsel to the utmost of his power, the knight prepared him for the road. Right heavy were his friends and kin, that he must go forth from amongst them.

Eliduc took with him ten knights of his household, and set out on his journey. His dame came with him so far as she was able, wringing her hands, and making much sorrow, at the departure of her husband. At the end he pledged good faith to her, as she to him, and so she returned to her own home. Eliduc went his way, till he came to a haven on the sea. He took ship, and sailed to the realm of Totenois, for many kings dwell in that country, and ever there were strife and war. Now, near to Exeter, in this land, there dwelt a King, right rich and strong, but old and very full of years. He had no son of his body, but one maid only, young, and of an age to wed. Since he would not bestow this damsel on a certain prince of his neighbours, this lord made mortal war upon his fellow, spoiling and wasting all his land. The ancient King, for surety, had set his daughter within a castle, fair and very strong. He had charged the sergeants not to issue forth from the gates, and for the rest there was none so bold as to seek to storm the keep, or even to joust about the barriers. When Eliduc was told of this quarrel, he needed to go no farther, and sojourned for awhile in the land. He turned over in his mind which of these princes dealt unjustly with his neighbour. Since he deemed that the agèd king was the more vexed and sorely pressed in the matter, he resolved to aid him to the best of his might, and to take arms in his service. Eliduc, therefore, wrote letters to the King, telling him that he had quitted his own country, and sought refuge in the King's realm. For his part he was willing to fight as a mercenary in the King's quarrel, and if a safe conduct were given him, he and the knights of his company would ride, forthwith, to their master's aid. This letter, Eliduc sent by the hands of his squires to the King. When the ancient lord had read the letter, he rejoiced

greatly, and made much of the messengers. He summoned his constable, and commanded him swiftly to
write out the safe conduct, that would bring the baron
to his side. For the rest he bade that the messengers
meetly should be lodged and apparelled, and that such
money should be given them as would be sufficient to
their needs. Then he sealed the safe conduct with his
royal seal, and sent it to Eliduc, straightway, by a sure
hand.

When Eliduc came in answer to the summons, he
was received with great honour by the King. His
lodging was appointed in the house of a grave and
courteous burgess of the city, who bestowed the fairest
chamber on his guest. Eliduc fared softly, both at bed
and board. He called to his table such good knights
as were in misease, by reason of prison or of war. He
charged his men that none should be so bold as to take
pelf or penny from the citizens of the town, during the
first forty days of their sojourn. But on the third day,
it was bruited about the streets, that the enemy were
near at hand. The country folk deemed that they
approached to invest the city, and to take the gates
by storm. When the noise and clamour of the fearful
burgesses came to the ears of Eliduc, he and his company
donned their harness, and got to horse, as quickly as
they might. Forty horsemen mounted with him; as
to the rest, many lay sick or hurt within the city, and
others were captives in the hands of the foe. These
forty stout sergeants waited for no sounding of trumpets;
they hastened to seek their captain at his lodging, and
rode at his back through the city gate.

"Sir," said they, "where you go, there we will follow,
and what you bid us, that shall we do."

"Friends," made answer the knight, "I thank you
for your fellowship. There is no man amongst us but

who wishes to molest the foe, and do them all the mischief that he is able. If we await them in the town, we defend ourselves with the shield, and not with the sword. To my mind it is better to fall in the field than to hide behind walls; but if any of you have a wiser counsel to offer, now let him speak."

"Sir," replied a soldier of the company, "through the wood, in good faith, there runs a path, right strict and narrow. It is the wont of the enemy to approach our city by this track. After their deeds of arms before the walls, it is their custom to return by the way they came, helmet on saddle bow, and hauberk unbraced. If we might catch them, unready in the path, we could trouble them very grievously, even though it be at the peril of our lives."

"Friends," answered Eliduc, "you are all the King's men, and are bound to serve him faithfully, even to the death. Come, now, with me where I will go, and do that thing which you shall see me do. I give you my word as a loyal gentleman, that no harm shall hap to any. If we gain spoil and riches from the foe, each shall have his lot in the ransom. At the least we may do them much hurt and mischief in this quarrel."

Eliduc set his men in ambush, near by that path, within the wood. He told over to them, like a cunning captain, the crafty plan he had devised, and taught them how to play their parts, and to call upon his name. When the foe had entered on that perilous path, and were altogether taken in the snare, Eliduc cried his name, and summoned his companions to bear themselves like men. This they did stoutly, and assailed their enemy so fiercely that he was dismayed beyond measure, and his line being broken, fled to the forest. In this fight was the constable taken, together with fifty and five other lords, who owned themselves prisoners, and were given to the keeping of the squires. Great was the spoil in horse and harness, and marvellous was the wealth they gained in gold and ransom. So having done such great deeds in so short a space, they returned to the city, joyous and content.

The King looked forth from a tower. He feared grievously for his men, and made his complaint of Eliduc, who—he deemed—had betrayed him in his need. Upon the road he saw a great company, charged and laden with spoil. Since the number of those who returned was more than those who went forth, the king knew not again his own. He came down from the tower, in doubt and sore trouble, bidding that the gates should be made fast, and that men should mount upon the walls. For such coil as this, there was slender warrant. A squire who was sent out, came back with all speed, and showed him of this adventure. He told over the story of the ambush, and the tale of the prisoners. He rehearsed how the constable was taken, and that many a knight was wounded, and many a brave man slain. When the King might give credence thereto, he had more joy than ever king before. He got him from his tower, and going before Eliduc, he praised him to his face, and rendered him the captives as a gift. Eliduc gave the King's bounty to his men. He bestowed on them besides, all the harness and the spoil; keeping, for his part, but three knights, who had won much honour in the battle. From this day the King loved and cherished Eliduc very dearly. He held the knight, and his company, for a full year in his service, and at the end of the year, such faith had he in the knight's loyalty, that he appointed him Seneschal and Constable of his realm.

Eliduc was not only a brave and wary captain; he was also a courteous gentleman, right goodly to behold. That fair maiden, the daughter of the King, heard tell

of his deeds, and desired to see his face, because of the
good men spake of him.   She sent her privy chamberlain
to the knight, praying him to come to her house, that
she might solace herself with the story of his deeds, for
greatly she wondered that he had no care for her friendship.   Eliduc gave answer to the chamberlain that
he would ride forthwith, since much he desired to
meet so high a dame.   He bade his squire to saddle
his destrier, and rode to the palace, to have speech
with the lady.   Eliduc stood without the lady's
chamber, and prayed the chamberlain to tell the dame
that he had come, according to her wish.   The chamberlain came forth with a smiling face, and straightway
led him in the chamber.   When the princess saw the
knight, she cherished him very sweetly, and welcomed
him in the most honourable fashion.   The knight
gazed upon the lady, who was passing fair to see.
He thanked her courteously, that she was pleased to
permit him to have speech with so high a princess.
Guillardun took Eliduc by the hand, and seated him
upon the bed, near her side.   They spake together of
many things, for each found much to say.   The maiden
looked closely upon the knight, his face and semblance ;
to her heart she said that never before had she beheld
so comely a man.   Her eyes might find no blemish in
his person, and Love knocked upon her heart, requiring
her to love, since her time had come.   She sighed, and her
face lost its fair colour ; but she cared only to hide her
trouble from the knight, lest he should think her the
less maidenly therefore.   When they had talked together
for a great space, Eliduc took his leave, and went
his way.   The lady would have kept him longer gladly,
but since she did not dare, she allowed him to depart.
Eliduc returned to his lodging, very pensive and deep
in thought.   He called to mind that fair maiden,

the daughter of his King, who so sweetly had bidden him to her side, and had kissed him farewell, with sighs that were sweeter still. He repented him right earnestly that he had lived so long a while in the land without seeking her face, but promised that often he would enter her palace now. Then he remembered the wife whom he had left in his own house. He recalled the parting between them, and the covenant he made, that good faith and stainless honour should be ever betwixt the twain. But the maiden, from whom he came, was willing to take him as her knight! If such was her will, might any pluck him from her hand?

All night long, that fair maiden, the daughter of the King, had neither rest nor sleep. She rose up, very early in the morning, and commanding her chamberlain, opened out to him all that was in her heart. She leaned her brow against the casement.

"By my faith," she said, "I am fallen into a deep ditch, and sorrow has come upon me. I love Eliduc, the good knight, whom my father made his Seneschal. I love him so dearly that I turn the whole night upon my bed, and cannot close my eyes, nor sleep. If he assured me of his heart, and loved me again, all my pleasure should be found in his happiness. Great might be his profit, for he would become King of this realm, and little enough is it for his deserts, so courteous is he and wise. If he have nothing better than friendship to give me, I choose death before life, so deep is my distress."

When the princess had spoken what it pleased her to say, the chamberlain, whom she had bidden, gave her loyal counsel.

"Lady," said he, "since you have set your love upon this knight, send him now—if so it please you—some goodly gift-girdle or scarf or ring. If he receive the gift with delight, rejoicing in your favour, you may be assured that he loves you. There is no Emperor, under Heaven, if he were tendered your tenderness, but would go the more lightly for your grace."

The damsel hearkened to the counsel of her chamberlain, and made reply,

"If only I knew that he desired my love! Did ever maiden woo her knight before, by asking whether he loved or hated her? What if he make of me a mock and a jest in the ears of his friends! Ah, if the secrets of the heart were but written on the face! But get you ready, for go you must, at once."

"Lady," answered the chamberlain, "I am ready to do your bidding."

"You must greet the knight a hundred times in my name, and will place my girdle in his hand, and this my golden ring."

When the chamberlain had gone upon his errand, the maiden was so sick at heart, that for a little she would have bidden him return. Nevertheless, she let him go his way, and eased her shame with words.

"Alas, what has come upon me, that I should put my heart upon a stranger. I know nothing of his folk, whether they be mean or high; nor do I know whether he will part as swiftly as he came. I have done foolishly, and am worthy of blame, since I have bestowed my love very lightly. I spoke to him yesterday for the first time, and now I pray him for his love. Doubtless he will make me a song! Yet if he be the courteous gentleman I believe him, he will understand, and not deal hardly with me. At least the dice are cast, and if he may not love me, I shall know myself the most woeful of ladies, and never taste of joy all the days of my life."

Whilst the maiden lamented in this fashion, the chamberlain hastened to the lodging of Eliduc. He came before the knight, and having saluted him in his lady's name, he gave to his hand the ring and the girdle. The knight thanked him earnestly for the gifts. He placed the ring upon his finger, and the girdle he girt about his body. He said no more to the chamberlain, nor asked him any questions; save only that he proffered him a gift. This the messenger might not have, and returned the way he came. The chamberlain entered in the palace and found the princess within her chamber. He greeted her on the part of the knight, and thanked her for her bounty.

"Diva, diva," cried the lady hastily, "hide nothing from me; does he love me, or does he not?"

"Lady," answered the chamberlain, "as I deem, he loves you, and truly. Eliduc is no cozener with words. I hold him for a discreet and prudent gentleman, who knows well how to hide what is in his heart. I gave him greeting in your name, and granted him your gifts. He set the ring upon his finger, and as to your girdle, he girt it upon him, and belted it tightly about his middle. I said no more to him, nor he to me; but if he received not your gifts in tenderness, I am the more deceived. Lady, I have told you his words: I cannot tell you his thoughts. Only, mark carefully what I am about to say. If Eliduc had not a richer gift to offer, he would not have taken your presents at my hand."

"It pleases you to jest," said the lady. "I know well that Eliduc does not altogether hate me. Since my only fault is to cherish him too fondly, should he hate me, he would indeed be blameworthy. Never again by you, or by any other, will I require him of aught, or look to him for comfort. He shall see that a maiden's love is no slight thing, lightly given, and lightly taken again—but, perchance, he will not dwell in the realm so long as to know of the matter."

" Lady, the knight has covenanted to serve the King, in all loyalty, for the space of a year. You have full leisure to tell, whatever you desire him to learn."

When the maiden heard that Eliduc remained in the country, she rejoiced very greatly. She was glad that the knight would sojourn awhile in her city, for she knew naught of the torment he endured, since first he looked upon her. He had neither peace nor delight, for he could not get her from his mind. He reproached himself bitterly. He called to remembrance the covenant he made with his wife, when he departed from his own land, that he would never be false to his oath. But his heart was a captive now, in a very strong prison. He desired greatly to be loyal and honest, but he could not deny his love for the maiden—Guillardun, so frank and so fair.

Eliduc strove to act as his honour required. He had speech and sight of the lady, and did not refuse her kiss and embrace. He never spoke of love, and was diligent to offend in nothing. He was careful in this, because he would keep faith with his wife, and would attempt no matter against his King. Very grievously he pained himself, but at the end he might do no more. Eliduc caused his horse to be saddled, and calling his companions about him, rode to the castle to get audience of the King. He considered, too, that he might see his lady, and learn what was in her heart. It was the hour of meat, and the King having risen from table, had entered in his daughter's chamber. The King was at chess, with a lord who had but come from over-sea. The lady sat near the board, to watch the movements of the game. When Eliduc came before the prince, he welcomed him gladly, bidding him to seat himself close at hand. Afterwards he turned to his daughter, and said,

"Princess, it becomes you to have a closer friendship with this lord, and to treat him well and worshipfully. Amongst five hundred, there is no better knight than he."

When the maiden had listened demurely to her father's commandment, there was no gayer lady than she. She rose lightly to her feet, and taking the knight a little from the others, seated him at her side. They remained silent, because of the greatness of their love. She did not dare to speak the first, and to him the maid was more dreadful than a knight in mail. At the end Eliduc thanked her courteously for the gifts she had sent him; never was grace so precious and so kind. The maiden made answer to the knight, that very dear to her was the use he had found for her ring, and the girdle with which he had belted his body. She loved him so fondly that she wished him for her husband. If she might not have her wish, one thing she knew well, that she would take no living man, but would die unwed. She trusted he would not deny her hope.

"Lady," answered the knight, "I have great joy in your love, and thank you humbly for the goodwill you bear me. I ought indeed to be a happy man, since you deign to show me at what price you value our friendship. Have you remembered that I may not remain always in your realm? I covenanted with the King to serve him as his man for the space of one year. Perchance I may stay longer in his service, for I would not leave him till his quarrel be ended. Then I shall return to my own land; so, fair lady, you permit me to say farewell."

The maiden made answer to her knight,

"Fair friend, right sweetly I thank you for your courteous speech. So apt a clerk will know, without more words, that he may have of me just what he would. It becomes my love to give faith to all you say."

The two lovers spoke together no further; each was

well assured of what was in the other's heart. Eliduc
rode back to his lodging, right joyous and content.
Often he had speech with his friend, and passing great
was the love which grew between the twain.

Eliduc pressed on the war so fiercely that in the end
he took captive the King who troubled his lord, and had
delivered the land from its foes. He was greatly praised
of all as a crafty captain in the field, and a hardy comrade with the spear. The poor and the minstrel counted
him a generous knight. About this time that King,
who had bidden Eliduc avoid his realm, sought diligently
to find him. He had sent three messengers beyond the
seas to seek his ancient Seneschal. A strong enemy
had wrought him much grief and loss. All his castles
were taken from him, and all his country was a spoil
to the foe. Often and sorely he repented him of the evil
counsel to which he had given ear. He mourned the
absence of his mightiest knight, and drove from his
councils those false lords who, for malice and envy,
had defamed him. These he outlawed for ever from his
realm. The King wrote letters to Eliduc, conjuring
him by the loving friendship that was once between
them, and summoning him as a vassal is required of
his lord, to hasten to his aid, in that his bitter need.
When Eliduc heard these tidings they pressed heavily
upon him, by reason of the grievous love he bore the
dame. She, too, loved him with a woman's whole heart.
Between the two there was nothing but the purest love
and tenderness. Never by word or deed had they spoiled
their friendship. To speak a little closely together ;
to give some fond and foolish gift ; this was the sum
of their love. In her wish and hope the maiden trusted
to hold the knight in her land, and to have him as her
lord. Naught she deemed that he was wedded to a wife
beyond the sea.

"Alas," said Eliduc, "I have loitered too long in this country, and have gone astray. Here I have set my heart on a maiden, Guillardun, the daughter of the King, and she, on me. If, now, we part, there is no help that one, or both, of us, must die. Yet go I must. My lord requires me by letters, and by the oath of fealty that I have sworn. My own honour demands that I should return to my wife. I dare not stay ; needs must I go. I cannot wed my lady, for not a priest in Christendom would make us man and wife. All things turn to blame. God, what a tearing asunder will our parting be ! Yet there is one who will ever think me in the right, though I be held in scorn of all. I will be guided by her wishes, and what she counsels that will I do. The King, her sire, is troubled no longer by any war. First, I will go to him, praying that I may return to my own land, for a little, because of the need of my rightful lord. Then I will seek out the maiden, and show her the whole business. She will tell me her desire, and I shall act according to her wish."

The knight hesitated no longer as to the path he should follow. He went straight to the King, and craved leave to depart. He told him the story of his lord's distress, and read, and placed in the King's hands, the letters calling him back to his home. When the King had read the writing, and knew that Eliduc purposed to depart, he was passing sad and heavy. He offered the knight the third part of his kingdom, with all the treasure that he pleased to ask, if he would remain at his side. He offered these things to the knight—these, and the gratitude of all his days besides.

"Do not tempt me, sire," replied the knight. "My lord is in such deadly peril, and his letters have come so great a way to require me, that go I must to aid him in his need. When I have ended my task, I will return very gladly, if you care for my services, and with me a goodly company of knights to fight in your quarrels."

The King thanked Eliduc for his words, and granted him graciously the leave that he demanded. He gave him, moreover, all the goods of his house; gold and silver, hound and horses, silken cloths, both rich and fair, these he might have at his will. Eliduc took of them discreetly, according to his need. Then, very softly, he asked one other gift. If it pleased the King, right willingly would he say farewell to the princess, before he went. The King replied that it was his pleasure, too. He sent a page to open the door of the maiden's chamber, and to tell her the knight's request. When she saw him, she took him by the hand, and saluted him very sweetly. Eliduc was the more fain of counsel than of claspings. He seated himself by the maiden's side, and as shortly as he might, commenced to show her of the business. He had done no more than read her of his letters, than her face lost its fair colour, and near she came to swoon. When Eliduc saw her about to fall, he knew not what he did, for grief. He kissed her mouth, once and again, and wept above her, very tenderly. He took, and held her fast in his arms, till she had returned from her swoon.

"Fair dear friend," said he softly, "bear with me while I tell you that you are my life and my death, and in you is all my comfort. I have bidden farewell to your father, and purposed to go back to my own land, for reason of this bitter business of my lord. But my will is only in your pleasure, and whatever the future brings me, your counsel I will do."

"Since you cannot stay," said the maiden, "take me with you, wherever you go. If not, my life is so joyless without you, that I would wish to end it with my knife."

Very sweetly made answer Sir Eliduc, for in honesty he loved honest maid,

"Fair friend, I have sworn faith to your father, and am his man. If I carried you with me, I should give the lie to my troth. Let this covenant be made between us. Should you give me leave to return to my own land I swear to you on my honour as a knight, that I will come again on any day that you shall name. My life is in your hands. Nothing on earth shall keep me from your side, so only that I have life and health."

Then she, who loved so fondly, granted her knight permission to depart, and fixed the term, and named the day for his return. Great was their sorrow that the hour had come to bid farewell. They gave rings of gold for remembrance, and sweetly kissed adieu. So they severed from each other's arms.

Eliduc sought the sea, and with a fair wind, crossed swiftly to the other side. His lord was greatly content to learn the tidings of his knight's return. His friends and his kinsfolk came to greet him, and the common folk welcomed him very gladly. But, amongst them all, none was so blithe at his home-coming as the fair and prudent lady who was his wife. Despite this show of friendship, Eliduc was ever sad, and deep in thought. He went heavily, till he might look upon his friend. He felt no happiness, nor made pretence of any, till he should meet with her again. His wife was sick at heart, because of the coldness of her husband. She took counsel with her soul, as to what she had done amiss. Often she asked him privily, if she had come short or offended in any measure, whilst he was without the realm. If she was accused by any, let him tell her the accusation, that she might purge herself of the offence.

"Wife," answered Eliduc, "neither I, nor any other, charge you with aught that is against your honour to do. The cause of my sorrow is in myself. I have pledged my faith to the King of that country, from whence I come, that I will return to help him in his need. When my lord the King has peace in his realm, within eight days I shall be once more upon the sea. Great travail I must endure, and many pains I shall suffer, in readiness for that hour. Return I must, and till then I have no mind for anything but toil ; for I will not give the lie to my plighted word."

Eliduc put his fief once more in the hands of his dame. He sought his lord, and aided him to the best of his might. By the counsel and prowess of the knight, the King came again into his own. When the term appointed by his lady, and the day she named for his return drew near, Eliduc wrought in such fashion that peace was accorded between the foes. Then the knight made him ready for his journey, and took thought to the folk he should carry with him. His choice fell on two of his nephews, whom he loved very dearly, and on a certain chamberlain of his household. These were trusted servitors, who were of his inmost mind, and knew much of his counsel. Together with these went his squires, these only, for Eliduc had no care to take many. All these, nephew and squire and chamberlain, Eliduc made to promise, and confirm by an oath, that they would reveal nothing of his business.

The company put to sea without further tarrying, and, crossing quickly, came to that land where Eliduc so greatly desired to be. The knight sought a hostel some distance from the haven, for he would not be seen of any, nor have it bruited that Eliduc was returned. He called his chamberlain, and sent him to his friend, bearing letters that her knight had come, according to the covenant that had been made. At nightfall, before the gates were made fast, Eliduc issued forth from the city, and followed after his messenger. He had clothed himself in mean apparel, and rode at a footpace straight to the city, where dwelt the daughter of the King. The chamberlain arrived before the palace, and by dint of asking and prying, found himself within the lady's chamber. He saluted the maiden, and told her that her lover was near. When Guillardun heard these tidings she was astonied beyond measure, and for joy and pity wept right tenderly. She kissed the letters of her friend, and the messenger who brought such welcome tidings. The chamberlain prayed the lady to attire and make her ready to join her friend. The day was spent in preparing for the adventure, according to such plan as had been devised. When dark was come, and all was still, the damsel stole forth from the palace, and the chamberlain with her. For fear that any man should know her again, the maiden had hidden, beneath a riding cloak, her silken gown, embroidered with gold. About the space of a bow shot from the city gate, there was a coppice standing within a fair meadow. Near by this wood, Eliduc and his comrades awaited the coming of Guillardun. When Eliduc saw the lady, wrapped in her mantle, and his chamberlain leading her by the hand, he got from his horse, and kissed her right tenderly. Great joy had his companions at so fair a sight. He set her on the horse, and climbing before her, took bridle in glove, and returned to the haven, with all the speed he might. He entered forthwith in the ship, which put to sea, having on board none, save Eliduc, his men, and his lady, Guillardun. With a fair wind, and a quiet hour, the sailors thought that they would swiftly come to shore. But when their journey was near its end, a sudden tempest arose on the sea. A mighty wind drove them far from their harbourage, so that their rudder was broken, and their sail torn from the mast. Devoutly they cried on St. Nicholas, St. Clement, and Madame St. Mary, to aid them in this peril. They implored the Mother that she would approach her Son, not to permit them to perish, but to bring them to the harbour where they would come. Without sail or oar, the ship drifted here and there, at the mercy of the storm. They were very close to death, when one of the company, with a loud voice began to cry,

" What need is there of prayers ! Sir, you have with you, her, who brings us to our death. We shall never win to land, because you, who already have a faithful wife, seek to wed this foreign woman, against God and His law, against honour and your plighted troth. Grant us to cast her in the sea, and straightway the winds and the waves will be still."

When Eliduc heard these words he was like to come to harm for rage.

" Bad servant and felon traitor," he cried, " you should pay dearly for your speech, if I might leave my lady."

Eliduc held his friend fast in his arms, and cherished her as well as he was able. When the lady heard that her knight was already wedded in his own realm, she swooned where she lay. Her face became pale and discoloured ; she neither breathed nor sighed, nor could any bring her any comfort. Those who carried her to a sheltered place, were persuaded that she was but dead, because of the fury of the storm. Eliduc was passing heavy. He rose to his feet, and hastening to his squire, smote him so grievously with an oar, that he fell senseless on the deck. He haled him by his legs to the side of the ship and flung the body in the sea, where it was swiftly swallowed by the waves. He went to the broken rudder, and governed the nave so skilfully, that it

presently drew to land. So, having come to their fair
haven, they cast anchor, and made fast their bridge to
the shore. Dame Guillardun lay yet in her swoon, and
seemed no other than if she were really dead. Eliduc's
sorrow was all the more, since he deemed that he had
slain her with his hand. He inquired of his companions
in what near place they might lay the lady to her rest,
" for I will not bid her farewell, till she is put in holy
ground with such pomp and rite as befit the obsequies
of the daughter of a King." His comrades answered
him never a word, for they were all bemused by reason
of what had befallen. Eliduc, therefore, considered
within himself to what place he should carry the lady.
His own home was so near the haven where he had
come, that very easily they could ride there before
evening. He called to mind that in his realm there was
a certain great forest, both long and deep. Within
this wood there was a little chapel, served by a holy
hermit for forty years, with whom Eliduc had oftimes
spoken.

" To this holy man," he said, " I will bear my lady.
In his chapel he shall bury her sweet body. I will endow
him so richly of my lands, that upon her chantry shall
be founded a mighty abbey. There some convent of
monks or nuns or canons shall ever hold her in remembrance, praying God to grant her mercy in His day."

Eliduc got to horse, but first took oath of his comrades
that never, by them, should be discovered, that which
they should see. He set his friend before him on the
palfrey, and thus the living and the dead rode together,
till they had entered the wood, and come before the
chapel. The squires called and beat upon the door, but
it remained fast, and none was found to give them any
answer. Eliduc bade that one should climb through a
window, and open the door from within. When they

had come within the chapel they found a new made tomb, and writ thereon, that the holy hermit having finished his course, was made perfect, eight days before Passing sad was Eliduc, and esmayed. His companions would have digged a second grave, and set therein, his friend ; but the knight would in no wise consent, for —he said—he purposed to take counsel of the priests of his country, as to building some church or abbey above her tomb. "At this hour we will but lay her body before the altar, and commend her to God His holy keeping." He commanded them to bring their mantles and make a bed upon the altar-pace. Thereon they laid the maiden, and having wrapped her close in her lover's cloak, left her alone. When the moment came for Eliduc to take farewell of his lady, he deemed that his own last hour had come. He kissed her eyes and her face.

"Fair friend," said he, "if it be pleasing to God, never will I bear sword or lance again, or seek the pleasures of this mortal world. Fair friend, in an ill hour you saw me ! Sweet lady, in a bitter hour you followed me to death ! Fairest, now were you a queen, were it not for the pure and loyal love you set upon me ? Passing sad of heart am I for you, my friend. The hour that I have seen you in your shroud, I will take the habit of some holy order, and every day, upon your tomb, I will tell over the chaplet of my sorrow."

Having taken farewell of the maiden, Eliduc came forth from the chapel, and closed the doors. He sent messages to his wife, that he was returning to his house, but weary and overborne. When the dame heard these tidings, she was happy in her heart, and made ready to greet him. She received her lord tenderly ; but little joy came of her welcome, for she got neither smiles in answer, nor tender words in return. She dared not inquire the reason, during the two days Eliduc remained in the house. The knight heard Mass very early in the morning, and then set forth on the road leading to the chapel where the maiden lay. He found her as he had parted, for she had not come back from her swoon, and there was neither stir in her, nor breath. He marvelled greatly, for he saw her, vermeil and white, as he had known her in life. She had lost none of her sweet colour, save that she was a little blanched. He wept bitterly above her, and entreated for her soul. Having made his prayer, he went again to his house.

On a day when Eliduc went forth, his wife called to her a varlet of her household, commanding him to follow his lord afar off, and mark where he went, and on what business. She promised to give him harness and horses, if he did according to her will. The varlet hid himself in the wood, and followed so cunningly after his lord, that he was not perceived. He watched the knight enter the chapel, and heard the cry and lamentation that he made. When Eliduc came out, the varlet hastened to his mistress, and told her what he had seen, the tears and dolour, and all that befell his lord within the hermitage. The lady summoned all her courage.

"We will go together, as soon as we may, to this hermitage. My lord tells me that he rides presently to the Court to speak with the King. I knew that my husband loved this dead hermit very tenderly, but I little thought that his loss would make him mad with grief."

The next day the dame let her lord go forth in peace. When, about noon, Eliduc rode to the Court to greet his King, the lady rose quickly, and carrying the varlet with her, went swiftly to the hermitage. She entered the chapel, and saw the bed upon the altar-pace, and the maiden thereon, like a new sprung rose. Stooping down the lady removed the mantle. She marked the rigid body, the long arms, and the frail white hands, with their slender fingers, folded on the breast. Thus she learned the secret of the sorrow of her lord. She called the varlet within the chapel, and showed him this wonder.

" Seest thou," she said, " this woman, who for beauty shineth as a gem! This lady, in her life, was the lover of my lord. It was for her that all his days were spoiled by grief. By my faith I marvel little at his sorrow, since I, who am a woman too, will—for pity's sake or love—never know joy again, having seen so fair a lady in the dust."

So the wife wept above the body of the maiden. Whilst the lady sat weeping, a weasel came from under the altar, and ran across Guillardun's body. The varlet smote it with his staff, and killed it as it passed. He took the vermin and flung it away. The companion of this weasel presently came forth to seek him. She ran to the place where he lay, and finding that he would not get him on his feet, seemed as one distraught. She went forth from the chapel, and hastened to the wood, from whence she returned quickly, bearing a vermeil flower beneath her teeth. This red flower she placed within the mouth of that weasel the varlet had slain, and immediately he stood upon his feet. When the lady saw this, she cried to the varlet,

" Throw, man, throw, and gain the flower."

The servitor flung his staff, and the weasels fled away, leaving that fair flower upon the floor. The lady rose. She took the flower, and returned with it swiftly to the altar pace. Within the mouth of the maiden, she set a flower that was more vermeil still. For a short space the dame and the damsel were alike breathless. Then the maiden came to herself, with a sigh. She opened her eyes, and commenced to speak.

"Diva," she said, "have I slept so long, indeed!"

When the lady heard her voice she gave thanks to God. She inquired of the maiden as to her name and degree. The damsel made answer to her,

"Lady, I was born in Logres, and am daughter to the King of that realm. Greatly there I loved a knight, named Eliduc, the seneschal of my sire. We fled together from my home, to my own most grievous fault. He never told me that he was wedded to a wife in his own country, and he hid the matter so cunningly, that I knew naught thereof. When I heard tell of his dame, I swooned for pure sorrow. Now I find that this false lover, has, like a felon, betrayed me in a strange land. What will chance to a maiden in so foul a plight ? Great is that woman's folly who puts her trust in man."

"Fair damsel," replied the lady, "there is nothing in the whole world that can give such joy to this felon, as to hear that you are yet alive. He deems that you are dead, and every day he beweeps your swoon in the chapel. I am his wife, and my heart is sick, just for looking on his sorrow. To learn the reason of his grief, I caused him to be followed, and that is why I have found you here. It is a great happiness for me to know that you live. You shall return with me to my home, and I will place you in the tenderness of your friend. Then I shall release him of his marriage troth, since it is my dearest hope to take the veil."

When the wife had comforted the maiden with such words, they went together to her own house. She called to her servitor, and bade him seek his lord. The varlet went here and there, till he lighted on Eliduc. He came before him, and showed him of all these things. Eliduc mounted straightway on his horse, and waiting

neither for squire or companion, that same night came
to his hall. When he found alive, her, who once was
dead, Eliduc thanked his wife for so dear a gift. He
rejoiced beyond measure, and of all his days, no day
was more happy than this. He kissed the maiden
often, and very sweetly she gave him again his kiss,
for great was the joy between the twain. The dame
looked on their happiness, and knew that her lord
meetly had bestowed his love. She prayed him, therefore,
that he would grant her leave to depart, since she would
serve God as a cloistered nun. Of his wealth she craved
such a portion as would permit her to found a convent.
He would then be able to wed the maiden on whom his
heart was set, for it was neither honest nor seemly that
a man should maintain a wife with either hand.

Eliduc could do no otherwise than consent. He gave
the permission she asked, and did all according to her
will. He endowed the lady of his lands, near by that
chapel and hermitage, within the wood. There he built
a church with offices and refectory, fair to see. Much
wealth he bestowed on the convent, in money and estate.
When all was brought to a good end, the lady took the
veil upon her head. Thirty other ladies entered in the
house with her, and long she ruled them as their Abbess,
right wisely and well.

Eliduc wedded with his friend, in great pomp, and
passing rich was the marriage feast. They dwelt in
unity together for many days, for ever between them
was perfect love. They walked uprightly, and gave
alms of their goods, till such a time as it became them
to turn to God. After much thought, Eliduc built a
great church close beside his castle. He endowed it
with all his gold and silver, and with the rest of his
land. He set priests there, and holy layfolk also, for
the business of the house, and the fair services of religion.

When all was builded and ordered, Eliduc offered himself, with them, that he—weak man—might serve the omnipotent God. He set with the Abbess Guildeluec —who once was his dame—that wife whom he loved so dearly well. The Abbess received her as a sister, and welcomed her right honourably. She admonished her in the offices of God, and taught her of the rules and practice of their holy Order. They prayed to God for their friend, that He would grant him mercy in His day. In turn, he entreated God for them. Messages came from convent and monastery as to how they fared, so that each might encourage the other in His way. Each strove painfully, for himself and his, to love God the more dearly, and to abide in His holy faith. Each made a good end, and the mercy of God was abundantly made clear to all.

Of the adventure of these three lovers, the courteous Bretons made this Lay for remembrance, since they deemed it a matter that men should not forget.

V.

THE LAY OF THE NIGHTINGALE

Now will I tell you a story, whereof the Breton harper already has made a Lay. Laustic, I deem, men name it in that country, which, being interpreted, means rossignol in French, and nightingale in good plain English.

In the realm of Brittany stands a certain rich and mighty city, called Saint Malo. There were citizens of this township two knights, so well spoken and reputed of all, that the city drew therefrom great profit and fame. The houses of these lords were very near the one to the other. One of the two knights had to wife a passing fair lady, right gracious of manner and sweet of tongue. Wondrous pleasure found this dame to array herself richly, after the wont and fashion of her time. The other knight was yet a bachelor. He was well accounted of amongst his fellows as a hardy knight and as an honourable man. He gave hospitality gladly. Largely he gained, largely he spent, and willingly bestowed gifts of all that he had.

This bachelor set his love upon his neighbour's wife. By reason of his urgent prayers, his long suit and service, and by reason that all men spake naught of him but praise—perchance, also, for reason that he was never far from her eye—presently this lady came to set her heart on him again. Though these two friends loved right tenderly, yet were they so private and careful in their

57

loves that none perceived what was in their hearts. No man pried on them, or disturbed their goings and comings. These were the more easy to devise since the bachelor and the lady were such near neighbours. Their two houses stood side by side, hall and cellar and combles. Only between the gardens was built a high and ancient wall, of worn gray stone. When the lady sat within her bower, by leaning from the casement she and her friend might speak together, he to her, and she to him. They could also throw messages in writing, and divers pretty gifts, the one to the other. Little enough had they to displease them, and greatly were they at their ease, save only that they might not take their pleasure together, so often as their hearts had wished. For the dame was guarded very straitly when her husband was abroad. Yet not so strictly but that they might have word and speech, the now by night and now by day. At least, however close the watch and ward, none might hinder that at times these fair lovers stood within their casements, and looked fondly on the other's face.

Now after these friends had loved for a great space it chanced that the season became warm and sweet. It was the time when meadow and copse are green ; when orchards grow white with bloom, and birds break into song as thickly as the bush to flower. It is the season when he who loves would win to his desire. Truly I tell you that the knight would have done all in his power to attain his wish, and the lady, for her part, yearned for sight and speech of her friend. At night, when the moon shone clearly in the sky, and her lord lay sleeping at her side, often the dame slipped softly from her bed, and hastening to the casement, leaned forth to have sight of him who watched. The greater part of the dark they kept vigil together, for very pleasant it is to look upon your friend, when sweeter things are denied.

This chanced so often, and the lady rose so frequently from her bed, that her lord was altogether wrathful, and many a time inquired the reason of her unrest.

" Husband," replied the dame, " there is no dearer joy in this world, than to hear the nightingale sing. It is to hearken to the song that rises so sweetly on the night, that I lean forth from the casement. What tune of harp or viol is half so fair! Because of my delight in his song, and of my desire to hear, I may not shut my eyes till it be morn."

When the husband heard the lady's words he laughed within himself for wrath and malice. He purposed that very soon the nightingale should sing within a net. So he bade the servants of his house to devise fillets and snares, and to set their cunning traps about the orchard. Not a chestnut tree nor hazel within the garth but was limed and netted for the caging of this bird. It was not long therefore ere the nightingale was taken, and the servants made haste to give him to the pleasure of their lord. Wondrous merry was the knight when he held him living in his hand. He went straightway to the chamber of his dame, and entering, said,

" Wife, are you within ? Come near, for I must speak with you. Here is the nightingale, all limed and taken, who made vigil of your sleeping hours. Take now your rest in peace, for he will never disturb you more."

When the lady understood these words she was marvellously sorrowful and heavy. She prayed her lord to grant her the nightingale for a gift. But for all answer he wrung his neck with both hands so fiercely that the head was torn from the body. Then, right foully, he flung the bird upon the knees of the dame, in such fashion that her breast was sprinkled with the blood. So he departed, incontinent, from the chamber in a rage.

The lady took the little body in her hands, and wept his evil fate. She railed on those who with nets and snares had betrayed the nightingale to his death; for anger and hate beyond measure had gained hold on her heart.

"Alas," cried she, "evil is come upon me. Never again may I rise from my bed in the night, and watch from the casement, so that I may see my friend. One thing I know full well, that he will deem my love is no more set upon him. Woe to her who has none to give her counsel. This I will do. I will bestow the nightingale upon him, and send him tidings of the chance that has befallen."

So this doleful lady took a fair piece of white samite, broidered with gold, and wrought thereon the whole story of this adventure. In this silken cloth she wrapped the body of the little bird, and calling to her a trusty servant of her house, charged him with the message, and bade him bear it to her friend. The varlet went his way to the knight, and having saluted him on the part of the lady, he told over to him the story, and bestowed the nightingale upon him. When all had been rehearsed and shown to him, and he had well considered the matter, the knight was very dolent; yet in no wise would he avenge himself wrongfully. So he caused a certain coffret to be fashioned, made not of iron or steel, but of fine gold and fair stones, most rich and precious, right strongly clasped and bound. In this little chest he set the body of the nightingale, and having sealed the shrine, carried it upon him whenever his business took him abroad.

This adventure could not long be hid. Very swiftly it was noised about the country, and the Breton folk made a Lay thereon, which they called the Lay of the Laustic, in their own tongue.

VI

THE LAY OF SIR LAUNFAL

I WILL tell you the story of another Lay. It relates the adventures of a rich and mighty baron, and the Breton calls it, the Lay of Sir Launfal.

King Arthur—that fearless knight and courteous lord—removed to Wales, and lodged at Caerleon-on-Usk, since the Picts and Scots did much mischief in the land. For it was the wont of the wild people of the north to enter in the realm of Logres, and burn and damage at their will. At the time of Pentecost, the King cried a great feast. Thereat he gave many rich gifts to his counts and barons, and to the Knights of the Round Table. Never were such worship and bounty shown before at any feast, for Arthur bestowed honours and lands on all his servants—save only on one. This lord, who was forgotten and misliked of the King, was named Launfal. He was beloved by many of the Court, because of his beauty and prowess, for he was a worthy knight, open of heart and heavy of hand. These lords, to whom their comrade was dear, felt little joy to see so stout a knight misprized. Sir Launfal was son to a King of high descent, though his heritage was in a distant land. He was of the King's household, but since Arthur gave him naught, and he was of too proud a mind to pray for his due, he had spent all that he had. Right heavy was Sir Launfal, when he considered these things,

for he knew himself taken in the toils. Gentles, marvel
not overmuch hereat. Ever must the pilgrim go heavily
in a strange land, where there is none to counsel and
direct him in the path.

Now, on a day, Sir Launfal got him on his horse,
that he might take his pleasure for a little. He came
forth from the city, alone, attended by neither servant
nor squire. He went his way through a green mead,
till he stood by a river of clear running water. Sir
Launfal would have crossed this stream, without thought
of pass or ford, but he might not do so, for reason that
his horse was all fearful and trembling. Seeing that he
was hindered in this fashion, Launfal unbitted his steed,
and let him pasture in that fair meadow, where they
had come. Then he folded his cloak to serve him as a
pillow, and lay upon the ground. Launfal lay in great
misease, because of his heavy thoughts, and the discomfort of his bed. He turned from side to side, and
might not sleep. Now as the knight looked towards
the river he saw two damsels coming towards him ;
fairer maidens Launfal had never seen. These two
maidens were richly dressed in kirtles closely laced and
shapen to their persons and wore mantles of a goodly
purple hue. Sweet and dainty were the damsels, alike
in raiment and in face. The elder of these ladies carried
in her hands a basin of pure gold, cunningly wrought
by some crafty smith—very fair and precious was the
cup ; and the younger bore a towel of soft white linen.
These maidens turned neither to the right hand nor to
the left, but went directly to the place where Launfal
lay. When Launfal saw that their business was with
him, he stood upon his feet, like a discreet and courteous
gentleman. After they had greeted the knight, one
of the maidens delivered the message with which she
was charged.

" Sir Launfal, my demoiselle, as gracious as she is fair, prays that you will follow us, her messengers, as she has a certain word to speak with you. We will lead you swiftly to her pavilion, for our lady is very near at hand. If you but lift your eyes you may see where her tent is spread."

Right glad was the knight to do the bidding of the maidens. He gave no heed to his horse, but left him at his provand in the meadow. All his desire was to go with the damsels, to that pavilion of silk and divers colours, pitched in so fair a place. Certainly neither Semiramis in the days of her most wanton power, nor Octavian, the Emperor of all the West, had so gracious a covering from sun and rain. Above the tent was set an eagle of gold, so rich and precious, that none might count the cost. The cords and fringes thereof were of silken thread, and the lances which bore aloft the pavilion were of refined gold. No King on earth might have so sweet a shelter, not though he gave in fee the value of his realm. Within this pavilion Launfal came upon the Maiden. Whiter she was than any altar lily, and more sweetly flushed than the new born rose in time of summer heat. She lay upon a bed with napery and coverlet of richer worth than could be furnished by a castle's spoil. Very fresh and slender showed the lady in her vesture of spotless linen. About her person she had drawn a mantle of ermine, edged with purple dye from the vats of Alexandria. By reason of the heat her raiment was unfastened for a little, and her throat and the rondure of her bosom showed whiter and more untouched than hawthorn in May. The knight came before the bed, and stood gazing on so sweet a sight. The Maiden beckoned him to draw near, and when he had seated himself at the foot of her couch, spoke her mind.

" Launfal," she said, " fair friend, it is for you that

I have come from my own far land. I bring you my love. If you are prudent and discreet, as you are goodly to the view, there is no emperor nor count, nor king, whose day shall be so filled with riches and with mirth as yours."

When Launfal heard these words he rejoiced greatly, for his heart was litten by another's torch.

"Fair lady," he answered, "since it pleases you to be so gracious, and to dower so graceless a knight with your love, there is naught that you may bid me do—right or wrong, evil or good—that I will not do to the utmost of my power. I will observe your commandment, and serve in your quarrels. For you I renounce my father and my father's house. This only I pray, that I may dwell with you in your lodging, and that you will never send me from your side."

When the Maiden heard the words of him whom so fondly she desired to love, she was altogether moved, and granted him forthwith her heart and her tenderness. To her bounty she added another gift besides. Never might Launfal be desirous of aught, but he would have according to his wish. He might waste and spend at will and pleasure, but in his purse ever there was to spare. No more was Launfal sad. Right merry was the pilgrim, since one had set him on the way, with such a gift, that the more pennies he bestowed, the more silver and gold were in his pouch.

But the Maiden had yet a word to say.

"Friend," she said, "hearken to my counsel. I lay this charge upon you, and pray you urgently, that you tell not to any man the secret of our love. If you show this matter, you will lose your friend, for ever and a day. Never again may you see my face. Never again will you have seisin of that body, which is now so tender in your eyes."

Launfal plighted faith, that right strictly he would observe this commandment. So the Maiden granted him her kiss and her embrace, and very sweetly in that fair lodging passed the day till evensong was come.

Right loath was Launfal to depart from the pavilion at the vesper hour, and gladly would he have stayed, had he been able, and his lady wished.

"Fair friend," said she, "rise up, for no longer may you tarry. The hour is come that we must part. But one thing I have to say before you go. When you would speak with me I shall hasten to come before your wish. Well I deem that you will only call your friend where she may be found without reproach or shame of men. You may see me at your pleasure; my voice shall speak softly in your ear at will; but I must never be known of your comrades, nor must they ever learn my speech."

Right joyous was Launfal to hear this thing. He sealed the covenant with a kiss, and stood upon his feet. Then there entered the two maidens who had led him to the pavilion, bringing with them rich raiment, fitting for a knight's apparel. When Launfal had clothed himself therewith, there seemed no goodlier varlet under heaven, for certainly he was fair and true. After these maidens had refreshed him with clear water, and dried his hands upon the napkin, Launfal went to meat. His friend sat at table with him, and small will had he to refuse her courtesy. Very serviceably the damsels bore the meats, and Launfal and the Maiden ate and drank with mirth and content. But one dish was more to the knight's relish than any other. Sweeter than the dainties within his mouth, was the lady's kiss upon his lips.

When supper was ended, Launfal rose from table, for his horse stood waiting without the pavilion. The destrier was newly saddled and bridled, and showed proudly in his rich gay trappings. So Launfal kissed, and bade farewell, and went his way. He rode back towards the city at a slow pace. Often he checked his steed, and looked behind him, for he was filled with amazement, and all bemused concerning this adventure. In his heart he doubted that it was but a dream. He was altogether astonished, and knew not what to do. He feared that pavilion and Maiden alike were from the realm of faery.

Launfal returned to his lodging, and was greeted by servitors, clad no longer in ragged raiment. He fared richly, lay softly, and spent largely, but never knew how his purse was filled. There was no lord who had need of a lodging in the town, but Launfal brought him to his hall, for refreshment and delight. Launfal bestowed rich gifts. Launfal redeemed the poor captive. Launfal clothed in scarlet the minstrel. Launfal gave honour where honour was due. Stranger and friend alike he comforted at need. So, whether by night or by day, Launfal lived greatly at his ease. His lady, she came at will and pleasure, and, for the rest, all was added unto him.

Now it chanced, the same year, about the feast of St. John, a company of knights came, for their solace, to an orchard, beneath that tower where dwelt the Queen. Together with these lords went Gawain and his cousin, Yvain the fair. Then said Gawain, that goodly knight, beloved and dear to all,

"Lords, we do wrong to disport ourselves in this pleasaunce without our comrade Launfal. It is not well to slight a prince as brave as he is courteous, and of a lineage prouder than our own."

Then certain of the lords returned to the city, and finding Launfal within his hostel, entreated him to take his pastime with them in that fair meadow. The Queen looked out from a window in her tower, she and three ladies of her fellowship. They saw the lords at their pleasure, and Launfal also, whom well they knew. So the Queen chose of her Court thirty damsels—the sweetest of face and most dainty of fashion—and commanded that they should descend with her to take their delight in the garden. When the knights beheld this gay company of ladies come down the steps of the perron, they rejoiced beyond measure. They hastened before to lead them by the hand, and said such words in their ear as were seemly and pleasant to be spoken. Amongst these merry and courteous lords hasted not Sir Launfal. He drew apart from the throng, for with him time went heavily, till he might have clasp and greeting of his friend. The ladies of the Queen's fellowship seemed but kitchen wenches to his sight, in comparison with the loveliness of the maiden. When the Queen marked Launfal go aside, she went his way, and seating herself upon the herb, called the knight before her. Then she opened out her heart.

" Launfal, I have honoured you for long as a worthy knight, and have praised and cherished you very dearly. You may receive a queen's whole love, if such be your care. Be content: he to whom my heart is given, has small reason to complain him of the alms."

" Lady," answered the knight, " grant me leave to go, for this grace is not for me. I am the King's man, and dare not break my troth. Not for the highest lady in the world, not even for her love, will I set this reproach upon my lord."

When the Queen heard this, she was full of wrath, and spoke many hot and bitter words.

" Launfal," she cried, " well I know that you think little of woman and her love. There are sins more black that a man may have upon his soul. Traitor you are, and false. Right evil counsel gave they to my lord, who prayed him to suffer you about his person. You remain only for his harm and loss."

Launfal was very dolent to hear this thing. He was not slow to take up the Queen's glove, and in his haste spake words that he repented long, and with tears.

"Lady," said he, "I am not of that guild of which you speak. Neither am I a despiser of woman, since I love, and am loved, of one who would bear the prize from all the ladies in the land. Dame, know now and be persuaded, that she, whom I serve, is so rich in state, that the very meanest of her maidens, excels you, Lady Queen, as much in clerkly skill and goodness, as in sweetness of body and face, and in every virtue."

The Queen rose straightway to her feet, and fled to her chamber, weeping. Right wrathful and heavy was she, because of the words that had besmirched her. She lay sick upon her bed, from which, she said, she would never rise, till the King had done her justice, and righted this bitter wrong. Now the King that day had taken his pleasure within the woods. He returned from the chase towards evening, and sought the chamber of the Queen. When the lady saw him, she sprang from her bed, and kneeling at his feet, pleaded for grace and pity. Launfal—she said—had shamed her, since he required her love. When she had put him by, very foully had he reviled her, boasting that his love was already set on a lady, so proud and noble, that her meanest wench went more richly, and smiled more sweetly, than the Queen. Thereat the King waxed marvellously wrathful, and swore a great oath that he would set Launfal within a fire, or hang him from a tree, if he could not deny this thing, before his peers.

Arthur came forth from the Queen's chamber, and called to him three of his lords. These he sent to seek the knight who so evilly had entreated the Queen. Launfal, for his part, had returned to his lodging, in a sad and sorrowful case. He saw very clearly that he had lost his friend, since he had declared their love to men. Launfal sat within his chamber, sick and heavy of thought. Often he called upon his friend, but the lady would not hear his voice. He bewailed his evil lot, with tears; for grief he came nigh to swoon; a hundred times he implored the Maiden that she would deign to speak with her knight. Then, since the lady yet refrained from speech, Launfal cursed his hot and unruly tongue. Very near he came to ending all this trouble with his knife. Naught he found to do but to wring his hands, and call upon the Maiden, begging her to forgive his trespass, and to talk with him again, as friend to friend.

But little peace is there for him who is harassed by a King. There came presently to Launfal's hostel those three barons from the Court. These bade the knight forthwith to go with them to Arthur's presence, to acquit him of this wrong against the Queen. Launfal went forth, to his own deep sorrow. Had any man slain him on the road, he would have counted him his friend. He stood before the King, downcast and speechless, being dumb by reason of that great grief, of which he showed the picture and image.

Arthur looked upon his captive very evilly.

" Vassal," said he, harshly, " you have done me a bitter wrong. It was a foul deed to seek to shame me in this ugly fashion, and to smirch the honour of the Queen. Is it folly or lightness which leads you to boast of that lady, the least of whose maidens is fairer, and goes more richly, than the Queen ? "

Launfal protested that never had he set such shame upon his lord. Word by word he told the tale of how he denied the Queen, within the orchard. But concerning that which he had spoken of the lady, he owned the truth, and his folly. The love of which he bragged was now lost to him, by his own exceeding fault. He cared little for his life, and was content to obey the judgment of the Court.

Right wrathful was the King at Launfal's words. He conjured his barons to give him such wise counsel herein, that wrong might be done to none. The lords did the King's bidding, whether good came of the matter, or evil. They gathered themselves together, and appointed a certain day that Launfal should abide the judgment of his peers. For his part Launfal must give pledge and surety to his lord, that he would come before this judgment in his own body. If he might not give such surety then he should be held captive till the appointed day. When the lords of the King's household returned to tell him of their counsel, Arthur demanded that Launfal should put such pledge in his hand, as they had said. Launfal was altogether mazed and bewildered at this judgment, for he had neither friend nor kindred in the land. He would have been set in prison, but Gawain came first to offer himself as his surety, and with him, all the knights of his fellowship. These gave into the King's hand as pledge, the fiefs and lands that they held of his Crown. The King having taken pledges from the sureties, Launfal returned to his lodging, and with him certain knights of his company. They blamed him greatly because of his foolish love, and chastened him grievously by reason of the sorrow he made before men. Every day they came to his chamber, to know of his meat and drink, for much they feared that presently he would become mad.

The lords of the household came together on the day appointed for this judgment. The King was on his chair, with the Queen sitting at his side. The sureties brought Launfal within the hall, and rendered him into the hands of his peers. Right sorrowful were they because of his plight. A great company of his fellowship did all that they were able to acquit him of this charge. When all was set out, the King demanded the judgment of the Court, according to the accusation and the answer. The barons went forth in much trouble and thought to consider this matter. Many amongst them grieved for the peril of a good knight in a strange land ; others held that it were well for Launfal to suffer, because of the wish and malice of their lord. Whilst they were thus perplexed, the Duke of Cornwall rose in the council, and said,

" Lords, the King pursues Launfal as a traitor, and would slay him with the sword, by reason that he bragged of the beauty of his maiden, and roused the jealousy of the Queen. By the faith that I owe this company, none complains of Launfal, save only the King. For our part we would know the truth of this business, and do justice between the King and his man. We would also show proper reverence to our own liege lord. Now, if it be according to Arthur's will, let us take oath of Launfal, that he seek this lady, who has put such strife between him and the Queen. If her beauty be such as he has told us, the Queen will have no cause for wrath. She must pardon Launfal for his rudeness, since it will be plain that he did not speak out of a malicious heart. Should Launfal fail his word, and not return with the lady, or should her fairness fall beneath his boast, then let him be cast off from our fellowship, and be sent forth from the service of the King."

This counsel seemed good to the lords of the household. They sent certain of his friends to Launfal, to acquaint him with their judgment, bidding him to pray his damsel to the Court, that he might be acquitted of this blame. The knight made answer that in no wise could he do this thing. So the sureties returned before the judges, saying that Launfal hoped neither for refuge nor for succour from the lady, and Arthur urged them to a speedy ending, because of the prompting of the Queen.

The judges were about to give sentence upon Launfal, when they saw two maidens come riding towards the palace, upon two white ambling palfreys. Very sweet and dainty were these maidens, and richly clothed in garments of crimson sendal, closely girt and fashioned to their bodies. All men, old and young, looked willingly upon them, for fair they were to see. Gawain, and three knights of his company, went straight to Launfal, and showed him these maidens, praying him to say which of them was his friend. But he answered never a word. The maidens dismounted from their palfreys, and coming before the daïs where the King was seated, spake him fairly, as they were fair.

" Sire, prepare now a chamber, hung with silken cloths, where it is seemly for my lady to dwell ; for she would lodge with you awhile."

This gift the King granted gladly. He called to him two knights of his household, and bade them bestow the maidens in such chambers as were fitting to their degree. The maidens being gone, the King required of his barons to proceed with their judgment, saying that he had sore displeasure at the slowness of the cause.

" Sire," replied the barons, " we rose from Council, because of the damsels who entered in the hall. We will at once resume the sitting, and give our judgment without more delay."

The barons again were gathered together, in much thought and trouble, to consider this matter. There was great strife and dissension amongst them, for they knew not what to do. In the midst of all this noise and tumult, there came two other damsels riding to the hall on two Spanish mules. Very richly arrayed were these damsels in raiment of fine needlework, and their kirtles were covered by fresh fair mantles, embroidered with gold. Great joy had Launfal's comrades when they marked these ladies. They said between themselves that doubtless they came for the succour of the good knight. Gawain, and certain of his company, made haste to Launfal, and said,

" Sir, be not cast down. Two ladies are near at hand, right dainty of dress, and gracious of person. Tell us truly, for the love of God, is one of these your friend ? "

But Launfal answered very simply that never before had he seen these damsels with his eyes, nor known and loved them in his heart.

The maidens dismounted from their mules, and stood before Arthur, in the sight of all. Greatly were they praised of many, because of their beauty, and of the colour of their face and hair. Some there were who deemed already that the Queen was overborne.

The elder of the damsels carried herself modestly and well, and sweetly told over the message wherewith she was charged.

" Sire, make ready for us chambers, where we may abide with our lady, for even now she comes to speak with thee."

The King commanded that the ladies should be led to their companions, and bestowed in the same honourable fashion as they. Then he bade the lords of his household to consider their judgment, since he would endure no further respite. The Court already had given too much time to the business, and the Queen was growing wrathful, because of the blame that was hers. Now the judges were about to proclaim their sentence, when, amidst the tumult of the town, there came riding to the palace the flower of all the ladies of the world. She came mounted upon a palfrey, white as snow, which carried her softly, as though she loved her burthen. Beneath the sky was no goodlier steed, nor one more gentle to the hand. The harness of the palfrey was so rich, that no king on earth might hope to buy trappings so precious, unless he sold or set his realm in pledge. The Maiden herself showed such as I will tell you. Passing slim was the lady, sweet of bodice and slender of girdle. Her throat was whiter than snow on branch, and her eyes were like flowers in the pallor of her face. She had a witching mouth, a dainty nose, and an open brow. Her eyebrows were brown, and her golden hair parted in two soft waves upon her head. She was clad in a shift of spotless linen, and above her snowy kirtle was set a mantle of royal purple, clasped upon her breast. She carried a hooded falcon upon her glove, and a greyhound followed closely after. As the Maiden rode at a slow pace through the streets of the city, there was none, neither great nor small, youth nor sergeant, but ran forth from his house, that he might content his heart with so great beauty. Every man that saw her with his eyes, marvelled at a fairness beyond that of any earthly woman. Little he cared for any mortal maiden, after he had seen this sight. The friends of Sir Launfal hastened to the knight, to tell him of his lady's succour, if so it were according to God's will.

" Sir comrade, truly is not this your friend ? This lady is neither black nor golden, mean nor tall. She is only the most lovely thing in all the world."

When Launfal heard this, he sighed, for by their words he knew again his friend. He raised his head, and as the blood rushed to his face, speech flowed from his lips.

"By my faith," cried he, "yes, she is indeed my friend. It is a small matter now whether men slay me, or set me free; for I am made whole of my hurt just by looking on her face."

The Maiden entered in the palace—where none so fair had come before—and stood before the King, in the presence of his household. She loosed the clasp of her mantle, so that men might the more easily perceive the grace of her person. The courteous King advanced to meet her, and all the Court got them on their feet, and pained themselves in her service. When the lords had gazed upon her for a space, and praised the sum of her beauty, the lady spake to Arthur in this fashion, for she was anxious to begone.

"Sire, I have loved one of thy vassals,—the knight who stands in bonds, Sir Launfal. He was always misprized in thy Court, and his every action turned to blame. What he said, that thou knowest; for over hasty was his tongue before the Queen. But he never craved her in love, however loud his boasting. I cannot choose that he should come to hurt or harm by me. In the hope of freeing Launfal from his bonds, I have obeyed thy summons. Let now thy barons look boldly upon my face, and deal justly in this quarrel between the Queen and me."

The King commanded that this should be done, and looking upon her eyes, not one of the judges but was persuaded that her favour exceeded that of the Queen. Since then Launfal had not spoken in malice against his lady, the lords of the household gave him again his sword. When the trial had come thus to an end the

Maiden took her leave of the King, and made her ready to depart. Gladly would Arthur have had her lodge with him for a little, and many a lord would have rejoiced in her service, but she might not tarry. Now without the hall stood a great stone of dull marble, where it was the wont of lords, departing from the Court, to climb into the saddle, and Launfal by the stone. The Maiden came forth from the doors of the palace, and mounting on the stone, seated herself on the palfrey, behind her friend. Then they rode across the plain together, and were no more seen.

The Bretons tell that the knight was ravished by his lady to an island, very dim and very fair, known as Avalon. But none has had speech with Launfal and his faery love since then, and for my part I can tell you no more of the matter.

VII

THE LAY OF THE TWO LOVERS

ONCE upon a time there lived in Normandy two lovers, who were passing fond, and were brought by Love to Death. The story of their love was bruited so abroad, that the Bretons made a song in their own tongue, and named this song the Lay of the Two Lovers.

In Neustria—that men call Normandy—there is verily a high and marvellously great mountain, where lie the relics of the Two Children. Near this high place the King of those parts caused to be built a certain fair and cunning city, and since he was lord of the Pistrians, it was known as Pistres. The town yet endures, with its towers and houses, to bear witness to the truth; moreover the country thereabouts is known to us all as the Valley of Pistres.

This King had one fair daughter, a damsel sweet of face and gracious of manner, very near to her father's heart, since he had lost his Queen. The maiden increased in years and favour, but he took no heed to her trothing, so that men—yea, even his own people—blamed him greatly for this thing. When the King heard thereof he was passing heavy and dolent, and considered within himself how he might be delivered from this grief. So then, that none should carry off his child, he caused it to be proclaimed, both far and near, by script and trumpet, that he alone should wed the maid, who would bear her in his arms to the pinnacle of the great and perilous

77

mountain, and that without rest or stay. When this news was noised about the country, many came upon the quest. But strive as they would they might not enforce themselves more than they were able. However mighty they were of body, at the last they failed upon the mountain, and fell with their burthen to the ground. Thus, for a while, was none so bold as to seek the high Princess.

Now in this country lived a squire, son to a certain count of that realm, seemly of semblance and courteous, and right desirous to win that prize, which was so coveted of all. He was a welcome guest at the Court, and the King talked with him very willingly. This squire had set his heart upon the daughter of the King, and many a time spoke in her ear, praying her to give him again the love he had bestowed upon her. So seeing him brave and courteous, she esteemed him for the gifts which gained him the favour of the King, and they loved together in their youth. But they hid this matter from all about the Court. This thing was very grievous to them, but the damoiseau thought within himself that it were good to bear the pains he knew, rather than to seek out others that might prove sharper still. Yet in the end, altogether distraught by love, this prudent varlet sought his friend, and showed her his case, saying that he urgently required of her that she would flee with him, for no longer could he endure the weariness of his days. Should he ask her of the King, well he knew that by reason of his love he would refuse the gift, save he bore her in his arms up the steep mount. Then the maiden made answer to her lover, and said,

"Fair friend, well I know you may not carry me to that high place. Moreover should we take to flight, my father would suffer wrath and sorrow beyond measure, and go heavily all his days. Certainly my love is too fond to plague him thus, and we must seek another counsel, for this is not to my heart. Hearken well. I have kindred in Salerno, of rich estate. For more than thirty years my aunt has studied there the art of medicine, and knows the secret gift of every root and herb. If you hasten to her, bearing letters from me, and show her your adventure, certainly she will find counsel and cure. Doubt not that she will discover some cunning simple, that will strengthen your body, as well as comfort your heart. Then return to this realm with your potion, and ask me at my father's hand. He will deem you but a stripling, and set forth the terms of his bargain, that to him alone shall I be given who knows how to climb the perilous mountain, without pause or rest, bearing his lady between his arms."

When the varlet heard this cunning counsel of the maiden, he rejoiced greatly, and thanking her sweetly for her rede, craved permission to depart. He returned to his own home, and gathering together a goodly store of silken cloths most precious, he bestowed his gear upon the pack horses, and made him ready for the road. So with a little company of men, mounted on swift palfreys, and most privy to his mind, he arrived at Salerno. Now the squire made no long stay at his lodging, but as soon as he might, went to the damsel's kindred to open out his mind. He delivered to the aunt the letters he carried from his friend, and bewailed their evil case. When the dame had read these letters with him, line by line, she charged him to lodge with her awhile, till she might do according to his wish. So by her sorceries, and for the love of her maid, she brewed such a potion that no man, however wearied and outworn, but by drinking this philtre, would not

be refreshed in heart and blood and bones. Such virtue
had this medicine, directly it were drunken. This simple
she poured within a little flacket, and gave it to the
varlet, who received the gift with great joy and delight,
and returned swiftly to his own land.

The varlet made no long sojourn in his home. He
repaired straightway to the Court, and, seeking out the
King, required of him his fair daughter in marriage,
promising, for his part, that were she given him, he
would bear her in his arms to the summit of the mount.
The King was no wise wrath at his presumption. He
smiled rather at his folly, for how should one so young
and slender succeed in a business wherein so many
mighty men had failed. Therefore he appointed a
certain day for this judgment. Moreover he caused letters
to be written to his vassals and his friends—passing
none by—bidding them to see the end of this adventure.
Yea, with public cry and sound of trumpet he bade all
who would, come to behold the stripling carry his fair
daughter to the pinnacle of the mountain. And from
every region round about men came to learn the issue
of this thing. But for her part the fair maiden did all
that she was able to bring her love to a good end. Ever
was it fast day and fleshless day with her, so that by
any means she might lighten the burthen that her
friend must carry in his arms.

Now on the appointed day this young dansellon came
very early to the appointed place, bringing the flacket
with him. When the great company were fully met
together, the King led forth his daughter before them ;
and all might see that she was arrayed in nothing but
her smock. The varlet took the maiden in his arms,
but first he gave her the flask with the precious brewage
to carry, since for pride he might not endure to drink
therefrom, save at utmost peril. The squire set forth

at a great pace, and climbed briskly till he was half-way up the mount. Because of the joy he had in clasping his burthen, he gave no thought to the potion. But she—she knew the strength was failing in his heart.

"Fair friend," said she, "well I know that you tire : drink now, I pray you, of the flacket, and so shall your manhood come again at need."

But the varlet answered,

"Fair love, my heart is full of courage ; nor for any reason will I pause, so long as I can hold upon my way. It is the noise of all this folk—the tumult and the shouting—that makes my steps uncertain. Their cries distress me, I do not dare to stand."

But when two thirds of the course was won, the grass-hopper would have tripped him off his feet. Urgently and often the maiden prayed him, saying,

"Fair friend, drink now of thy cordial."

But he would neither hear, nor give credence to her words. A mighty anguish filled his bosom. He climbed upon the summit of the mountain, and pained himself grievously to bring his journey to an end. This he might not do. He reeled and fell, nor could he rise again, for the heart had burst within his breast.

When the maiden saw her lover's piteous plight, she deemed that he had swooned by reason of his pain. She kneeled hastily at his side, and put the enchanted brewage to his lips, but he could neither drink nor speak, for he was dead, as I have told you. She bewailed his evil lot, with many shrill cries, and flung the useless flacket far away. The precious potion bestrewed the ground, making a garden of that desolate place. For many saving herbs have been found there since that day by the simple folk of that country, which from the magic philtre derived all their virtue.

But when the maiden knew that her lover was dead, she made such wondrous sorrow, as no man had ever seen. She kissed his eyes and mouth, and falling upon his body, took him in her arms, and pressed him closely to her breast. There was no heart so hard as not to be touched by her sorrow; for in this fashion died a dame, who was fair and sweet and gracious, beyond the wont of the daughters of men.

Now the King and his company, since these two lovers came not again, presently climbed the mountain to learn their end. But when the King came upon them lifeless, and fast in that embrace, incontinent he fell to the ground, bereft of sense. After his speech had returned to him, he was passing heavy, and lamented their doleful case, and thus did all his people with him.

Three days they kept the bodies of these two fair children from earth, with uncovered face. On the third day they sealed them fast in a goodly coffin of marble, and by the counsel of all men, laid them softly to rest on that mountain where they died. Then they departed from them, and left them together, alone.

Since this adventure of the Two Children this hill is known as the Mountain of the Two Lovers, and their story being bruited abroad, the Breton folk have made a Lay thereof, even as I have rehearsed before you.

VIII

THE LAY OF THE WERE-WOLF

AMONGST the tales I tell you once again, I would not forget the Lay of the Were-Wolf. Such beasts as he are known in every land. Bisclavaret he is named in Brittany; whilst the Norman calls him Garwal.

It is a certain thing, and within the knowledge of all, that many a christened man has suffered this change, and ran wild in woods, as a Were-Wolf. The Were-Wolf is a fearsome beast. He lurks within the thick forest, mad and horrible to see. All the evil that he may, he does. He goeth to and fro, about the solitary place, seeking man, in order to devour him. Hearken, now, to the adventure of the Were-Wolf, that I have to tell.

In Brittany there dwelt a baron who was marvellously esteemed of all his fellows. He was a stout knight, and a comely, and a man of office and repute. Right private was he to the mind of his lord, and dear to the counsel of his neighbours. This baron was wedded to a very worthy dame, right fair to see, and sweet of semblance. All his love was set on her, and all her love was given again to him. One only grief had this lady. For three whole days in every week her lord was absent from her side. She knew not where he went, nor on what errand. Neither did any of his house know the business which called him forth.

On a day when this lord was come again to his house, altogether joyous and content, the lady took him to task, right sweetly, in this fashion,

"Husband," said she, " and fair, sweet friend, I have a certain thing to pray of you. Right willingly would I receive this gift, but I fear to anger you in the asking. It is better for me to have an empty hand, than to gain hard words."

When the lord heard this matter, he took the lady in his arms, very tenderly, and kissed her.

"Wife," he answered, " ask what you will. What would you have, for it is yours already ?"

"By my faith," said the lady, "soon shall I be whole. Husband, right long and wearisome are the days that you spend away from your home. I rise from my bed in the morning, sick at heart, I know not why. So fearful am I, lest you do aught to your loss, that I may not find any comfort. Very quickly shall I die for reason of my dread. Tell me now, where you go, and on what business ! How may the knowledge of one who loves so closely, bring you to harm ?"

"Wife," made answer the lord, " nothing but evil can come if I tell you this secret. For the mercy of God do not require it of me. If you but knew, you would withdraw yourself from my love, and I should be lost indeed."

When the lady heard this, she was persuaded that her baron sought to put her by with jesting words. Therefore she prayed and required him the more urgently, with tender looks and speech, till he was overborne, and told her all the story, hiding naught.

"Wife, I become Bisclavaret. I enter in the forest, and live on prey and roots, within the thickest of the wood."

After she had learned his secret, she prayed and entreated the more as to whether he ran in his raiment, or went spoiled of vesture.

"Wife," said he, "I go naked as a beast."

"Tell me, for hope of grace, what you do with your clothing?"

"Fair wife, that will I never. If I should lose my raiment, or even be marked as I quit my vesture, then a Were-Wolf I must go for all the days of my life. Never again should I become man, save in that hour my clothing were given back to me. For this reason never will I show my lair."

"Husband," replied the lady to him, "I love you better than all the world. The less cause have you for doubting my faith, or hiding any tittle from me. What savour is here of friendship? How have I made forfeit of your love; for what sin do you mistrust my honour? Open now your heart, and tell what is good to be known."

So at the end, outwearied and overborne by her importunity, he could no longer refrain, but told her all.

"Wife," said he, "within this wood, a little from the path, there is a hidden way, and at the end thereof an ancient chapel, where oftentimes I have bewailed my lot. Near by is a great hollow stone, concealed by a bush, and there is the secret place where I hide my raiment, till I would return to my own home."

On hearing this marvel the lady became sanguine of visage, because of her exceeding fear. She dared no longer to lie at his side, and turned over in her mind, this way and that, how best she could get her from him. Now there was a certain knight of those parts, who, for a great while, had sought and required this lady for her love. This knight had spent long years in her service, but little enough had he got thereby, not even fair words, or a promise. To him the dame wrote a letter, and meeting, made her purpose plain.

" Fair friend," said she, " be happy. That which you have coveted so long a time, I will grant without delay. Never again will I deny your suit. My heart, and all I have to give, are yours, so take me now as love and dame."

Right sweetly the knight thanked her for her grace, and pledged her faith and fealty. When she had confirmed him by an oath, then she told him all this business of her lord—why he went, and what he became, and of his ravening within the wood. So she showed him of the chapel, and of the hollow stone, and of how to spoil the Were-Wolf of his vesture. Thus, by the kiss of his wife, was Bisclavaret betrayed. Often enough had he ravished his prey in desolate places, but from this journey he never returned. His kinsfolk and acquaintance came together to ask of his tidings, when this absence was noised abroad. Many a man, on many a day, searched the woodland, but none might find him, nor learn where Bisclavaret was gone.

The lady was wedded to the knight who had cherished her for so long a space. More than a year had passed since Bisclavaret disappeared. Then it chanced that the King would hunt in that self-same wood where the Were-Wolf lurked. When the hounds were unleashed they ran this way and that, and swiftly came upon his scent. At the view the huntsman winded on his horn, and the whole pack were at his heels. They followed him from morn to eve, till he was torn and bleeding, and was all adread lest they should pull him down. Now the King was very close to the quarry, and when Bisclavaret looked upon his master, he ran to him for pity and for grace. He took the stirrup within his paws, and fawned upon the prince's foot. The King was very fearful at this sight, but presently he called his courtiers to his aid.

"Lords," cried he, "hasten hither, and see this marvellous thing. Here is a beast who has the sense of man. He abases himself before his foe, and cries for mercy, although he cannot speak. Beat off the hounds, and let no man do him harm. We will hunt no more to-day, but return to our own place, with the wonderful quarry we have taken."

The King turned him about, and rode to his hall, Bisclavaret following at his side. Very near to his master the Were-Wolf went, like any dog, and had no care to seek again the wood. When the King had brought him safely to his own castle, he rejoiced greatly, for the beast was fair and strong, no mightier had any man seen. Much pride had the King in his marvellous beast. He held him so dear, that he bade all those who wished for his love, to cross the Wolf in naught, neither to strike him with a rod, but ever to see that he was richly fed and kennelled warm. This commandment the Court observed willingly. So all the day the Wolf sported with the lords, and at night he lay within the chamber of the King. There was not a man who did not make much of the beast, so frank was he and debonair. None had reason to do him wrong, for ever was he about his master, and for his part did evil to none. Every day were these two companions together, and all perceived that the King loved him as his friend.

Hearken now to that which chanced.

The King held a high Court, and bade his great vassals and barons, and all the lords of his venery to the feast. Never was there a goodlier feast, nor one set forth with sweeter show and pomp. Amongst those who were bidden, came that same knight who had the wife of Bisclavaret for dame. He came to the castle, richly

gowned, with a fair company, but little he deemed
whom he would find so near. Bisclavaret marked his
foe the moment he stood within the hall. He ran
towards him, and seized him with his fangs, in the
King's very presence, and to the view of all. Doubtless
he would have done him much mischief, had not the
King called and chidden him, and threatened him with a
rod. Once, and twice, again, the Wolf set upon the
knight in the very light of day. All men marvelled at
his malice, for sweet and serviceable was the beast,
and to that hour had shown hatred of none. With one
consent the household deemed that this deed was done
with full reason, and that the Wolf had suffered at the
knight's hand some bitter wrong. Right wary of his
foe was the knight until the feast had ended, and all
the barons had taken farewell of their lord, and departed,
each to his own house. With these, amongst the very
first, went that lord whom Bisclavaret so fiercely had
assailed. Small was the wonder that he was glad to go.

No long while after this adventure it came to pass
that the courteous King would hunt in that forest where
Bisclavaret was found. With the prince came his wolf,
and a fair company. Now at nightfall the King abode
within a certain lodge of that country, and this was
known of that dame who before was the wife of Bisclavaret. In the morning the lady clothed her in her
most dainty apparel, and hastened to the lodge, since
she desired to speak with the King, and to offer him
a rich present. When the lady entered in the chamber,
neither man nor leash might restrain the fury of the Wolf.
He became as a mad dog in his hatred and malice.
Breaking from his bonds he sprang at the lady's face,
and bit the nose from her visage. From every side
men ran to the succour of the dame. They beat off
the wolf from his prey, and for a little would have cut

him in pieces with their swords. But a certain wise
counsellor said to the King,

"Sire, hearken now to me. This beast is always
with you, and there is not one of us all who has not
known him for long. He goes in and out amongst us,
nor has molested any man, neither done wrong or felony
to any, save only to this dame, one only time as we have
seen. He has done evil to this lady, and to that knight,
who is now the husband of the dame. Sire, she was
once the wife of that lord who was so close and private
to your heart, but who went, and none might find where
he had gone. Now, therefore, put the dame in a sure
place, and question her straitly, so that she may tell—
if perchance she knows thereof—for what reason this
Beast holds her in such mortal hate. For many a strange
deed has chanced, as well we know, in this marvellous
land of Brittany."

The King listened to these words, and deemed the
counsel good. He laid hands upon the knight, and put
the dame in surety in another place. He caused them
to be questioned right straitly, so that their torment
was very grievous. At the end, partly because of her
distress, and partly by reason of her exceeding fear,
the lady's lips were loosed, and she told her tale. She
showed them of the betrayal of her lord, and how his
raiment was stolen from the hollow stone. Since then
she knew not where he went, nor what had befallen
him, for he had never come again to his own land.
Only, in her heart, well she deemed and was persuaded,
that Bisclavaret was he.

Straightway the King demanded the vesture of his
baron, whether this were to the wish of the lady, or
whether it were against her wish. When the raiment
was brought him, he caused it to be spread before
Bisclavaret, but the Wolf made as though he had not

seen. Then that cunning and crafty counsellor took the King apart, that he might give him a fresh rede.

"Sire," said he, "you do not wisely, nor well, to set this raiment before Bisclavaret, in the sight of all. In shame and much tribulation must he lay aside the beast, and again become man. Carry your wolf within your most secret chamber, and put his vestment therein. Then close the door upon him, and leave him alone for a space. So we shall see presently whether the ravening beast may indeed return to human shape."

The King carried the Wolf to his chamber, and shut the doors upon him fast. He delayed for a brief while, and taking two lords of his fellowship with him, came again to the room. Entering therein, all three, softly together, they found the knight sleeping in the King's bed, like a little child. The King ran swiftly to the bed and taking his friend in his arms, embraced and kissed him fondly, above a hundred times. When man's speech returned once more, he told him of his adventure. Then the King restored to his friend the fief that was stolen from him, and gave such rich gifts, moreover, as I cannot tell. As for the wife who had betrayed Bisclavaret, he bade her avoid his country, and chased her from the realm. So she went forth, she and her second lord together, to seek a more abiding city, and were no more seen.

The adventure that you have heard is no vain fable. Verily and indeed it chanced as I have said. The Lay of the Were-Wolf, truly, was written that it should ever be borne in mind.

IX

THE LAY OF THE ASH TREE

Now will I tell you the Lay of the Ash Tree, according to the story that I know.

In ancient days there dwelt two knights in Brittany, who were neighbours and close friends. These two lords were brave and worthy gentlemen, rich in goods and lands, and near both in heart and home. Moreover each was wedded to a dame. One of these ladies was with child, and when her time was come, she was delivered of two boys. Her husband was right happy and content. For the joy that was his, he sent messages to his neighbour, telling that his wife had brought forth two sons, and praying that one of them might be christened with his name. The rich man was at meat when the messenger came before him. The servitor kneeled before the daïs, and told his message in his ear. The lord thanked God for the happiness that had befallen his friend, and bestowed a fair horse on the bringer of good tidings. His wife, sitting at board with her husband, heard the story of the messenger, and smiled at his news. Proud she was, and sly, with an envious heart, and a rancorous tongue. She made no effort to bridle her lips, but spoke lightly before the servants of the house, and said,

" I marvel greatly that so reputable a man as our neighbour, should publish his dishonour to my lord. It is a shameful thing for any wife to have two children at a birth. We all know that no woman brings forth two at one bearing, except two husbands have aided her therein."

Her husband looked upon her in silence for awhile, and when he spoke it was to blame her very sternly.

"Wife," he said, "be silent. It is better to be dumb, than to utter such words as these. As you know well, there is not a breath to tarnish this lady's good name."

The folk of the house, who listened to these words, stored them in their hearts, and told abroad the tale, spoken by their lady. Very soon it was known throughout Brittany. Greatly was the lady blamed for her evil tongue, and not a woman who heard thereof—whether she were rich or poor—but who scorned her for her malice. The servant who carried the message, on his return repeated to his lord of what he had seen and heard. Passing heavy was the knight, and knew not what to do. He doubted his own true wife, and suspected her the more sorely, because she had done naught that was in any way amiss.

The lady, who so foully slandered her fellow, fell with child in the same year. Her neighbour was avenged upon her, for when her term was come, she became the mother of two daughters. Sick at heart was she. She was right sorrowful, and lamented her evil case.

"Alas," she said, "what shall I do, for I am dishonoured for all my days. Shamed I am, it is the simple truth. When my lord and his kinsfolk shall hear of what has chanced, they will never believe me a stainless wife. They will remember how I judged all women in my plight. They will recall how I said before my house, that my neighbour could not have been doubly a mother, unless she had first been doubly a wife. I have the best reason now to know that I was wrong, and I am caught in my own snare. She who digs a pit for another,

cannot tell that she may not fall into the hole herself.
If you wish to speak loudly concerning your neighbour,
it is best to say nothing of him but in praise. The only
way to keep me from shame, is that one of my children
should die. It is a great sin ; but I would rather trust
to the mercy of God, than suffer scorn and reproach for
the rest of my life."

The women about her comforted her as best they
might in this trouble. They told her frankly that they
would not suffer such wrong to be done, since the slaying
of a child was not reckoned a jest. The lady had a
maiden near her person, whom she had long held and
nourished. The damsel was a freeman's daughter, and
was greatly loved and cherished of her mistress. When
she saw the lady's tears, and heard the bitterness of
her complaint, anguish went to her heart, like a knife.
She stooped over her lady, striving to bring her comfort.

" Lady," she said, " take it not so to heart. Give
over this grief, for all will yet be well. You shall deliver
me one of these children, and I will put her so far from
you, that you shall never see her again, nor know shame
because of her. I will carry her safe and sound to the
door of a church. There I will lay her down. Some
honest man shall find her, and—please God—will be
at the cost of her nourishing."

Great joy had the lady to hear these words. She
promised the maiden that in recompense of her service,
she would grant her such guerdon as she should wish.
The maiden took the babe—yet smiling in her sleep—
and wrapped her in a linen cloth. Above this she set
a piece of sanguine silk, brought by the husband of
this dame from a bazaar in Constantinople—fairer was
never seen. With a silken lace they bound a great ring
to the child's arm. This ring was of fine gold, weighing
fully an ounce, and was set with garnets most precious.

Letters were graven thereon, so that those who found the maid might understand that she came of a good house. The damsel took the child, and went out from the chamber. When night was come, and all was still, she left the town, and sought the high road leading through the forest. She held on her way, clasping the baby to her breast, till from afar, to her right hand, she heard the howling of dogs and the crowing of cocks. She deemed that she was near a town, and went the lighter for the hope, directing her steps, there, whence the noises came. Presently the damsel entered in a fair city, where was an Abbey, both great and rich. This Abbey was worshipfully ordered, with many nuns in their office and degree, and an Abbess in charge of all. The maiden gazed upon the mighty house, and considered its towers and walls, and the church with its belfry. She went swiftly to the door, and setting the child upon the ground, kneeled humbly to make her prayer.

"Lord," said she, "for the sake of Thy Holy Name, if such be Thy will, preserve this child from death."

Her petition ended, the maiden looked about her, and saw an ash tree, planted to give shadow in a sunny place. It was a fair tree, thick and leafy, and was divided into four strong branches. The maiden took the child again in her arms, and running to the ash, set her within the tree. There she left her, commending her to the care of God. So she returned to her mistress, and told her all that she had done.

Now in this Abbey was a porter, whose duty it was to open the doors of the church, before folk came to hear the service of God. This night he rose at his accustomed hour, lighted candles and lamps, rang the bells, and set wide the doors. His eyes fell upon the silken stuff within the ash. He thought at first that some

The Lay of the Ash Tree 95

bold thief had hidden his spoil within the tree. He felt
with his hand to discover what it might be, and found
that it was a little child. The porter praised God for
His goodness ; he took the babe, and going again to his
house, called to his daughter, who was a widow, with an
infant yet in the cradle.

"Daughter," he cried, " get from bed at once ; light
your candle, and kindle the fire. I bring you a little
child, whom I have found within our ash. Take her
to your breast ; cherish her against the cold, and bathe
her in warm water."

The widow did according to her father's will. She
kindled a fire, and taking the babe, washed and cherished
her in her need. Very certain she was, when she saw
that rich stuff of crimson samite, and the golden ring
about the arm, that the girl was come of an honourable
race. The next day, when the office was ended, the
porter prayed the Abbess that he might have speech
with her as she left the church. He related his story,
and told of the finding of the child. The Abbess bade
him to fetch the child, dressed in such fashion as she
was discovered in the ash. The porter returned to his
house, and showed the babe right gladly to his dame.
The Abbess observed the infant closely, and said that
she would be at the cost of her nourishing, and would
cherish her as a sister's child. She commanded the
porter strictly to forget that he took her from the ash.
In this manner it chanced that the maiden was tended
of the Abbess. The lady considered the maid as her
niece, and since she was taken from the ash, gave her
the name of Frêne. By this name she was known of all,
within the Abbey precincts, where she was nourished.

When Frêne came to that age in which a girl turns to
woman, there was no fairer maiden in Brittany, nor
so sweet a damsel. Frank, she was, and open, but

discreet in semblance and in speech.   To see her was to
love her, and to prize her smile above the beauty of
the world.   Now at Dol there lived a lord of whom much
good was spoken.   I will tell you his name.   The folk
of his country called him Buron.   This lord heard speak
of the maiden, and began to love her, for the sweetness
men told of her.   As he rode home from some tournament, he passed near the convent, and prayed the Abbess
that he might look upon her niece.   The Abbess gave
him his desire.   Greatly was the maiden to his mind.
Very fair he found her, sweetly schooled and fashioned,
modest and courteous to all.   If he might not win her
to his love, he counted himself the more forlorn.   This
lord was at his wits end, for he knew not what to do.
If he repaired often to the convent, the Abbess would
consider of the cause of his comings, and he would never
again see the maiden with his eyes.   One thing only
gave him a little hope.   Should he endow the Abbey
of his wealth, he would make it his debtor for ever.
In return he might ask a little room, where he might
abide to have their fellowship, and, at times, withdraw
him from the world.   This he did.   He gave richly of
his goods to the Abbey.   Often, in return, he went to
the convent, but for other reasons than for penitence
and peace.   He besought the maiden, and with prayers
and promises, persuaded her to set upon him her love.
When this lord was assured that she loved him, on a
certain day he reasoned with her in this manner.

" Fair friend," said he, " since you have given me
your love, come with me, where I can cherish you
before all the world.   You know, as well as I, that if
your aunt should perceive our friendship, she would
be passing wrath, and grieve beyond measure.   If my
counsel seems good, let us flee together, you with me,
and I with you.   Certes, you shall never have cause to

regret your trust, and of my riches you shall have the half."

When she who loved so fondly heard these words, she granted of her tenderness what it pleased him to have, and followed after where he would. Frêne fled to her lover's castle, carrying with her that silken cloth and ring, which might do her service on a day. These the Abbess had given her again, telling her how one morning at prime she was found upon an ash, this ring and samite her only wealth, since she was not her niece. Right carefully had Frêne guarded her treasure from that hour. She shut them closely in a little chest, and this coffret she bore with her in her flight, for she would neither lose them nor forget.

The lord, with whom the maiden fled, loved and cherished her very dearly. Of all the men and servants of his house, there was not one—either great or small—but who loved and honoured her for her simplicity. They lived long together in love and content, till the fair days passed, and trouble came upon this lord. The knights of his realm drew together, and many a time urged that he should put away his friend, and wed with some rich gentlewoman. They would be joyous if a son were born, to come after to his fief and heritage. The peril was too great to suffer that he remained a bachelor, and without an heir. Never more would they hold him as lord, or serve him with a good heart, if he would not do according to their will.

There being naught else to do, the lord deferred to this counsel of his knights, and begged them to name the lady whom he needs must wed.

" Sir," answered they, " there is a lord of these parts, privy to our counsel, who has but one child, a maid, his only heir. Broad lands will he give as her dowry. This damsel's name is Coudre, and in all this country

there is none so fair. Be advised : throw away the
ash rod you carry, and take the hazel as your staff.[1]
The ash is a barren stock ; but the hazel is thick with
nuts and delight. We shall be content if you take this
maiden as your wife, so it be to the will of God, and
she be given you of her kinsfolk."

Buron demanded the hand of the lady in marriage,
and her father and kin betrothed her to the lord. Alas !
it was hid from all, that these two were twin sisters.
It was Frêne's lot to be doubly abandoned, and to see
her lover become her sister's husband. When she
learned that her friend purposed taking to himself a
wife, she made no outcry against his falseness. She
continued to serve her lord faithfully, and was diligent
in the business of his house. The sergeant and the varlet
were marvellously wrathful, when they knew that she
must go from amongst them. On the day appointed for
the marriage, Buron bade his friends and acquaintance
to the feast. Together with these came the Archbishop,
and those of Dol who held of him their lands. His
betrothed was brought to his home by her mother.
Great dread had the mother because of Frêne, for she
knew of the love that the lord bore the maiden, and
feared lest her daughter should be a stranger in her own
hall. She spoke to her son-in-law, counselling him to
send Frêne from his house, and to find her an honest
man for her husband. Thus there would be quittance
between them. Very splendid was the feast. Whilst
all was mirth and jollity, the damsel visited the chambers,
to see that each was ordered to her lord's pleasure.
She hid the torment in her heart, and seemed neither
troubled nor downcast. She compassed the bride with
every fair observance, and waited upon her right daintily.

[1] This is a play on words; Frêne in the French, meaning ash, and Coudre
meaning hazel.

Her courage was marvellous to that company of lords and ladies, who observed her curiously. The mother of the bride regarded her also, and praised her privily. She said aloud that had she known the sweetness of this lady, she would not have taken her lover from her, nor spoiled her life for the sake of the bride. The night being come the damsel entered in the bridal chamber to deck the bed against her lord. She put off her mantle, and calling the chamberlains, showed them how their master loved to lie. His bed being softly arrayed, a coverlet was spread upon the linen sheets. Frêne looked upon the coverlet: in her eyes it showed too mean a garnishing for so fair a lord. She turned it over in her mind, and going to her coffret she took therefrom that rich stuff of sanguine silk, and set it on the couch. This she did not only in honour of her friend, but that the Archbishop might not despise the house, when he blessed the marriage bed, according to the rite. When all was ready the mother carried the bride to that chamber where she should lie, to disarray her for the night. Looking upon the bed she marked the silken coverlet, for she had never seen so rich a cloth, save only that in which she wrapped her child. When she remembered of this thing, her heart turned to water. She summoned a chamberlain.

"Tell me," she said, "tell me in good faith where this garniture was found."

"Lady," he made reply, "that you shall know. Our damsel spread it on the bed, because this dossal is richer than the coverlet that was there before."

The lady called for the damsel. Frêne came before her in haste, being yet without her mantle. All the mother moved within her, as she plied her with questions.

"Fair friend, hide it not a whit from me. Tell me truly where this fair samite was found; whence came it ; who gave it to you ? Answer swiftly, and tell me who bestowed on you this cloth ? "

The damsel made answer to her:

" Lady, my aunt, the Abbess, gave me this silken stuff, and charged me to keep it carefully. At the same time she gave me a ring, which those who put me forth, had bound upon me."

" Fair friend, may I see this ring ? "

" Certes, lady, I shall be pleased to show it."

The lady looked closely on the ring, when it was brought. She knew again her own, and the crimson samite flung upon the bed. No doubt was in her mind. She knew and was persuaded that Frêne was her very child. All words were spoken, and there was nothing more to hide.

" Thou art my daughter, fair friend."

Then for reason of the pity that was hers, she fell to the ground, and lay in a swoon. When the lady came again to herself, she sent for her husband, who, all adread, hastened to the chamber. He marvelled the more sorely when his wife fell at his feet, and embracing him closely, entreated pardon for the evil that she had done.

Knowing nothing of her trespass, he made reply,

" Wife, what is this ? Between you and me there is nothing to call for forgiveness. Pardon you may have for whatever fault you please. Tell me plainly what is your wish."

" Husband, my offence is so black, that you had better give me absolution before I tell you the sin. A long time ago, by reason of lightness and malice, I spoke evil of my neighbour, whenas she bore two sons at a birth. I fell afterwards into the very pit that I had digged. Though I told you that I was delivered of a daughter, the truth is that I had borne two maids. One of these I wrapped in our stuff of samite, together with the ring you gave me the first time we met, and caused her to be laid beside a church.   Such a sin will out.   The cloth and the ring I have found, and I have recognised our maid, whom I had lost by my own folly.   She is this very damsel—so fair and amiable to all—whom the knight so greatly loved. Now we have married the lord to her sister."

The husband made answer,

" Wife, if your sin be double, our joy is manifold. Very tenderly hath God dealt with us, in giving us back our child.   I am altogether joyous and content to have two daughters for one.   Daughter, come to your father's side."

The damsel rejoiced greatly to hear this story.   Her father tarried no longer, but seeking his son-in-law, brought him to the Archbishop, and related the adventure.   The knight knew such joy as was never yet.   The Archbishop gave counsel that on the morrow he would part him and her whom he had joined together.   This was done, for in the morning he severed them, bed and board.   Afterwards he married Frêne to her friend, and her father accorded the damsel with a right good heart. Her mother and sister were with her at the wedding, and for dowry her father gave her the half of his heritage. When they returned to their own realm they took Coudre, their daughter, with them.   There she was granted to a lord of those parts, and rich was the feast.

When this adventure was bruited abroad, and all the story, the Lay of the Ash Tree was written, so called of the lady, named Frêne.

X

THE LAY OF THE HONEYSUCKLE

W<small>ITH</small> a glad heart and right good mind will I tell the
Lay that men call Honeysuckle; and that the truth may
be known of all it shall be told as many a minstrel has
sung it to my ear, and as the scribe hath written it
for our delight. It is of Tristan and Isoude, the Queen.
It is of a love which passed all other love, of love from
whence came wondrous sorrow, and whereof they died
together in the self-same day.

King Mark was sorely wrath with Tristan, his sister's
son, and bade him avoid his realm, by reason of the
love he bore the Queen. So Tristan repaired to his own
land, and dwelt for a full year in South Wales, where
he was born. Then since he might not come where
he would be, Tristan took no heed to his ways, but
let his life run waste to Death. Marvel not overmuch
thereat, for he who loves beyond measure must ever
be sick in heart and hope, when he may not win according
to his wish. So sick in heart and mind was Tristan that
he left his kingdom, and returned straight to the realm
of his banishment, because that in Cornwall dwelt the
Queen. There he hid privily in the deep forest, withdrawn from the eyes of men; only when the evening
was come, and all things sought their rest, he prayed
the peasant and other mean folk of that country, of their
charity to grant him shelter for the night. From the
serf he gathered tidings of the King. These gave again

to him what they, in turn, had taken from some outlawed knight. Thus Tristan learned that when Pentecost
was come King Mark purposed to hold high Court at
Tintagel, and keep the feast with pomp and revelry;
moreover that thither would ride Isoude, the Queen.

When Tristan heard this thing he rejoiced greatly,
since the Queen might not adventure through the forest,
except he saw her with his eyes. After the King had
gone his way, Tristan entered within the wood, and
sought the path by which the Queen must come. There
he cut a wand from out a certain hazel-tree, and having
trimmed and peeled it of its bark, with his dagger he
carved his name upon the wood. This he placed upon
her road, for well he knew that should the Queen but
mark his name she would bethink her of her friend.
Thus had it chanced before. For this was the sum of
the writing set upon the wand, for Queen Isoude's heart
alone : how that in this wild place Tristan had lurked
and waited long, so that he might look upon her face,
since without her he was already dead. Was it not with
them as with the Honeysuckle and the Hazel tree she
was passing by ! So sweetly laced and taken were they
in one close embrace, that thus they might remain
whilst life endured. But should rough hands part so
fond a clasping, the hazel would wither at the root,
and the honeysuckle must fail. Fair friend, thus is
the case with us, nor you without me, nor I without you.

Now the Queen fared at adventure down the forest
path. She spied the hazel wand set upon her road, and
well she remembered the letters and the name. She bade
the knights of her company to draw rein, and dismount
from their palfreys, so that they might refresh themselves a little. When her commandment was done she
withdrew from them a space, and called to her Brang-
waine, her maiden, and own familiar friend. Then she

hastened within the wood, to come on him whom more she loved than any living soul. How great the joy between these twain, that once more they might speak together softly, face to face. Isoude showed him her delight. She showed in what fashion she strove to bring peace and concord betwixt Tristan and the King, and how grievously his banishment had weighed upon her heart. Thus sped the hour, till it was time for them to part ; but when these lovers freed them from the other's arms, the tears were wet upon their cheeks. So Tristan returned to Wales, his own realm, even as his uncle bade. But for the joy that he had had of her, his friend, for her sweet face, and for the tender words that she had spoken, yea, and for that writing upon the wand, to remember all these things, Tristan, that cunning harper, wrought a new Lay, as shortly I have told you. Goatleaf, men call this song in English. Chèvrefeuille it is named in French ; but Goatleaf or Honeysuckle, here you have the very truth in the Lay that I have spoken.

XI

THE LAY OF EQUITAN

In ancient days many a noble lord lived in Brittany
beyond the Seas. By reason of their courtesy and nobleness they would gladly keep in remembrance the deeds
that were done in the land. That these marvellous
things should not be forgotten they fashioned them into
Lays. Amongst these Lays I have heard tell of one
which is not made to die as though it had never been.

Equitan, lord of Nantes, was a loyal and courteous
gentleman, of great worth, beloved by all in his own
country. He was set on pleasure, and was Love's lover,
as became a gentle knight. Like many others who dote
on woman, he observed neither sense nor measure in
love. But it is in the very nature of Love that pro-
portion cannot enter into the matter.

Equitan had for seneschal a right brave and loyal
knight, who was captain of his army, and did justice
in his realm. He was often abroad upon his master's
business, for the King would not forego his delight for
any reason whatever. To dance, to hunt, to fish within
the river—this was all his joy. This seneschal was married
to a wife, by whom great evil came upon the land.
Very desirable was the lady ; passing tender of body,
and sweet of vesture, coiffed and fretted with gold. Her
eyes were blue ; her face warmly coloured, with a
fragrant mouth, and a dainty nose. Certainly she had
no peer in all the realm. The King had heard much

in praise of this lady and many a time saluted her upon
the way. He had also sent her divers gifts. Often he
considered in his mind how best he might get speech
with the dame. For his privy pleasure this amorous
King went to chase in that country where the seneschal
had his castle. The lady being in her own house,
Equitan craved a lodging for the night. By this means
when the hunt was done, he could speak with her, and
show what was in his heart. Equitan found the lady
as discreet as courteous. He looked closely upon her,
for she was fair of face and person, and sweet of semblance and address. Love bound him captive to his
car. The god loosed a shaft which entered deeply in his
breast. The arrow pierced to his heart, and from thence-
forth he cared nothing for measure, or kingship, or
delight. Equitan was so surprised of the lady, that he
remained silent and pensive. He heard nothing, and
nothing he could do. All night he lay in unrest upon
the bed, reproaching himself for what had come to pass.

" Alas," said he, " what evil fate has led me into
this land ! The sight only of this lady has put such
anguish into my heart that my members fail beneath
me. It is Love, I deem, who rides me thus cruelly.
But if I love this lady I shall do a great wrong. She
is the wife of my seneschal, and it is my duty to keep
the same love and faith to him as I would wish him
to observe with me. If by any means I could know
what is in her mind, I should be the easier, for torment
is doubled that you bear alone. There is not a dame,
however curst, but would rather love than not; for if
she were a contemner of love where would be her courtesy ? But if she loves, there is not a woman under the
sky who would not suck thereout all the advantage
that she may. If the matter came to the ears of the
seneschal, he ought not to think too hardly of me. He

cannot hope to keep such treasure for himself alone; and, certes, I shall claim my portion."

Equitan tossed on his bed, and sighed. His thoughts were still on the lady, so that in a little he said,

"I think of the ford, before I come to the river. I go too quickly, for I know not yet whether the lady will take me as her friend. But know I will as swiftly as I can, since I cannot get rest or sleep. I will come before her as soon as it is day, and if she feels as I feel, the sooner I shall be rid of my pain."

The King kept vigil till the daylight came at last. He arose and went forth, as if to the chase. He returned presently, telling that he was sick, and going straight to his chamber, lay upon his bed. The seneschal was very troubled, for he could not imagine the sickness of which his master felt the pangs. He counselled his wife to seek their guest, that she might cheer and comfort him in his trouble. When they were alone the King opened to her his heart. He told her that he was dying for her love, and that if she had no more than friendship to offer, he preferred death before life.

"Sire," replied the dame, "I require a little time to think of what you say, for I cannot answer yes or no, without thought, in a business of this moment. I am not of your wealth, and you are too high a lord, for your love to do more than rest lightly on me. When you have had your desire, it will as lightly fly away. My sorrow would be overlong, if I should love you, and grant you what you wish. It is much the best that between you and me love should not be spoken of. You are a puissant prince; my husband is one of your vassals, and faith and trust should bind us—not the dangerous bond of love. Love is only lasting between like and like. Better is the love of an honest man— so he be of sense and worth—than that of a prince or king, with no loyalty in him. She who sets her love more highly than she can reach, may pluck no fruit from the tree. The rich man deems that love is his of right. He prays little of his friend, for he thinks none dare take her from his hand, and that her tenderness is his by prize of lordship."

When she had ceased, Equitan made answer,

"Lady, I can offer you but short thanks for your words, since they savour of scant courtesy. You speak of love as a burgess makes a bargain. Those who desire to get, rather than to give, often find that they have the worser half of the business. There is no lady under heaven—so she be courteous and kind and of a good heart—but would grant her grace to a true lover, even though she have beneath her cloak only a rich prince in his castle. Those who care but for a fresh face—tricksters in love as a cozener with dice—are justly flouted and deceived, as oftentimes we see. None wastes pity on him who receives the stripes he deserves. Dear lady, let me make myself plain. Do not regard me as your King; look on me as your servant and your friend. I give my word and plight my troth that all my happiness shall be found in your pleasure. Let me not die for your love. You shall be the Dame, and I the page; you shall be the scornful beauty, and I the prayer at your knee."

The King prayed the lady so urgently, so tenderly he sued for grace, that at the last she assured him of her love, and gave him the gift of her heart. They granted rings one to another, and pledged affiance between them. They kept this faith, and guarded this love, till they died together, and there was an end to all.

Equitan and the lady loved for a great while without it coming to the ears of any. When the King desired to have speech of his friend, he told his household that he would be alone, since it was the day appointed for his bleeding. The King having shut the doors of his chamber, there was none so bold as to enter therein, save he were bidden of his lord. Whilst he was busied in this fashion, the seneschal sat in open court to hear the pleas and right the wrong. He was as much to the King's mind, as his wife was to the King's heart. The lord was so assotted upon the lady that he would neither take to himself a wife, nor listen to a word upon the matter. His people blamed him loudly, so loudly that it came to the ears of the lady. She was passing heavy, for she feared greatly that the barons would have their way. When next she had speech with Equitan, in place of the kiss and sweetness of her customary greeting, she came before him making great sorrow and in tears. The King inquiring the reason of her dolour, the lady replied,

"Sire, I lament our love, and the trouble I always said would be mine. You are about to wed the daughter of some King, and my good days are over. Everybody says so, and I know it to be true. What will become of me when you put me away! I will die, rather than lose you, for I may have no other comfort."

The King made answer very tenderly,

"Fair friend, you need not fear. There will never be wife of mine to put you from me. I shall never wed, except your husband die, and then it is you who would be my queen and lady. I will leave you for no other dame."

The lady thanked him sweetly for his words. Much was she beholden to him in her heart. Since she was assured that he would not leave her for any other, she turned over swiftly in her mind the profit that would come from her husband's death. Much happiness might be bought at a little cost, if Equitan would lend his aid.

The King made answer that he would do her will to the utmost of his power, whether her counsel were for good or evil.

"Sire," said the lady, "let it please you to hunt the forest within the country where I dwell. You can lodge in my lord's castle, and there you must be bled. Three days after your surgery is done, you must call for your bath. My lord shall be bled with you, so that he may go to his bathing at the same time. It will be your part to keep him at your side, and make him your constant companion. It will be mine to heat the water, and to carry the baths to your chamber. My husband's bath shall boil so fiercely, that no breathing man, having entered therein, may come forth living. When he is dead you must call for your people, and show them how the seneschal has died suddenly in his bath."

Because of his love the King granted her desire, and promised to do according to her will. Before three months were done the King rode to the chase within the lady's realm. He caused surgeons to bleed him for his health, and the seneschal with him. He said that he would take his bath on the third day, and the seneschal required his, too, to be made ready. The lady caused the water to be heated, and carried the baths to the chamber. According to her device she set a bath beside each bed, filling with boiling water that bath which her lord should enter. Her lord had gone forth for a little, so for a space the King and the lady were alone. They sat on the husband's bed, and looked tenderly each on the other, near by that heated bath. The door of the chamber was kept by a young damsel to give them warning. The seneschal made haste to return, and would have struck on the door of the chamber, but was stayed by the maiden. He put her by, and in his impatience flung the door wide open. Entering he found his master and his wife clasped in each other's arms. When the King saw the seneschal he had no thought but to hide his dishonour. He started up, and sprang with joined feet in the bath that was filled with boiling water. There he perished miserably, in the very snare he had spread for another, who was safe and sound. The seneschal marked what had happened to the King. In his rage he turned to his wife, and laying hands upon her thrust her, head first, in the self-same bath. So they died together, the King first, and the lady afterwards, with him.

Those who are willing to listen to fair words, may learn from this ensample, that he who seeks another's ill often brings the evil upon himself.

As I have told you before, of this adventure the Bretons made the Lay of Equitan, the lady whom he loved, and of their end.

XII

THE LAY OF MILON

He who would tell divers tales must know how to vary
the tune. To win the favour of any, he must speak to
the understanding of all. I purpose in this place to
show you the story of Milon, and—since few words are
best—I will set out the adventure as briefly as I may.

Milon was born in South Wales. So great was his
prowess that from the day he was dubbed knight there
was no champion who could stand before him in the lists.
He was a passing fair knight, open and brave, courteous
to his friends, and stern to his foes. Men praised his
name in whatever realm they talked of gallant deeds—
Ireland, Norway, and Wales, yea, from Jutland even
to Albania. Since he was praised by the frank, he was
therefore envied of the mean. Nevertheless, by reason of
his skill with the spear, he was counted a very worshipful
knight, and was honourably entreated by many a prince
in divers lands.

In Milon's own realm there lived a lord whose name
has gone from mind. With this baron dwelt his daughter,
a passing fair and gracious damsel. Much talk had this
maiden heard of Milon's knightly deeds, so that she
began to set her thoughts upon him, because of the good
men spoke of him. She sent him a message by a sure
hand, saying that if her love was to his mind, sweetly
would it be to her heart. Milon rejoiced greatly when
he knew this thing. He thanked the lady for her words,

giving her love again in return for her own, and swearing
that he would never depart therefrom any day of his days.
Beyond this courteous answer Milon bestowed on the messenger costly gifts, and made him promises that were
richer still.

" Friend," said he, " of your charity I pray you that I
may have speech with my friend, in such a fashion
that none shall know of our meeting.   Carry her this, my
golden ring.   Tell her, on my part, that so she pleases she
shall come to me, or, if it be her better pleasure, I will go
to her."

The messenger bade farewell, and returned to his lady.
He placed the ring in her hand, saying that he had
done her will, as he was bidden to do.

Right joyous was the damsel to know that Milon's love
was tender as her own.   She required her friend to come
for speech within the private garden of her house, where
she was wont to take her delight.   Milon came at her
commandment.   He came so often, and so dearly she
loved him, that in the end she gave him all that maid may
give.   When the damsel perceived how it was with her,
she sent messages to her friend, telling him of her case,
and making great sorrow.

" I have lost my father and all his wealth," said the
lady, " for when he hears of this matter he will make
of me an example.   Either I shall be tormented with
the sword, or else he will sell me as a slave in a far
country."

(For such was the usage of our fathers in the days
of this tale).

Milon grieved sorely, and made answer that he would
do the thing the damsel thought most seemly to be done.

" When the child is born," replied the lady, " you must
carry him forthwith to my sister.   She is a rich dame,
pitiful and good, and is wedded to a lord of North-

umberland. You will send messages with the babe—both
in writing and by speech—that the little innocent is her
sister's child. Whether it be a boy or girl his mother will
have suffered much because of him, and for her sister's
sake you will pray her to cherish the babe. Beyond this
I shall set your signet by a lace about his neck, and write
letters wherein shall be made plain the name of his sire,
and the sad story of his mother. When he shall have
grown tall, and of an age to understand these matters,
his aunt will give him your ring, and rehearse to him the
letter. If this be done, perchance the orphan will not be
fatherless all his days."

Milon approved the counsel of the lady, and when her
time had come she was brought to bed of a boy. The old
nurse who tended her mistress was privy to the damsel's
inmost mind. So warily she went to work, so cunning was
she in gloss and concealment, that none within the palace
knew that there was aught to hide. The damsel looked
upon her boy, and saw that he was very fair. She laced
the ring about his neck, and set the letter that it were
death to find, within a silken chatelaine. The child
was then placed in his cradle, swathed close in white
linen. A pillow of feathers was put beneath his head,
and over all was laid a warm coverlet, wadded with
fur. In this fashion the ancient nurse gave the babe to
his father, who awaited him within the garden. Milon
commended the child to his men, charging them to carry
him loyally, by such towns as they knew, to that lady
beyond the Humber. The servitors set forth, bearing the
infant with them. Seven times a day they reposed them
in their journey, so that the women might nourish the
babe, and bathe and tend him duly. They served their
lord so faithfully, keeping such watch upon the way,
that at the last they won to the lady to whom they
were bidden. The lady received them courteously, as

became her breeding. She broke the seal of the letter, and when she was assured of what was therein, marvellously she cherished the infant. These having bestowed the boy in accordance with their lord's commandment, returned to their own land.

Milon went forth from his realm to serve beyond the seas for guerdon. His friend remained within her house and was granted by her father in marriage to a right rich baron of that country. Though this baron was a worthy knight, justly esteemed of all his fellows, the damsel was grieved beyond measure when she knew her father's will. She called to mind the past, and regretted that Milon had gone from the country, since he would have helped her in her need.

"Alas!" said the lady, "what shall I do? I doubt that I am lost, for my lord will find that his bride is not a maid. If this becomes known they will make me a bondwoman for all my days. Would that my friend were here to free me from this coil. It were good for me to die rather than to live, but by no means can I escape from their hands. They have set warders about me, men, old and young, whom they call my chamberlains, contemners of love, who delight themselves in sadness. But endure it I must, for, alas, I know not how to die."

So on the appointed day the lady was wedded to the baron, and her husband took her to dwell with him in his fief.

When Milon returned to his own country he was right heavy and sorrowful to learn of this marriage. He lamented his wretched case, but in this he found comfort, that he was not far from the realm where the lady abode whom so tenderly he loved. Milon commenced to think within himself how best he might send letters to the damsel that he was come again to his home, yet so that none should have knowledge thereof.   He wrote a letter, and sealed it with his seal.   This message he made fast to the neck, and hid within the plumage of a swan that was long his, and was greatly to his heart.   He bade his squire to come, and made him his messenger.

"Change thy raiment swiftly," said he, " and hasten to the castle of my friend.   Take with thee my swan, and see that none, neither servant nor handmaid, delivers the bird to my lady, save thyself alone."

The squire did according to his lord's commandment. He made him ready quickly, and went forth, bearing the swan with him.   He went by the nearest road, and passing through the streets of the city, came before the portal of the castle.   In answer to his summons the porter drew near.

"Friend," said he, " hearken to me.   I am of Caerleon, and a fowler by craft.   Within my nets I have snared the most marvellous swan in the world.   This wondrous bird I would bestow forthwith upon your lady, but perforce I must offer her the gift with my own hand."

"Friend," replied the porter, " fowlers are not always welcomed of ladies.   If you come with me I will bring you where I may know whether it pleases my lady to have speech with you and to receive your gift."

The porter entered in the hall, where he found none but two lords seated at a great table, playing chess for their delight.   He swiftly returned on his steps, and the fowler with him, so furtively withal that the lords were not disturbed at their game, nor perceived aught of the matter. They went therefore to the chamber of the lady.   In answer to their call the door was opened to them by a maiden, who led them before her dame.   When the swan was proffered to the lady it pleased her to receive the gift. She summoned a varlet of her household and gave the bird to his charge, commanding him to keep it safely, and to see that it ate enough and to spare.

"Lady," said the servitor, "I will do your bidding. We shall never receive from any fowler on earth such another bird as this. The swan is fit to serve at a royal table, for the bird is plump as he is fair."

The varlet put the swan in his lady's hands. She took the bird kindly, and smoothing his head and neck, felt the letter that was hidden beneath its feathers. The blood pricked in her veins, for well she knew that the writing was sent her by her friend. She caused the fowler to be given of her bounty, and bade the men to go forth from her chamber. When they had parted the lady called a maiden to her aid. She broke the seal, and unfastening the letter, came upon the name of Milon at the head. She kissed the name a hundred times through her tears. When she might read the writing she learned of the great pain and dolour that her lover suffered by day and by night. In you—he wrote—is all my pleasure, and in your white hands it lies to heal me or to slay. Strive to find a plan by which we may speak as friend to friend, if you would have me live. The knight prayed her in his letter to send him an answer by means of the swan. If the bird were well guarded, and kept without provand for three days, he would of a surety fly back to the place from whence he came, with any message that the lady might lace about his neck.

When the damsel had considered the writing, and understood what was put therein, she commanded that her bird should be tended carefully, and given plenteously to eat and to drink. She held him for a month within her chamber, but this was less from choice, than for the craft that was necessary to obtain the ink and parchment requisite for her writing. At the end she wrote a letter according to her heart, and sealed it with her ring. The lady caused the swan to fast for three full days ; then having concealed the message about his neck, let him take his flight. The bird was all anhungered for food, and remembering well the home from which he drew, he returned thither as quickly as his wings might bear him.

He knew again his town, and his master's house, and descended to the ground at Milon's very feet. Milon rejoiced greatly when he marked his own. He caught the bird by his wings, and crying for his steward, bade him give the swan to eat. The knight removed the missive from the messenger's neck. He glanced from head to head of the letter, seeking the means that he hoped to find, and the salutation he so tenderly wished. Sweet to his heart was the writing, for the lady wrote that without him there was no joy in her life, and since it was his desire to hear by the swan, it would be her pleasure also.

For twenty years the swan was made the messenger of these two lovers, who might never win together. There was no speech between them, save that carried by the bird. They caused the swan to fast for three days, and then sent him on his errand. He to whom the letter came, saw to it that the messenger was fed to heart's desire. Many a time the swan went upon his journey, for however strictly the lady was held of her husband, there was none who had suspicion of a bird.

The dame beyond the Humber nourished and tended the boy committed to her charge with the greatest care. When he was come to a fitting age she made him to be knighted of her lord, for goodly and serviceable was the lad. On the same day the aunt read over to him the letter, and put in his hand the ring. She told him the name of his mother, and his father's story. In all the world there was no worthier knight, nor a more chivalrous and gallant gentleman. The lad hearkened diligently to the lady's tale. He rejoiced greatly to hear

of his father's prowess, and was proud beyond measure of
his renown. He considered within himself, saying to his
own heart, that much should be required of his father's
son, and that he would not be worthy of his blood if he
did not endeavour to merit his name. He determined
therefore that he would leave his country, and seek
adventure as a knight errant, beyond the sea. The
varlet delayed no longer than the evening. On the morrow
he bade farewell to his aunt, who having warned and
admonished him for his good, gave him largely of her
wealth, to bring him on his way. He rode to South-
ampton, that he might find a ship equipped for sea,
and so came to Barfleur. Without any tarrying the lad
went straight to Brittany, where he spent his money and
himself in feasts and in tourneys. The rich men of the
land were glad of his friendship, for there was none who
bore himself better in the press with spear or with sword.
What he took from the rich he bestowed on such knights
as were poor and luckless. These loved him greatly,
since he gained largely and spent freely, granting of his
wealth to all. Wherever this knight sojourned in the
realm he bore away the prize. So debonair was he and
chivalrous that his fame and praise crossed the water,
and were noised abroad in his own land. Folk told how a
certain knight from beyond the Humber, who had passed
the sea in quest of wealth and honour, had so done, that
by reason of his prowess, his liberality, and his modesty,
men called him the Knight Peerless, since they did not
know his name.

This praise of the good knight, and of his deeds, came
to be heard of Milon. Very dolent was he and sorely
troubled that so young a knight should be esteemed above
his fathers. He marvelled greatly that the stout spears
of the past had not put on their harness and broken a
lance for their ancient honour. One thing he determined,

that he would cross the sea without delay, so that he might joust with the dansellon, and abate his pride. In wrath and anger he purposed to fight, to beat his adversary from the saddle, and bring him at last to shame. After this was ended he would seek his son, of whom he had heard nothing, since he had gone from his aunt's castle. Milon caused his friend to know of his wishes. He opened out to her all his thought, and craved her permission to depart. This letter he sent by the swan, commending the bird to her care.

When the lady heard of her lover's purpose, she thanked him for his courtesy, for greatly was his counsel to her mind. She approved his desire to quit the realm for the sake of his honour, and far from putting let and hindrance in his path, trusted that in the end he would bring again her son. Since Milon was assured of his friend's goodwill, he arrayed himself richly, and crossing the sea to Normandy, came afterwards into the land of the Bretons. There he sought the friendship of the lords of that realm, and fared to all the tournaments of which he might hear. Milon bore himself proudly, and gave graciously of his wealth, as though he were receiving a gift. He sojourned till the winter was past in that land, he, and a brave company of knights whom he held in his house with him. When Easter had come, and the season that men give to tourneys and wars and the righting of their private wrongs, Milon considered how he could meet with the knight whom men called Peerless. At that time a tournament was proclaimed to be held at Mont St. Michel. Many a Norman and Breton rode to the game; knights of Flanders and of France were there in plenty, but few fared from England. Milon drew to the lists amongst the first. He inquired diligently of the young champion, and all men were ready to tell from whence he came, and of his harness, and of the blazon on his shield. At length the knight appeared in the lists and Milon looked upon the adversary he so greatly desired to see. Now in this tournament a knight could joust with that lord who was set over against him, or he could seek to break a lance with his chosen foe. A player must gain or lose, and he might find himself opposed either by his comrade or his enemy. Milon did well and worshipfully in the press, and was praised of many that day. But the Knight Peerless carried the cry from all his fellows, for none might stand before him, nor rival him in skill and address. Milon observed him curiously. The lad struck so heavily, he thrust home so shrewdly, that Milon's hatred changed to envy as he watched. Very comely showed the varlet, and much to Milon's mind. The older knight set himself over against the champion, and they met together in the centre of the field. Milon struck his adversary so fiercely, that the lance splintered in his gauntlet; but the young knight kept his seat without even losing a stirrup. In return his spear was aimed with such cunning that he bore his antagonist to the ground. Milon lay upon the earth bareheaded, for his helmet was unlaced in the shock. His hair and beard showed white to all, and the varlet was heavy to look on him whom he had overthrown. He caught the destrier by the bridle, and led him before the stricken man.

" Sir," said he, " I pray you to get upon your horse. I am right grieved and vexed that I should have done this wrong. Believe me that it was wrought unwittingly."

Milon sprang upon his steed. He approved the courtesy of his adversary, and looking upon the hand that held his bridle, he knew again his ring. He made inquiry of the lad.

" Friend," said he, " hearken to me. Tell me now the name of thy sire. How art thou called; who is

thy mother ? I have seen much, and gone to and fro
about the world. All my life I have journeyed from realm
to realm, by reason of tourneys and quarrels and princes'
wars, yet never once by any knight have I been borne
from my horse. This day I am overthrown by a boy,
and yet I cannot help but love thee."

The varlet answered,

" I know little of my father. I understand that his
name is Milon, and that he was a knight of Wales.
He loved the daughter of a rich man, and was loved
again. My mother bore me in secret, and caused me
to be carried to Northumberland, where I was taught and
tended. An old aunt was at the costs of my nourishing.
She kept me at her side, till of all her gifts she gave me
horse and arms, and sent me here, where I have remained.
In hope and wish I purpose to cross the sea, and return
to my own realm. There I would seek out my father,
and learn how it stands between him and my mother.
I will show him my golden ring, and I will tell him
of such privy matters that he may not deny our
kinship, but must love me as a son, and ever hold me
dear."

When Milon heard these words he could endure
them no further. He got him swiftly from his horse,
and taking the lad by the fringe of his hauberk, he
cried,

" Praise be to God, for now am I healed. Fair friend,
by my faith thou art my very son, for whom I came
forth from my own land, and have sought through all
this realm."

The varlet climbed from the saddle, and stood upon
his feet. Father and son kissed each other tenderly,
with many comfortable words. Their love was fair to
see, and those who looked upon their meeting, wept
for joy and pity.

Milon and his son departed from the tournament so soon as it came to an end, for the knight desired greatly to speak to the varlet at leisure, and to open before him all his mind. They rode to their hostel, and with the knights of their fellowship, passed the hours in mirth and revelry. Milon spoke to the lad of his mother. He told him of their long love, and how she was given by her father in marriage to a baron of his realm. He rehearsed the years of separation, accepted by both with a good heart, and of the messenger who carried letters between them, when there was none they dared to trust in, save only the swan.

The son made answer,

"In faith, fair father, let us return to our own land. There I will slay this husband, and you shall yet be my mother's lord."

This being accorded between them, on the morrow they made them ready for the journey, and bidding farewell to their friends, set forth for Wales. They embarked in a propitious hour, for a fair wind carried the ship right swiftly to its haven. They had not ridden far upon their road, when they met a certain squire of the lady's household on his way to Brittany, bearing letters to Milon. His task was done long before sundown in chancing on the knight. He gave over the sealed writing with which he was charged, praying the knight to hasten to his friend without any tarrying, since her husband was in his grave. Milon rejoiced greatly when he knew this thing. He showed the message to his son, and pressed forward without pause or rest. They made such speed, that at the end they came to the castle where the lady had her lodging. Light of heart was she when she clasped again her child. These two fond lovers sought neither countenance of their kin, nor counsel of any man. Their son handselled them together, and gave the mother to his sire. From the day they were wed they dwelt in wealth and in sweetness to the end of their lives.

Of their love and content the minstrel wrought this Lay. I, also, who have set it down in writing, have won guerdon enough just by telling over the tale.

XIII

THE LAY OF YONEC

Since I have commenced I would not leave any of these Lays untold. The stories that I know I would tell you forthwith. My hope is now to rehearse to you the story of Yonec, the son of Eudemarec, his mother's first born child.

In days of yore there lived in Britain a rich man, old and full of years, who was lord of the town and realm of Chepstow. This town is builded on the banks of the Douglas, and is renowned by reason of many ancient sorrows which have there befallen. When he was well stricken in years this lord took to himself a wife, that he might have children to come after him in his goodly heritage. The damsel, who was bestowed on this wealthy lord, came of an honourable house, and was kind and courteous, and passing fair. She was beloved by all because of her beauty, and none was more sweetly spoken of from Chepstow to Lincoln, yea, or from there to Ireland. Great was their sin who married the maiden to this agèd man. Since she was young and gay, he shut her fast within his tower, that he might the easier keep her to himself. He set in charge of the damsel his elder sister, a widow, to hold her more surely in ward. These two ladies dwelt alone in the tower, together with their women, in a chamber by themselves. There the damsel might have speech of none, except at the bidding of the ancient dame. More than seven years passed in this fashion. The lady had no children for her solace, and she never went forth from the castle to greet her kinsfolk and her friends. Her husband's jealousy was such that when she sought her bed, no chamberlain or usher was permitted in her chamber to light the candles. The lady became passing heavy. She spent her days in sighs and tears. Her loveliness began to fail, for she gave no thought to her person. Indeed at times she hated the very shadow of that beauty which had spoiled all her life.

Now when April had come with the gladness of the birds, this lord rose early on a day to take his pleasure in the woods. He bade his sister to rise from her bed to make the doors fast behind him. She did his will, and going apart, commenced to read the psalter that she carried in her hand. The lady awoke, and shamed the brightness of the sun with her tears. She saw that the old woman was gone forth from the chamber, so she made her complaint without fear of being overheard.

"Alas," said she, "in an ill hour was I born. My lot is hard to be shut in this tower, never to go out till I am carried to my grave. Of whom is this jealous lord fearful that he holds me so fast in prison? Great is a man's folly always to have it in mind that he may be deceived. I cannot go to church, nor hearken to the service of God. If I might talk to folk, or have a little pleasure in my life, I should show the more tenderness to my husband, as is my wish. Very greatly are my parents and my kin to blame for giving me to this jealous old man, and making us one flesh. I cannot even look to become a widow, for he will never die. In place of the waters of baptism, certainly he was plunged in the flood of the Styx. His nerves are like iron, and his veins quick with blood as those of a young man. Often have I heard that in years gone by things chanced to the sad, which brought their sorrows to an end. A knight would meet with a maiden, fresh and fair to his desire. Damsels took to themselves lovers, discreet and brave, and were blamed of none. Moreover since these ladies were not seen of any, except their friends, who was there to count them blameworthy! Perchance I deceive myself, and in spite of all the tales, such adventures happened to none. Ah, if only the mighty God would but shape the world to my wish!"

When the lady had made her plaint, as you have known, the shadow of a great bird darkened the narrow window, so that she marvelled what it might mean. This falcon flew straightway into the chamber, jessed and hooded from the glove, and came where the dame was seated. Whilst the lady yet wondered upon him, the tercel became a young and comely knight before her eyes. The lady marvelled exceedingly at this sorcery. Her blood turned to water within her, and because of her dread she hid her face in her hands. By reason of his courtesy the knight first sought to persuade her to put away her fears.

"Lady," said he, " be not so fearful. To you this hawk shall be as gentle as a dove. If you will listen to my words I will strive to make plain what may now be dark. I have come in this shape to your tower that I may pray you of your tenderness to make of me your friend. I have loved you for long, and in my heart have esteemed your love above anything in the world. Save for you I have never desired wife or maid, and I shall find no other woman desirable, until I die. I should have sought you before, but I might not come, nor even leave my own realm, till you called me in your need. Lady, in charity, take me as your friend."

The lady took heart and courage whilst she hearkened to these words. Presently she uncovered her face, and made answer. She said that perchance she would be willing to give him again his hope, if only she had assurance of his faith in God. This she said because of her fear, but in her heart she loved him already by reason of his great beauty. Never in her life had she beheld so goodly a youth, nor a knight more fair.

"Lady," he replied, "you ask rightly. For nothing that man can give would I have you doubt my faith and affiance. I believe truly in God, the Maker of all, who redeemed us from the woe brought on us by our father Adam, in the eating of that bitter fruit. This God is and was and ever shall be the life and light of us poor sinful men. If you still give no credence to my word, ask for your chaplain; tell him that since you are sick you greatly desire to hear the Service appointed by God to heal the sinner of his wound. I will take your semblance, and receive the Body of the Lord. You will thus be certified of my faith, and never have reason to mistrust me more."

When the sister of that ancient lord returned from her prayers to the chamber, she found that the lady was awake. She told her that since it was time to get her from bed, she would make ready her vesture. The lady made answer that she was sick, and begged her to warn the chaplain, for greatly she feared that she might die. The agèd dame replied,

"You must endure as best you may, for my lord has gone to the woods, and none will enter in the tower, save me."

Right distressed was the lady to hear these words. She called a woman's wiles to her aid, and made seeming to swoon upon her bed. This was seen by the sister of her lord, and much was she dismayed. She set wide the doors of the chamber, and summoned the priest. The chaplain came as quickly as he was able, carrying

with him the Lord's Body. The knight received the
Gift, and drank of the Wine of that chalice; then the
priest went his way, and the old woman made fast the
door behind him.

The knight and the lady were greatly at their ease;
a comelier and a blither pair were never seen. They
had much to tell one to the other, but the hours passed
till it was time for the knight to go again to his own
realm. He prayed the dame to give him leave to depart,
and she sweetly granted his prayer, yet so only that he
promised to return often to her side.

"Lady," he made answer, "so you please to require
me at any hour, you may be sure that I shall hasten at
your pleasure. But I beg you to observe such
measure in the matter, that none may do us wrong.
This old woman will spy upon us night and day, and if
she observes our friendship, will certainly show it to
her lord. Should this evil come upon us, for both it
means separation, and for me, most surely, death."

The knight returned to his realm, leaving behind
him the happiest lady in the land. On the morrow
she rose sound and well, and went lightly through the
week. She took such heed to her person, that her former
beauty came to her again. The tower that she was wont
to hate as her prison, became to her now as a pleasant
lodging, that she would not leave for any abode and
garden on earth. There she could see her friend at will,
when once her lord had gone forth from the chamber.
Early and late, at morn and eve, the lovers met together.
God grant her joy was long, against the evil day that
came.

The husband of the lady presently took notice of
the change in his wife's fashion and person. He was
troubled in his soul, and misdoubting his sister, took
her apart to reason with her on a day. He told her of

his wonder that his dame arrayed her so sweetly, and inquired what this should mean. The crone answered that she knew no more than he, " for we have very little speech one with another. She sees neither kin nor friend ; but, now, she seems quite content to remain alone in her chamber."

The husband made reply,

" Doubtless she is content, and well content. But by my faith, we must do all we may to discover the cause. Hearken to me. Some morning when I have risen from bed, and you have shut the doors upon me, make pretence to go forth, and let her think herself alone. You must hide yourself in a privy place, where you can both hear and see. We shall then learn the secret of this new found joy."

Having devised this snare the twain went their ways. Alas, for those who were innocent of their counsel, and whose feet would soon be tangled in the net.

Three days after, this husband pretended to go forth from his house. He told his wife that the King had bidden him by letters to his Court, but that he should return speedily. He went from the chamber, making fast the door. His sister arose from her bed, and hid behind her curtains, where she might see and hear what so greedily she desired to know. The lady could not sleep, so fervently she wished for her friend. The knight came at her call, but he might not tarry, nor cherish her more than one single hour. Great was the joy between them, both in word and tenderness, till he could no longer stay. All this the crone saw with her eyes, and stored in her heart. She watched the fashion in which he came, and the guise in which he went. But she was altogether fearful and amazed that so goodly a knight should wear the semblance of a hawk. When the husband returned to his house—for he was

near at hand—his sister told him that of which she was
the witness, and of the truth concerning the knight.
Right heavy was he and wrathful. Straightway he
contrived a cunning gin for the slaying of this bird. He
caused four blades of steel to be fashioned, with point
and edge sharper than the keenest razor. These he
fastened firmly together, and set them securely within
that window, by which the tercel would come to his
lady. Ah, God, that a knight so fair might not see nor
hear of this wrong, and that there should be none to
show him of such treason.

On the morrow the husband arose very early, at day-
break, saying that he should hunt within the wood.
His sister made the doors fast behind him, and returned
to her bed to sleep, because it was yet but dawn. The
lady lay awake, considering of the knight whom she
loved so loyally. Tenderly she called him to her side.
Without any long tarrying the bird came flying at her
will. He flew in at the open window, and was entangled
amongst the blades of steel. One blade pierced his
body so deeply, that the red blood gushed from the
wound. When the falcon knew that his hurt was to
death, he forced himself to pass the barrier, and coming
before his lady fell upon her bed, so that the sheets
were dabbled with his blood. The lady looked upon
her friend and his wound, and was altogether anguished
and distraught.

" Sweet friend," said the knight, " it is for you that
my life is lost. Did I not speak truly that if our loves
were known, very surely I should be slain ? "

On hearing these words the lady's head fell upon the
pillow, and for a space she lay as she were dead. The
knight cherished her sweetly. He prayed her not to
sorrow overmuch, since she should bear a son who would
be her exceeding comfort. His name should be called

Yonec. He would prove a valiant knight, and would avenge both her and him by slaying their enemy. The knight could stay no longer, for he was bleeding to death from his hurt. In great dolour of mind and body he flew from the chamber. The lady pursued the bird with many shrill cries. In her desire to follow him she sprang forth from the window. Marvellous it was that she was not killed outright, for the window was fully twenty feet from the ground. When the lady made her perilous leap she was clad only in her shift. Dressed in this fashion she set herself to follow the knight by the drops of blood which dripped from his wound. She went along the road that he had gone before, till she lighted on a little lodge. This lodge had but one door, and it was stained with blood. By the marks on the lintel she knew that Eudemarec had refreshed him in the hut, but she could not tell whether he was yet within. The damsel entered in the lodge, but all was dark, and since she might not find him, she came forth, and pursued her way. She went so far that at the last the lady came to a very fair meadow. She followed the track of blood across this meadow, till she saw a city near at hand. This fair city was altogether shut in with high walls. There was no house, nor hall, nor tower, but shone bright as silver, so rich were the folk who dwelt therein. Before the town lay a still water. To the right spread a leafy wood, and on the left hand, near by the keep, ran a clear river. By this broad stream the ships drew to their anchorage, for there were above three hundred lying in the haven. The lady entered in the city by the postern gate. The gouts of freshly fallen blood led her through the streets to the castle. None challenged her entrance to the city; none asked of her business in the streets; she passed neither man nor woman upon her way. Spots of red blood lay on the staircase of the palace. The lady entered and found herself within a low ceiled room, where a knight was sleeping on a pallet. She looked upon his face and passed beyond. She came within a larger room, empty, save for one lonely couch, and for the knight who slept thereon. But when the lady entered in the third chamber she saw a stately bed, that well she knew to be her friend's. This bed was of inwrought gold, and was spread with silken cloths beyond price. The furniture was worth the ransom of a city, and waxen torches in sconces of silver lighted the chamber, burning night and day. Swiftly as the lady had come she knew again her friend, directly she saw him with her eyes. She hastened to the bed, and incontinently swooned for grief. The knight clasped her in his arms, bewailing his wretched lot, but when she came to her mind, he comforted her as sweetly as he might.

"Fair friend, for God's love I pray you get from hence as quickly as you are able. My time will end before the day, and my household, in their wrath, may do you a mischief if you are found in the castle. They are persuaded that by reason of your love I have come to my death. Fair friend, I am right heavy and sorrowful because of you."

The lady made answer,

"Friend, the best thing that can befall me is that we shall die together. How may I return to my husband? If he finds me again he will certainly slay me with the sword."

The knight consoled her as he could. He bestowed a ring upon his friend, teaching her that so long as she wore the gift, her husband would think of none of these things, nor care for her person, nor seek to revenge him for his wrongs. Then he took his sword and rendered it to the lady, conjuring her by their great love, never to give it to the hand of any, till their son should be counted a brave and worthy knight. When that time was come she and her lord would go—together with the son—to a feast. They would lodge in an Abbey, where should be seen a very fair tomb. There her son must be told of this death; there he must be girt with this sword. In that place shall be rehearsed the tale of his birth, and his father, and all this bitter wrong. And then shall be seen what he will do.

When the knight had shown his friend all that was in his heart, he gave her a bliaut, passing rich, that she might clothe her body, and get her from the palace. She went her way, according to his command, bearing with her the ring, and the sword that was her most precious treasure. She had not gone half a mile beyond the gate of the city when she heard the clash of bells, and the cries of men who lamented the death of their lord. Her grief was such that she fell four separate times upon the road, and four times she came from out her swoon. She bent her steps to the lodge where her friend had refreshed him, and rested for awhile. Passing beyond she came at last to her own land, and returned to her husband's tower. There, for many a day, she dwelt in peace, since—as Eudemarec foretold—her lord gave no thought to her outgoings, nor wished to avenge him, neither spied upon her any more.

In due time the lady was delivered of a son, whom she named Yonec. Very sweetly nurtured was the lad. In all the realm there was not his like for beauty and generosity, nor one more skilled with the spear. When he was of a fitting age the King dubbed him knight. Hearken now, what chanced to them all, that self-same year.

It was the custom of that country to keep the feast of St. Aaron with great pomp at Caerleon, and many

another town besides. The husband rode with his
friends to observe the festival, as was his wont. Together with him went his wife and her son, richly
apparelled. As the roads were not known of the company, and they feared to lose their way, they took with
them a certain youth to lead them in the straight path.
The varlet brought them to a town ; in all the world
was none so fair. Within this city was a mighty Abbey,
filled with monks in their holy habit. The varlet craved
a lodging for the night, and the pilgrims were welcomed
gladly of the monks, who gave them meat and drink
near by the Abbot's table. On the morrow, after Mass,
they would have gone their way, but the Abbot prayed
them to tarry for a little, since he would show them his
chapter house and dormitory, and all the offices of the
Abbey. As the Abbot had sheltered them so courteously,
the husband did according to his wish.

Immediately that the dinner had come to an end,
the pilgrims rose from table, and visited the offices of
the Abbey. Coming to the chapter house they entered
therein, and found a fair tomb, exceeding great, covered
with a silken cloth, banded with orfreys of gold. Twenty
torches of wax stood around this rich tomb, at the head,
the foot, and the sides. The candlesticks were of fine
gold, and the censer swung in that chantry was fashioned
from an amethyst. When the pilgrims saw the great
reverence vouchsafed to this tomb, they inquired of
the guardians as to whom it should belong, and of the
lord who lay therein. The monks commenced to weep,
and told with tears, that in that place was laid the body
of the best, the bravest, and the fairest knight who ever
was, or ever should be born. " In his life he was King
of this realm, and never was there so worshipful a lord.
He was slain at Caerwent for the love of a lady of those
parts. Since then the country is without a King. Many

a day have we waited for the son of these luckless lovers
to come to our land, even as our lord commanded us
to do."

When the lady heard these words she cried to her
son with a loud voice before them all.

"Fair son," said she, "you have heard why God
has brought us to this place. It is your father who lies
dead within this tomb. Foully was he slain by this
ancient Judas at your side."

With these words she plucked out the sword, and
tendered him the glaive that she had guarded for so
long a season. As swiftly as she might she told the
tale of how Eudemarec came to have speech with his
friend in the guise of a hawk; how the bird was betrayed
to his death by the jealousy of her lord; and of Yonec
the falcon's son. At the end she fell senseless across
the tomb, neither did she speak any further word until
the soul had gone from her body. When the son saw
that his mother lay dead upon her lover's grave, he
raised his father's sword and smote the head of that
ancient traitor from his shoulders. In that hour he
avenged his father's death, and with the same blow
gave quittance for the wrongs of his mother. As soon
as these tidings were published abroad, the folk of that
city came together, and setting the body of that fair
lady within a coffin, sealed it fast, and with due rite
and worship placed it beside the body of her friend.
May God grant them pardon and peace. As to Yonec,
their son, the people acclaimed him for their lord, as
he departed from the church.

Those who knew the truth of this piteous adventure,
after many days shaped it to a Lay, that all men might
learn the plaint and the dolour that these two friends
suffered by reason of their love.

XIV

THE LAY OF THE THORN

WHOSOEVER counts these Lays as fable, may be assured that I am not of his mind. The dead and past stories that I have told again in divers fashions, are not set down without authority. The chronicles of these far off times are yet preserved in the land. They may be read by the curious at Caerleon, or in the monastery of St. Aaron. They may be heard in Brittany, and in many another realm besides. To prove how the remembrance of such tales endures, I will now relate to you the adventure of the Two Children, making clear what has remained hidden to this very hour.

In Brittany there lived a prince, high of spirit, fair of person, courteous and kind to all. This Childe was a King's son, and there were none to cherish him but his father and his father's wife, for his mother was dead. The King held him dearer than aught else in the world, and close he was to the lady's heart. The lady, for her part, had a daughter by another husband than the King. Very dainty was the maiden, sweet of colour and of face, passing young and fair. Both these children, born to so high estate, were right tender of age, for the varlet, who was the elder of the twain, was but seven years. The two children loved together very sweetly. Nothing seemed of worth to one, if it were not shared with the other. They were nourished at the same table, went their ways together, and lived side by side. The guardians who held them in ward, seeing their great love, made no effort to put them apart, but allowed them to have all things in common. The love of these children increased with their years, but Dame Nature brought another love to youth and maid than she gave to the child. They delighted no more in their old frolic and play. Such sport gave place to clasp and kisses, to many words, and to long silences. To savour their friendship they took refuge in an attic of the keep, but all the years they had passed together, made the new love flower more sweetly in their hearts, as each knew well. Very pure and tender was their love, and good would it have been if they could have hidden it from their fellows. This might not be, for in no great while they were spied upon, and seen.

It chanced upon a day that this prince, so young and debonair, came home from the river with an aching head, by reason of the heat. He entered in a chamber, and shutting out the noise and clamour, lay upon his bed, to ease his pain. The Queen was with her daughter in a chamber, instructing her meetly in that which it becomes a maid to know. Closer to a damsel's heart is her lover than her kin. So soon as she heard that her friend was come again to the house, she stole forth from her mother, without saying word to any, and accompanied by none, went straight to the chamber where he slept. The prince welcomed her gladly, for they had not met together that day. The lady, who thought no wrong, condoled with him in his sickness, and of her sweetness gave him a hundred kisses to soothe his hurt. Too swiftly sped the time in this fashion. Presently the Queen noticed that the damsel was no longer with her at her task. She rose to her feet, and going quickly to the chamber of the prince, entered therein without call or knock, for the door was unfastened on the latch.

When the Queen saw these two lovers fondly laced in each other's arms, she knew and was certified of their love. Right wrathful was the Queen. She caught the maiden by the wrist, and shut her fast in her room. She prayed the King to govern his son more strictly, and to hold him in such ward about the Court that he might get no speech with the damsel. Since he could have neither sight nor word of his friend, save only the sound of weeping from her chamber, the prince determined to tarry no further in the palace. He sought his father the self-same hour, and showed him what was in his mind.

"Sire," said he, "I crave a gift. If it pleases you to be a father to your son, make me now a knight. I desire to seek another realm, and to serve some prince for guerdon. The road calls me, for many a knight has won much riches with his sword."

The King did not refuse the lad's request, but accorded it should be even as he wished. He prayed the prince to dwell for a year about the Court, that he might the more readily assist at such tourneys and follow such feats of arms as were proclaimed in the kingdom. This the prince agreed to do—the more readily because there was nothing else to be done. He remained therefore at the Court, moving ever by his father's side. The maiden, for her part, was in the charge of her mother, who reproached her always for that she had done amiss. The Queen did not content herself with reproaches and threats. She used the sharp discipline upon her, so that the maiden suffered grievously in her person. Sick at heart was the varlet whilst he hearkened to the beatings, the discipline and the chastisement wherewith her mother corrected the damsel. He knew not what to do, for well he understood that his was the fault, and that by reason of him was her neck bowed down in her youth. More and more was he tormented because of his friend.

More and more the stripes with which she was afflicted became heavier for him to bear. He shut himself close within his chamber, and making fast the door, gave his heart over to tears.

"Alas," cried he, "what shall I do! How may the ill be cured that I have brought on us by my lightness and folly! I love her more than life, and, certes, if I may not have my friend I will prove that I can die for her, though I cannot live without her."

Whilst the prince made this lamentation, the Queen came before the King.

"Sir," said she, "I pledge my oath and word as a crowned lady that I keep my daughter as strictly as I may. Think to your own son, and see to it that he cannot set eyes on the maid. He considers none other thing but how to get clasp and speech of his friend."

For this reason the King guarded his son about the Court as closely as the Queen held the maiden in her chamber. So vigilant was the watch that these pitiful lovers might never have word together. They had no leisure to meet; they never looked one on the other; nor heard tidings of how they did, whether by letter or by sergeant.

They lived this death in life till the same year—eight days before the Feast of St. John—the varlet was dubbed knight. The King spent the day in the chase, and returning, brought with him great store of fowl and venison that he had taken. After supper, when the tables were removed, the King seated himself for his delight upon a carpet spread before the daïs, his son and many a courteous lord with him. The fair company gave ear to the Lay of Alys, sweetly sung by a minstrel from Ireland, to the music of his rote. When his story was ended, forthwith he commenced another, and related the Lay of Orpheus; none being so bold as to disturb the singer, or to let his mind wander from the song. Afterwards the knights spoke together amongst themselves. They told of adventures which in ancient days had chanced to many, and were noised about Brittany. Amongst these lords sat a damsel, passing sweet of tongue. In her turn she told of a certain adventure which awaited the adventurous at the Ford of the Thorn, once every year, on the vigil of St. John, " but much I doubt whether now there be knights so bold as to dare the perils of that passage." When the newly made knight heard these words his pride quickened within him. He considered that although he was belted with the sword, he had as yet done no deed to prove his courage in the eyes of men. He deemed the time had come to show his hardihood, and to put to silence the malicious lips. He stood upon his feet, calling upon damsel, King and barons to hearken to his voice, and spake out manfully in the ears of great and small.

" Lords," cried he, " whatever says the maiden, I boast before you all that on St. John's Eve I will ride alone to the Ford of the Thorn, and dare this adventure, whether it bring me gain or whether it bring me loss."

The King was right heavy to hear these words. He thought them to be the gab and idle speech of a boy.

" Fair son," said he, " put this folly from your mind."

But when the King was persuaded that whether it were foolishness or wisdom the lad was determined to go his way, and abide the issue of the adventure,

" Go swiftly," said he, " in the care of God. Since risk your life you must, play it boldly like a pawn, and may God grant you heart's desire and happy hours."

The self-same night, whilst the lad lay sleeping in his bed, that fair lady, his friend, was in much unrest in hers. The tidings of her lover's boast had been carried quickly to her chamber, and sorely was she adread for what might chance. When the Eve of St. John was come, and the day drew towards evening, the varlet, with all fair hopes, made him ready to ride to the Ford Adventurous. He had clad himself from basnet to shoes in steel, and mounted on a strong destrier, went his road to essay the Passage of the Thorn. Whilst he took his path the maiden took hers. She went furtively to the orchard, that she might importune God to bring her friend again, safe and sound to his own house. She seated herself on the roots of a tree, and with sighs and tears lamented her piteous case.

"Father of Heaven," said the girl, "Who was and ever shall be, be pitiful to my prayer. Since it is not to Thy will that any man should be wretched, be merciful to a most unhappy maid. Fair Sire, give back the days that are gone, when my friend was at my side, and grant that once again I may be with him. Lord God of Hosts, when shall I be healed? None knows the bitterness of my sorrow, for none may taste thereof, save such as set their heart on what they may not have. These only, Lord, know the wormwood and the gall."

Thus prayed the maiden, seated on the roots of that ancient tree, her feet upon the tender grass. At the time of her orisons much was she sought and inquired after in the palace, but none might find where she had hidden. The damsel herself was given over altogether to her love and her sorrow, and had no thought for anything, save for prayers and tears. The night wore through, and dawn already laced the sky, when she fell on a little slumber, in the tree where she was sheltered. She woke with a start, but returned to her sleep more deeply than before. She had not slept long, when herseemed she was ravished from the tree—but I cannot make this plain for I know no wizardry—to that Ford of the Thorn, where her friend and lover had repaired. The

knight looked upon the sleeping maiden, and marvelled
at so fair a sight. All adread was the lady when she
came from her slumber, for she knew not where she
lay, and wondered greatly. She covered her head by
reason of her exceeding fear, but the knight consoled
her courteously.

"Diva," said he, "there is no reason for terror. If
you are an earthly woman, speaking with a mortal
tongue, tell me your story. Tell me in what guise and
manner you came so suddenly to this secret place."

The maiden began to be of more courage, till she
remembered that she was no longer in the orchard of
the castle. She inquired of the knight to what haunt
she had come.

"Lady," he made answer, " you are laid at the Ford
of the Thorn, where adventures chance to the seeker,
sometimes greatly against the mind, and sometimes
altogether according to the heart."

"Ah, dear God," cried the lady, " now shall I be made
whole. Sir, look a little closer upon me, for I have been
your friend. Thanks be to God, Who so soon has heard
my prayer."

This was the beginning of adventures which happened
that night to the seeker. The maiden hastened to
embrace her lover. He got him nimbly from his horse,
and taking her softly between his arms, kissed her with
more kisses than I can tell. Then they sat together
beneath the thorn, and the damsel told how she fell
asleep within that old tree in the pleasaunce, of how
she was rapt from thence in her slumber, and of how,
yet sleeping, he came upon her by the Ford. When the
knight had hearkened to all that she had to say, he
looked from her face, and glancing across the river,
marked a lord, with lifted lance, riding to the ford.
This knight wore harness of a fair vermeil colour, and

bestrode a horse white of body, save for his two ears, which were red as the rider's mail. Slender of girdle was this knight, and he made no effort to enter the river, but drew rein upon the other side of the passage, and watched. The varlet said to his friend that it became his honour to essay some feats of arms with this adversary. He got to horse, and rode to the river, leaving the maiden beneath the thorn. Had she but found another horse at need, very surely would she have ridden to his aid. The two knights drew together as swiftly as their steeds could bear them. They thrust so shrewdly with the lance, that their shields were split and broken. The spears splintered in the gauntlet, and both champions were unhorsed by the shock, rolling on the sand; but nothing worse happened to them. Since they had neither squire nor companion to help them on their feet, they pained them grievously to get them from the ground. When they might climb upon their steeds, they hung again the buckler about the neck, and lowered their ashen spears. Passing heavy was the varlet, for shame that his friend had seen him thrown. The two champions met together in the onset, but the prince struck his adversary so cunningly with the lance, that the laces of his buckler were broken, and the shield fell from his body. When the varlet saw this he rejoiced greatly, for he knew that the eyes of his friend were upon him. He pressed his quarrel right fiercely, and tumbling his foe from the saddle, seized his horse by the bridle.[1]

The two knights passed the ford, and the prince feared sorely because of the skill and mightiness of his adversary. He could not doubt that if they fell upon him together he would perish at their hands. He put the thought from mind, for he would not suspect them of conduct so unbecoming to gentle knight, and so

[1] There is here some omission in the manuscript.

contrary to the laws of chivalry. If they desired some passage of arms, doubtless they would joust as gentlemen, and each for himself alone. When these three knights were mounted on their steeds, they crossed the ford with courtesy and order, each seeking to give precedence to his companion. Having come to the bank the stranger knights prayed the prince to run a course for their pleasure. He answered that it was his wish, too, and made him ready for the battle. The prince rejoiced greatly when he saw one of these two adversaries ride a little apart, that he might the more easily observe the combat. He was assured that he would suffer no felony at their hands. For their part the two knights were persuaded that they had to do with an errant who had ridden to the ford for no other gain than honour and praise. The two adversaries took their places within the lists. They lowered their lance, and covering their bodies with the shield, smote fiercely together. So rude was the shock that the staves of the spears were broken, and the strong destriers were thrown upon their haunches. Neither of the good knights had lost his saddle. Each of the combatants got him to his feet, and drawing the sword, pressed upon his fellow, till the blood began to flow. When the knight who judged this quarrel saw their prowess, he came near, and commanded that the battle should cease. The adversaries drew apart, and struck no further blow with the sword. Right courteously and with fair words he spake to the prince.

" Friend," said the knight, " get to your horse, and break a lance with me. Then we can go in peace, for our time grows short. You must endure till the light be come if you hope to gain the prize. Do your devoir, valiantly, for should you chance to be thrown in this course, or slain by misadventure, you have lost your desire. None will ever hear of this adventure; all your life you will remain little and obscure. Your maiden will be led away by the victor, seated on the good Castilian horse you have gained by right of courage. Fight bravely. The trappings of the destrier are worth the spoil of a king's castle, and as for the horse himself he is the swiftest and the fairest in the world. Be not amazed that I tell you of these matters. I have watched you joust, and know you for a hardy knight and a gallant gentleman. Besides I stand to lose horse and harness equally with you."

The prince listened to these words, and accorded that the knight spoke wisely and well. He would willingly have taken counsel of the maiden, but first, as surely he knew, he must joust with this knight. He gathered the reins in his glove, and choosing a lance with an ashen staff, opposed himself to his adversary. The combatants met together so fiercely that the lance pierced the steel of the buckler; yet neither lost stirrup by the shock. When the prince saw this he smote the knight so shrewdly that he would have fallen from the saddle, had he not clung to the neck of his destrier. Of his courtesy the prince passed on, and refrained his hand until his enemy had recovered his seat. On his return he found the knight full ready to continue his devoir. Each of the champions plucked forth his sword, and sheltered him beneath his shield. They struck such mighty blows that the bucklers were hewn in pieces, but in spite of all they remained firm in the saddle. The maiden was aghast whilst she watched the melée. She had great fear for her friend, lest mischief should befall him, and she cried loudly to the knight that, for grace, he should give over this combat, and go his way. Very courteous was the knight, and meetly schooled in what was due to maidens. He saluted the damsel, and, together with his companion, rode straightway from the ford. The prince watched them pass for a little, then without further tarrying he went swiftly to the maiden, where, all fearful and trembling, she knelt beneath the thorn. The lady stood upon her feet as her lover drew near. She climbed behind him on the saddle, for well she knew that their pains were done. They fared so fast that when it was yet scarce day they came again to the palace. The King saw them approach, and rejoiced greatly at his son's prowess; but at this he marvelled much, that he should return with the daughter of the Queen.

The self-same day of this homecoming—as I have heard tell—the King had summoned to Court his barons and vassals because of a certain quarrel betwixt two of his lords. This quarrel being accorded between them, and come to a fair end, the King related to that blithe company the story of this adventure. He told again that which you know, of how the prince defended the Ford, of the finding of the maiden beneath the thorn, of the mighty joust, and of that white horse which was taken from the adversary.

The prince both then and thereafter caused the horse to be entreated with the greatest care. He received the maiden to wife, and cherished her right tenderly. She, and the steed on which she would always ride, were his richest possessions. The destrier lived many years in much honour, but on a day when his master was taking the harness from his head, he fell and died forthwith.

Of the story which has been set before you the Bretons wrought a Lay. They did not call the song the Lay of the Ford, although the adventure took place at a river; neither have they named it The Lay of the Two Children. For good or ill the rhyme is known as the Lay of the Thorn. It begins well and endeth better, for these kisses find their fruition in marriage.

XV

THE LAY OF GRAELENT

Now will I tell you the adventure of **Graelent**, even as it was told to me, for the Lay is sweet to hear, and the tune thereof lovely to bear in mind.

Graelent was born in Brittany of a gentle and noble house, very comely of person and very frank of heart. The King who held Brittany in that day, made mortal war upon his neighbours, and commanded his vassals to take arms in his quarrel. Amongst these came Graelent, whom the King welcomed gladly, and since he was a wise and hardy knight greatly was he honoured and cherished by the Court. So Graelent strove valiantly at tourney and at joust, and pained himself mightily to do the enemy all the mischief that he was able. The Queen heard tell the prowess of her knight, and loved him in her heart for reason of his feats of arms and of the good men spoke of him. So she called her chamberlain apart, and said,

"Tell me truly, hast thou not often heard speak of that fair knight, Sir Graelent, whose praise is in all men's mouths?"

"Lady," answered the chamberlain, "I know him for a courteous gentleman, well spoken of by all."

"I would he were my friend," replied the lady, "for I am in much unrest because of him. Go thou, and bid him come to me, so he would be worthy of my love."

" Passing gracious and rich is your gift, lady, and doubtless he will receive it with marvellous joy. Why, from here to Troy there is no priest even, however holy, who in looking on your face would not lose Heaven in your eyes."

Thereupon the chamberlain took leave of the Queen, and seeking Graelent within his lodging saluted him courteously, and gave him the message, praying him to come without delay to the palace.

" Go before, fair friend," answered the knight, " for I will follow you at once."

So when the chamberlain was gone Graelent caused his grey horse to be saddled, and mounting thereon, rode to the castle, attended by his squire. He descended without the hall, and passing before the King entered within the Queen's chamber. When the lady saw him she embraced him closely, and cherished and honoured him sweetly. Then she made the knight to be seated on a fair carpet, and to his face praised him for his exceeding comeliness. But he answered her very simply and courteously, saying nothing but what was seemly to be said. Then the Queen kept silence for a great while, considering whether she should require him to love her for the love of love; but at the last, made bold by passion, she asked if his heart was set on any maid or dame.

" Lady," said he, " I love no woman, for love is a serious business, not a jest. Out of five hundred who speak glibly of love, not one can spell the first letter of his name. With such it is idleness, or fulness of bread, or fancy, masking in the guise of love. Love requires of his servants chastity in thought, in word and in deed. If one of two lovers is loyal, and the other jealous and false, how may their friendship last, for Love is slain! But sweetly and discreetly love passes from person to person, from heart to heart, or it is nothing worth. For what the lover would, that would the beloved; what she would ask of him that should he go before to grant. Without accord such as this, love is but a bond and a constraint. For above all things Love means sweetness, and truth, and measure; yea, loyalty to the loved one and to your word. And because of this I dare not meddle with so high a matter."

The Queen heard Graelent gladly, finding him so tripping of tongue, and since his words were wise and courteous, at the end she discovered to him her heart.

" Friend, Sir Graelent, though I am a wife, yet have I never loved my lord. But I love you very dearly, and what I have asked of you will you not go before to grant ? "

" Lady," said he, " give me pity and forgiveness, but this may not be. I am the vassal of the King, and on my knees have pledged him loyalty and faith, and sworn to defend his life and honour. Never shall he have shame because of me."

With these words Sir Graelent took his leave of the Queen, and went his way.

Seeing him go in this fashion the Queen commenced to sigh. She was grieved in her heart, and knew not what to do. But whatever chanced she would not renounce her passion, so often she required his love by means of soft messages and costly gifts, but he refused them all. Then the Queen turned from love to hate, and the greatness of her passion became the measure of her wrath, for very evilly she spoke of Graelent to the King. So long as the war endured Graelent remained in that realm. He spent all that he had upon his company, for the King grudged wages to his men. The Queen persuaded the King to this, counselling him that by withholding the pay of the sergeants, Graelent might in no wise flee the country, nor take service with another lord. So at the end Graelent was wonderfully downcast, nor was it strange that he was sad, for there remained nothing which he might pledge, but one poor steed, and when this was gone, no horse had he to carry him from the country.

It was now the month of May, when the hours are long and warm. The burgess, with whom Graelent lodged, had risen early in the morning, and with his wife had gone to eat with neighbours in the town. No one was in the house except Graelent, no squire, nor archer, nor servant, save only the daughter of his host, a very courteous maid. When the hour for dinner was come she prayed the knight that they might sit at board together. But he had no heart for mirth, and seeking out his squire bade him bridle and saddle his horse, for he had no care to eat.

" I have no saddle," replied the squire.

" Friend," said the demoiselle, " I will lend you bridle and saddle as well."

So when the harness was done upon him, Graelent mounted his horse, and went his way through the town, clad in a cloak of sorry fur, which he had worn overlong already. The townsfolk in the street turned and stared upon him, making a jest of his poverty, but of their jibes he took no heed, for such act but after their kind, and seldom show kindliness or courtesy.

Now without the town there spread a great forest, thick with trees, and through the forest ran a river. Towards this forest Graelent rode, deep in heavy thought, and very dolent. Having ridden for a little space beneath the trees, he spied within a leafy thicket a fair white hart, whiter even than snow on winter branches. The hart fled before him, and Graelent followed so closely in her track that man and deer presently came

together to a grassy lawn, in the midst of which sprang
a fountain of clear, sweet water. Now in this fountain
a demoiselle disported herself for her delight. Her
raiment was set on a bush near by, and her two maidens
stood on the bank busied in their lady's service. Graelent
forgot the chase at so sweet a sight, since never in his
life had he seen so lovely a dame. For the lady was
slender in shape and white, very gracious and dainty
of colour, with laughing eyes and an open brow, certainly the most beautiful thing in all the world. Graelent
dared not draw nigh the fountain for fear of troubling
the dame, so he came softly to the bush to set hands
upon her raiment. The two maidens marked his
approach, and at their fright the lady turned, and calling
him by name, cried with great anger,

"Graelent, put my raiment down, for it will profit
you little even if you carry it away, and leave me naked
in this wood. But if you are indeed too greedy of gain
to remember your knighthood, at least return me my
shift, and content yourself with my mantle, since it
will bring you money, as it is very good."

"I am not a merchant's son," answered Graelent
merrily, "nor am I a huckster to sell mantles in a booth.
If your cloak were worth the spoil of three castles I
would not now carry it from the bush. Come forth
from your bathing, fair friend, and clothe yourself in
your vesture, for you have to say a certain word to
me."

"I will not trust myself to your hand, for you might
seize upon me," answered the lady, "and I tell you
frankly that I put no faith in your word, nor have had
any dealings with your school."

Then Graelent answered still more merrily,

"Lady, needs must I suffer your wrath. But at
least I will guard your raiment till you come forth

from the well and, fairest, very dainty is your body in my eyes."

When the lady knew that Graelent would not depart, nor render again her raiment, then she demanded surety that he would do her no hurt. This thing was accorded between them, so she came forth from the fountain, and did her vesture upon her. Then Graelent took her gently by the left hand, and prayed and required of her that she would grant him love for love. But the lady answered,

" I marvel greatly that you should dare to speak to me in this fashion, for I have little reason to think you discreet. You are bold, sir knight, and overbold, to seek to ally yourself with a woman of my lineage."

Sir Graelent was not abashed by the dame's proud spirit, but wooed and prayed her gently and sweetly, promising that if she granted him her love he would serve her in all loyalty, and never depart therefrom all the days of his life. The demoiselle hearkened to the words of Graelent, and saw plainly that he was a valiant knight, courteous and wise. She thought within herself that should she send him from her, never might she find again so sure a friend. Since, then, she knew him worthy of her love, she kissed him softly, and spoke to him in this manner,

" Graelent, I will love you none the less truly, though we have not met until this day. But one thing is needful that our love may endure. Never must you speak a word by which this hidden thing may become known. I will furnish you with deniers in your purse, with cloth of silk, with silver and with gold. Night and day will I stay with you, and great shall be the love between us twain. You shall see me riding at your side ; you may talk and laugh with me at your pleasure, but I must never be seen of your comrades, nor must they know aught concerning your bride. Graelent, you are loyal, brave, and courteous, and comely enough to the view. For you I spread my snare at the fountain; for you shall I suffer heavy pains, as well I knew before I set forth on this adventure. Now must I trust to your discretion, for if you speak vainly and boastfully of this thing then am I undone. Remain now for a year in this country, which shall be for you a home that your lady loves well. But noon is past, and it is time for you to go. Farewell, and a messenger shortly shall tell you that which I would have you do."

Graelent took leave of the lady, and she sweetly clasped and kissed him farewell. He returned to his lodging, dismounted from his steed, and entering within a chamber, leaned from the casement, considering this strange adventure. Looking towards the forest he saw a varlet issue therefrom riding upon a palfrey. He drew rein before Graelent's door, and taking his feet from the stirrup, saluted the knight. So Graelent inquired from whence he rode, and of his name and business.

"Sir," answered he, "I am the messenger of your lady. She sends you this destrier by my hand, and would have me enter in your service, to pay your servitors their wages and to take charge of your lodging."

When Graelent heard this message he thought it both good and fair. He kissed the varlet upon the cheek, and accepting his gift, caused the destrier—which was the noblest, the swiftest and the most speedy under the sun—to be led to the stable. Then the varlet carried his baggage to his master's chamber, and took therefrom a large cushion and a rich coverlet which he spread upon the couch. After this he drew thereout a purse containing much gold and silver, and stout cloth fitting for the knight's apparel. Then he sent for the host, and paying him what was owing, called upon him

to witness that he was recompensed most largely for
the lodging. He bade him also to seek out such knights
as should pass through the town to refresh and solace
themselves in the company of his lord. The host was
a worthy man. He made ready a plenteous dinner,
and inquired through the town for such poor knights as
were in misease by reason of prison or of war. These he
brought to the hostelry of Sir Graelent, and comforted
them with instruments of music, and with all manner
of mirth. Amongst them sat Graelent at meat, gay and
debonair, and richly apparelled. Moreover, to these
poor knights and the harpers Graelent gave goodly
gifts, so that there was not a citizen in all the town
who did not hold him in great worship, and regard him
as his lord.

From this moment Graelent lived greatly at his ease,
for not a cloud was in his sky. His lady came at will
and pleasure; all day long they laughed and played
together, and at night she lay softly at his side. What
truer happiness might he know than this ? Often,
besides, he rode to such tournaments of the land as he
was able, and all men esteemed him for a stout and worthy
knight. Very pleasant were his days, and his love, and
if such things might last for ever he had nothing else
to ask of life.

When a full year had passed by, the season drew to
the Feast of Pentecost. Now it was the custom of the
King to summon at that tide his barons and all who
held their fiefs of him to his Court for a rich banquet.
Amongst these lords was bidden Sir Graelent. After
men had eaten and drunk the whole day, and all were
merry, the King commanded the Queen to put off her
royal robes, and to stand forth upon the daïs. Then he
boasted before the company,

"Lord barons, how seems it to you ? Beneath the

sky is there a lovelier Queen than mine, be she maid, lady or demoiselle ? "

So all the lords made haste to praise the Queen, and to cry and affirm that in all the world was neither maid nor wife so dainty, fresh and fair. Not a single voice but bragged of her beauty, save only that of Graelent. He smiled at their folly, for his heart remembered his friend, and he held in pity all those who so greatly rejoiced in the Queen. So he sat with covered head, and with face bent smiling to the board. The Queen marked his discourtesy, and drew thereto the notice of the King.

" Sire, do you observe this dishonour ! Not one of these mighty lords but has praised the beauty of your wife, save Graelent only, who makes a mock of her. Always has he held me in envy and despite."

The King commanded Graelent to his throne, and in the hearing of all bade the knight to tell, on his faith as vassal to his liege, for what reason he had hid his face and laughed.

" Sire," answered Graelent to the King, " Sire, hearken to my words. In all the world no man of your lineage does so shameful a deed as this. You make your wife a show upon a stage. You force your lords to praise her just with lies, saying that the sun does not shine upon her peer. One man will tell the truth to your face, and say that very easily can be found a fairer dame than she."

Right heavy was the King when he heard these words. He conjured Graelent to tell him straightly if he knew a daintier dame.

" Yes, Sire, and thirty times more gracious than the Queen."

The Queen was marvellously wrathful to hear this thing, and prayed her husband of his grace to compel the knight to bring that woman to the Court of whose beauty he made so proud a boast.

" Set us side by side, and let the choice be made between us. Should she prove the fairer let him go in peace ; but if not, let justice be done on him for his calumny and malice."

So the King bade his guards to lay hands on Graelent, swearing that between them never should be love nor peace, nor should the knight issue forth from prison, until he had brought before him her whose beauty he had praised so much.

Graelent was held a captive. He repented him of his hasty words, and begged the King to grant him respite. He feared to have lost his friend, and sweated grievously with rage and mortification. But though many of the King's house pitied him in his evil case, the long days brought him no relief, until a full year went by, and once again the King made a great banquet to his barons and his lieges. Then was Graelent brought to hall, and put to liberty on such terms that he would return bringing with him her whose loveliness he had praised before the King. Should she prove so desirable and dear, as his boast, then all would be well, for he had naught to fear. But if he returned without his lady, then he must go to judgment, and his only hope would be in the mercy of the King.

Graelent mounted his good horse, and parted from the Court sad and wrathful. He sought his lodging, and inquired for his servant, but might not find him. He called upon his friend, but the lady did not heed his voice. Then Graelent gave way to despair, and preferred death to life. He shut himself within his chamber, crying upon his dear one for grace and mercy, but from her he got neither speech nor comfort. So seeing that his love had withdrawn herself from him by reason of his grievous fault, he took no rest by night or day, and held his life in utter despite. For a full year he lived in this piteous case, so that it was marvellous to those about him that he might endure his life.

On the day appointed the sureties brought Graelent where the King was set in hall with his lords. Then the King inquired of Graelent where was now his friend.

"Sire," answered the knight, "she is not here, for in no wise might I find her. Now do with me according to your will."

"Sir Graelent," said the King, "very foully have you spoken. You have slandered the Queen, and given all my lords the lie. When you go from my hands never will you do more mischief with your tongue."

Then the King spoke with a high voice to his barons.

"Lords, I pray and command you to give judgment in this matter. You heard the blame that Graelent set upon me before all my Court. You know the deep dishonour that he fastened on the Queen. How may such a disloyal vassal deal honestly with his lord, for as the proverb tells, 'Hope not for friendship from the man who beats your dog!'"

The lords of the King's household went out from before him, and gathered themselves together to consider their judgment. They kept silence for a great space, for it was grievous to them to deal harshly with so valiant a knight. Whilst they thus refrained from words a certain page hastened unto them, and prayed them not to press the matter, for (said he) "even now two young maidens, the freshest maids in all the realm, seek the Court. Perchance they bring succour to the good knight, and, so it be the will of God, may deliver him from peril." So the lords waited right gladly, and presently they saw two damsels come riding to the palace. Very young were these maidens, very slender and gracious, and daintily cloaked in two fair mantles. So when the pages had hastened to hold their stirrup and bridle, the maidens dismounted from their palfreys and entering within the hall came straight before the King.

"Sire," said one of the two damsels, "hearken now to me. My lady commands us to pray you to put back this cause for a while, nor to deliver judgment therein, since she comes to plead with you for the deliverance of this knight."

When the Queen heard this message she was filled with shame, and made speed to get her from the hall Hardly had she gone than there entered two other damsels, whiter and more sweetly flushed even than their fellows. These bade the King to wait for a little, since their mistress was now at hand. So all men stared upon them, and praised their great beauty, saying that if the maid was so fair, what then must be the loveliness of the dame. When, therefore, the demoiselle came in her turn, the King's household stood upon their feet to give her greeting. Never did woman show so queenly to men's sight as did this lady riding to the hall. Passing sweet she was to see, passing simple and gracious of manner, with softer eyes and a daintier face than girl of mother born. The whole Court marvelled at her beauty, for no spot or blemish might be found in her body. She was richly dressed in a kirtle of vermeil silk, broidered with gold, and her mantle was worth the spoil of a king's castle. Her palfrey was of good race, and speedy; the harness and trappings upon him were worth a thousand livres in minted coin. All men pressed about her, praising her face and person, her simplicity and queenlihead. She came at slow pace before the King, and dismounting from the palfrey, spoke very courteously in this fashion.

" Sire," said she, " hearken to me, and you, lord
barons, give heed to my pleading. You know the words
Graelent spake to the King, in the ears of men, when
the Queen made herself a show before the lords, saying
that often had he seen a fairer lady. Very hasty and
foolish was his tongue, since he provoked the King to
anger. But at least he told the truth when he said that
there is no dame so comely but that very easily may be
found one more sweet than she. Look now boldly upon
my face, and judge you rightly in this quarrel between
the Queen and me. So shall Sir Graelent be acquitted
of this blame."

Then gazing upon her, all the King's household, lord
and lackey, prince and page, cried with one voice that
her favour was greater than that of the Queen. The
King himself gave judgment with his barons that this
thing was so ; therefore Sir Graelent was acquitted of
his blame, and declared a free man.

When judgment was given the lady took her leave of
the King, and attended by her four damsels departed
straightway from the hall upon her palfrey. Sir Graelent
caused his white horse to be saddled, and mounting,
followed hotly after her through the town. Day after
day he rode in her track, pleading for pity and pardon,
but she gave him neither good words nor bad in answer.
So far they fared that at last they came to the forest,
and taking their way through a deep wood rode to the
bank of a fair, clear stream. The lady set her palfrey
to the river, but when she saw that Graelent also would
enter therein she cried to him,

" Stay, Graelent, the stream is deep, and it is death
for you to follow."

Graelent took no heed to her words, but forced his
horse to enter the river, so that speedily the waters
closed above his head. Then the lady seized his bridle,

and with extreme toil brought horse and rider back again to land.

"Graelent," said she, "you may not pass this river, however mightily you pain yourself, therefore must you remain alone on this bank."

Again the lady set her palfrey to the river, but Graelent could not suffer to see her go upon her way alone. Again he forced his horse to enter the water; but the current was very swift and the stream was very deep, so that presently Graelent was torn from his saddle, and being borne away by the stream came very nigh to drown. When the four maidens saw his piteous plight they cried aloud to their lady, and said,

"Lady, for the love of God, take pity on your poor friend. See, how he drowns in this evil case. Alas, cursed be the day you spake soft words in his ear, and gave him the grace of your love. Lady, look how the current hurries him to his death. How may your heart suffer him to drown whom you have held so close! Aid him, nor have the sin on your soul that you endured to let the man who loved you die without your help."

When the lady heard the complaint of her maidens, no longer could she hide the pity she felt in her heart. In all haste she turned her palfrey to the river, and entering the stream clutched her lover by the belt. Thus they won together to the bank. There she stripped the drowned man of his raiment, and wrapping him fast in her own dry mantle cherished him so meetly that presently he came again to life. So she brought him safely into her own land, and none has met Sir Graelent since that day.

But the Breton folk still hold firmly that Graelent yet liveth with his friend. His destrier, when he escaped him from the perilous river, grieved greatly for his master's loss. He sought again the mighty forest, yet never was at rest by night or day. No peace might he find, but ever pawed he with his hoofs upon the ground, and neighed so loudly that the noise went through all the country round about. Many a man coveted so noble a steed, and sought to put bit and bridle in his mouth, yet never might one set hands upon him, for he would not suffer another master. So each year in its season the forest was filled with the cry and the trouble of this noble horse which might not find its lord.

This adventure of the good steed and of the stout knight, who went to the land of faery with his love, was noised abroad throughout all Brittany, and the Bretons made a Lay thereof which was sung in the ears of many people, and was called a Lay of the Death of Sir Graelent.

XVI

A STORY OF BEYOND THE SEA

In times gone by there lived a Count of Ponthieu, who loved chivalry and the pleasures of the world beyond measure, and moreover was a stout knight and a gallant gentleman. In the self-same day there lived a Count of St. Pol, who was lord of much land, and a right worthy man. One grief he had, that there was no heir of his body; but a sister was his, a prudent woman and a passing good gentlewoman, who was dame of Dommare in Ponthieu. This lady had a son, Thibault by name, who was heir to this County of St. Pol, but he was a poor man so long as his uncle lived. He was a prudent knight, valiant and skilled with the spear, noble and fair. Greatly was he loved and honoured of all honest people, for he was of high race and gentle birth.

The Count of Ponthieu, of whom the tale hath spoken, had to wife a very worthy lady. He and his dame had but one child, a daughter, very good and gracious, who increased with her days in favour and in virtues; and the maid was of some sixteen years. The third year after her birth her mother died, whereof she was sorely troubled and right heavy. The Count, her father, took to himself another wife with no long tarrying, a dame of gentle race and breeding. Of this lady he got him quickly a son; very near was the boy to his father's heart. The lad grew with his years in stature and in valour, and gave promise to increase in all good qualities.

The Count of Ponthieu marked my lord Thibault of
Dommare. He summoned the knight to his castle,
and made him of his house for guerdon. When Sir
Thibault was of his fellowship he rejoiced greatly, for
the Count prospered in goods and in praise by reason
of his servant's deeds. As they came from a tournament
on a day, the Count and my lord Thibault together,
the Count required of his companion and said,

"Thibault, by the aid of God tell me truly which
jewel of my crown shines the fairest in your eyes!"

"Sir," replied Messire Thibault, "I am only a beggar,
but so help me God, of all the jewels in your crown I
love and covet none, save only my demoiselle, your
daughter."

When he heard this thing the Count had great content.
He laughed in his heart and said,

"Thibault, I will grant her to the beggar, if it be to
her mind."

"Sir," answered he, "thanks and gramercy. May
God make it up to you."

Then went the Count to his daughter, and said,

"Fair daughter, I have promised you in marriage,
so it go not against your heart."

"Sir," inquired the maid, "to whom?"

"In the name of God, to a loyal man, and a true
man, of whom much is hoped; to a knight of my own
household, Thibault of Dommare."

"Dear sir," answered the maiden sweetly, "if your
county were a kingdom, and I were the king's only
child, I would choose him as my husband, and gladly
give him all that I had."

"Daughter," said the Count, "blessed be your pretty
person, and the hour that you were born."

Thus was this marriage made. The Count of Ponthieu
and the Count of St. Pol were at the feast, and many

another honourable man besides. Great was the joy
in which they met, fair was the worship, and marvellous
the delight. The bride and groom lived together in all
happiness for five years. This was their only sorrow,
that it pleased not our Lord Jesus Christ that they
should have an heir to their flesh.

On a night Sir Thibault lay in his bed. He considered
within himself and said,

"Lord, whence cometh it that I love this dame so
fondly, and she me, yet we may have no heir of our
bodies to serve God and to do a little good in the world ? "

Then he remembered my lord St. James, the Apostle
of Spain, who gives to the fervent supplicant that which
rightly he desires. Earnestly, to his own heart, he
promised that he would walk a pilgrim in his way.
His wife lay sleeping at his side, but when she came from
out her sleep, he took her softly in his arms, and required
of her that she would bestow on him a gift.

"Sir," said the lady, "what gift would you
have ? "

"Wife," he made answer, "that you shall know when
it is mine."

"Husband," said she, "if it be mine to grant, I will
give it you, whatever the price."

"Wife," he said, "I pray you to grant me leave to
seek my lord St. James the Apostle, that he may intercede
with our Lord Jesus Christ to bestow on us an heir
of our flesh, whereby God may be served in this world
and Holy Church glorified."

"Sir," cried the lady, "sweet and dear it is that you
should crave such bounty, and I grant the permission
you desire right willingly."

Deep and long was the tenderness that fell betwixt
these twain. Thus passed a day, and another day, and
yet a third. On this third day it chanced that they lay

together in their bed, and it was night. Then said the
dame,

"Husband, I pray and require of you a gift."

"Wife," he replied, "ask, and I will give it you, if
by any means I can."

"Husband," she said, "I require leave to come with
you on this errand and journey."

When Messire Thibault heard this thing he was right
sorrowful, and said,

"Wife, grievous would be the journey to your body,
for the way is very long, and the land right strange and
perilous."

Said she,

"Husband, be not in doubt because of me. You
shall be more hindered of your squire than of your wife."

"Dame," said he, "as God wills and as you wish."

The days went, and these tidings were so noised
abroad that the Count of Ponthieu heard thereof. He
commanded my lord Sir Thibault to his house, and said,

"Thibault, you are a vowed pilgrim, as I hear, and
my daughter too!"

"Sir," answered he, "that is verily and truly so."

"Thibault," replied the Count, "as to yourself what
pleases you is to my mind also, but concerning my
daughter that is another matter."

"Sir," made answer Sir Thibault, "go she must, and
I cannot deny her."

"Since this is so," said the Count, "part when you
will. Make ready for the road your steeds, your palfreys,
and the pack horses, and I will give you riches and gear
enough for the journey."

"Sir," said Messire Thibault, "thanks and gramercy."

Thus these pilgrims arrayed them, and sought that
shrine with marvellous joy. They fared so speedily
upon the way, that at length they came near to my

lord St. James, by less than two days faring. That
night they drew to a goodly town. After they had eaten
in the hostel, Sir Thibault called for the host and inquired
of him the road for the morrow, how it ran, and whether
it were smooth.

"Fair sir," replied the innkeeper to the knight, "at
the gate of this town you will find a little wood. Beyond
the wood a strong smooth road runs for the whole day's
journey."

Hearing this they asked no more questions, but the
beds being laid down, they went to their rest. The
morrow broke full sweetly. The pilgrims rose lightly
from their beds as soon as it was day, and made much
stir and merriment. Sir Thibault rose also, since he
might not sleep, but his head was heavy. He therefore
called his chamberlain, and said,

"Rise quickly, and bid the company to pack the
horses and go their way. Thou shalt remain with me,
and make ready our harness, for I am a little heavy
and disquieted."

The chamberlain made known to the sergeants the
pleasure of their lord, so that presently they took the
road. In no great while Messire Thibault and his dame
got them from the bed, and arraying their persons,
followed after their household. The chamberlain folded
the bed linen, and it was yet but dawn, though warm
and fair. The three went forth through the gate of
the city, those three together, with no other companion
save God alone, and drew near to the forest. When they
came close they found two roads, the one good, the
other ill; so that Sir Thibault said to his chamberlain,

"Put spurs to your horse, and ride swiftly after our
people. Bid them await our coming, for foul it is for
lady and knight to pass through this wood with so
little company."

The servitor went speedily, and Messire Thibault entered the forest. He drew rein beside the two roads, for he knew not which to follow.

"Wife," he said, "which way is ours?"

"Please God, the good," she answered.

Now in this wood were robbers, who spoiled the fair way, and made wide and smooth the false, so that pilgrims should mistake and wander from the path. Messire Thibault lighted from his horse. He looked from one to the other, and finding the wrong way broader and more smooth than the true, he cried,

"Wife, come now; in the name of God, this."

They had proceeded along this road for some quarter of a mile when the path grew strict and narrow, and boughs made dark the way.

"Wife," said the knight, "I fear that we fare but ill."

When he had thus spoken he looked before him, and marked four armed thieves, seated on four strong horses, and each bore lance in hand. Thereupon he glanced behind him, and, lo, four other robbers, armed and set in ambush, so he said,

"Dame, be not affrighted of aught that you may see from now."

Right courteously Sir Thibault saluted the robbers in his path, but they gave no answer to his greeting. Afterwards he sought of them what was in their mind, and one replied that he should know anon. The thief, who had thus spoken, drew towards my lord Thibault, with outstretched sword, thinking to smite him in the middle. Messire Thibault saw the blow about to fall, and it was no marvel if he feared greatly. He sprang forward nimbly, as best he might, so that the glaive smote the air. Then as the robber staggered by, Sir Thibault seized him fiercely, and wrested the sword from his hand. The knight advanced stoutly against those three from whom the thief had come. He struck the foremost amidst the bowels, so that he perished miserably. Then he turned and went again to that one who had first come against him with the sword, and slew him also. Now it was decreed of God that after the knight had slain three of this company of robbers, that the five who were left, encompassed him round about, and killed his palfrey. Sir Thibault tumbled flat upon his back, although he was not wounded to his hurt. Since he had neither sword nor other harness he could do no more. The thieves therefore stripped him to his very shirt, his boots and hosen, and binding him hand and foot with a baldrick, cast him into a thorn bush, right thick and sharp. When they had done this they hastened to the lady. From her they took her palfrey and her vesture, even to the shift. Passing fair was the lady ; she wept full piteously, and never was dame more sorrowful than she. Now one of these bold robbers stared upon the lady, and saw that she was very fair. He spoke to his companions in this fashion,

"Comrades, I have lost my brother in this broil. I will take this woman for his blood money."

But the others made answer,

"I, too, have lost my kin. I claim as much as you, and my right is good as yours."

So said a third, and a fourth, and a fifth. Then spake yet another.

"In keeping of the lady will be found neither peace nor profit. Rather let us lead her from here within the forest, there do our pleasure upon her, and then put her again upon the path, so that she may go her way."

Thus they did as they had devised together, and left her on the road.

Right sick at heart was Messire Thibault when he saw her so entreated, but nothing could he do. He bore no malice against his wife by reason of that which had befallen, for well he knew that it was by force, and not according to her will. When he saw her again, weeping bitterly and altogether shamed, he called to her, and said,

"Wife, for God's love unloose me from these bonds, and deliver me from the torment that I suffer, for these thorns are sharper than I can endure."

The lady hastened to the place where Sir Thibault lay, and marked a sword flung behind the bush, belonging to one of those felons that were slain. She took the glaive, and went towards her lord, filled full of wrath and evil thoughts because of what had chanced to her. She feared greatly lest her husband should bear malice for that which he had seen, reproaching her upon a day, and taunting her for what was past. She said,

"Sir, you are out of your pain already."

She raised the sword, and came towards her husband, thinking to strike him midmost the body. When he marked the falling glaive he deemed that his day had come, for he was a naked man, clad in nought but his shirt and hosen. He trembled so sorely that his bonds were loosed, and the lady struck so feebly that she wounded him but little, severing that baldrick with which his hands were made fast. Thereat the knight brake the cords about his legs, and leaping upon his feet, cried,

"Dame, by the grace of God it is not to-day that you shall slay me with the sword."

Then she made answer,

"Truly, sir, the sorer grief is mine."

Sir Thibault took the sword, and set it again in the sheath, afterwards he put his hand upon the lady's shoulder, and brought her back by the path they had

fared. At the fringe of the woodland he found a large
part of his fellowship, who were come to meet him. When
these saw their lord and lady so spoiled and disarrayed
they inquired of them,

" Sir, who hath put you in this case ? "

He set them by, saying that they had fallen amongst
felons who had done them much mischief.

Mightily the sergeants lamented ; but presently they
fetched raiment from the packs, and arrayed them, for
enough they had and to spare. So they climbed into
the saddle, and continued their journey.

They rode that day, nor for aught that had chanced
did Messire Thibault show sourer countenance to the
lady. At nightfall they came to a goodly town, and
there took shelter in an inn. Messire Thibault sought
of his host if there was any convent of nuns in those
parts where a lady might repose her. The host made
answer to him,

"Sir, you are served to your wish. Just beyond the walls
is a right fair religious house, with many holy women."

On the morrow Messire Thibault went to this house, and
heard Mass. Afterwards he spoke to the Abbess and her
chapter, praying that he might leave his lady in their
charge, until his return ; and this they accorded very
willingly. Messire Thibault bestowed the lady in this
convent, with certain of his house to do her service,
and went his way to bring his pilgrimage to a fair end.
When he had knelt before the shrine, and honoured the
Saint, he came again to the convent and the lady. He
gave freely of his wealth to the house, and taking to
himself his wife, returned with her to their own land, in the
same joy and honour as he had brought her forth, save
only that they lay not together.

Great was the gladness of the folk of that realm when
Sir Thibault returned to his home. The Count of

Ponthieu, the father of his wife was there, and there, too, was his uncle the Count of St. Pol. Many worthy and valiant gentlemen came for his welcome, and a fair company of dames and maidens likewise honoured the lady. That day the Count of Ponthieu sat at meat with my lord Thibault, and ate from the same dish, the two together. Then it happed that the Count spake to him,

"Thibault, fair son, he who journeys far hears many a strange matter and sees many strange sights, which are hidden from those who sit over the fire. Tell me therefore, of your favour, something of all you have seen and heard since you went from amongst us."

Messire Thibault answered shortly that he knew no tale worth the telling. The Count would take no denial, but plagued him so sorely, begging him of his courtesy to tell over some adventure, that at the last he was overborne.

"Sir, I will narrate a story, since talk I must; but at least let it be in your private ear, if you please, and not for the mirth of all."

The Count replied that his pleasure was the same. After meat, when men had eaten their fill, the Count rose in his chair, and taking my lord Thibault by the hand, entreated,

"Tell me now, I pray, that which it pleases you to tell, for there are few of the household left in hall."

Then Messire Thibault began to relate that which chanced to a knight and a dame, even as it has been rehearsed before you in this tale; only he named not the persons to whom this lot was appointed. The Count, who was wise and sober of counsel, inquired what the knight had done with the lady. Thibault made answer that the knight had brought the lady back by the way she went, with the same joy and worship as he led her forth, save only that they slept not together.

"Thibault," said the Count, "your knight walked another road than I had trod. By my faith in God and my love for you, I had hanged this dame by her tresses to a tree. The laces of her gown would suffice if I could find no other cord."

"Sir," said Messire Thibault, "you have but my word. The truth can only be assured if the lady might bear witness and testify with her own mouth."

"Thibault," said the Count, "know you the name of this knight ? "

"Sir," cried Messire Thibault, "I beg you again to exempt me from naming the knight to whom this sorrow befell. Know of a truth that his name will bring no profit."

"Thibault," said the Count, "it is my pleasure that his name should not be hid."

"Sir," answered Thibault, "tell I must, as you will not acquit me ; but I take you to witness that I speak only under compulsion, since gladly I would have kept silence, had this been your pleasure, for in the telling there is neither worship nor honour."

"Thibault," replied the Count, "without more words I would know forthwith who was the knight to whom this adventure chanced. By the faith that you owe to your God and to me, I conjure you to tell me his name, since it is in your mind."

"Sir," replied Messire Thibault, "I will answer by the faith I owe my God and you, since you lay this charge upon me. Know well, and be persuaded, that I am the knight on whom this sorrow lighted. Hold it for truth that I was sorely troubled and sick of heart. Be assured that never before have I spoken to any living man about the business, and moreover that gladly would I have held my peace, had such been your will."

When the Count heard this adventure he was sore astonied, and altogether cast down. He kept silence for a great space, speaking never a word. At the last he said,

"Thibault, was it indeed my child who did this thing?"

"Sir, it is verily and truly so."

"Thibault," said the Count, "sweet shall be your vengeance, since you have given her again to my hand."

Because of his exceeding wrath the Count sent straightway for his daughter, and demanded of her if those things were true of which Messire Thibault had spoken. She inquired of the accusation, and her father answered,

"That you would have slain him with the sword, even as he has told me?"

"Sir, of a surety."

"And wherefore would you slay your husband?"

"Sir, for reason that I am yet heavy that he is not dead."

When the Count heard the lady speak in this fashion, he answered her nothing, but suffered in silence until the guests had departed. After these were gone, the Count came on a day to Rue-sur-Mer, and Messire Thibault with him, and the Count's son. With them also went the lady. Then the Count caused a ship to be got ready, very stout and speedy, and he made the dame to enter in the boat. He set also on the ship an untouched barrel, very high and strong. These three lords climbed into the nave, with no other company, save those sailors who should labour at the oar. The Count commanded the mariners to put the ship to sea, and all marvelled greatly as to what he purposed, but there was none so bold as to ask him any questions. When they had rowed a great way from the land, the Count bade them to strike the head from out the barrel. He took that dame, his own child, who was so dainty and so fair, and thrust her in the tun, whether she would or whether she would not. This being done he caused the cask to be made fast again with staves and wood, so that the water might in no manner enter therein. Afterwards he dragged the barrel to the edge of the deck, and with his own hand cast it into the sea, saying,

" I commend thee to the wind and waves."

Passing heavy was Messire Thibault at this, and the lady's brother also, and all who saw. They fell at the Count's feet, praying him of his grace that she might be delivered from the barrel. So hot was his wrath that he would not grant their prayer, for aught that they might do or say. They therefore left him to his rage, and turning to the Heavenly Father, besought our Lord Jesus Christ that of His most sweet pity He would have mercy on her soul, and give her pardon for her sins.

The ship came again to land, leaving the lady in sore peril and trouble, even as the tale has told you. But our Lord Jesus Christ, who is Lord and Father of all, and desireth not the death of a sinner, but rather that he should turn from his wickedness and live—as each day He showeth us openly by deed, by example and by miracle—sent succour to this lady, even as you shall hear. For a ship from Flanders, laden with merchandise, marked this barrel drifting at the mercy of winds and waters, before ever the Count and his companions were come ashore. One of the merchants said to his comrades,

" Friends, behold a barrel drifting in our course. If we may reach it, perchance we may find it to our gain."

This ship was wont to traffic with the Saracens in their country, so the sailors rowed towards the barrel, and partly by cunning and partly by strength, at the

last got it safely upon the deck. The merchants looked
long at the cask. They wondered greatly what it could
be, and wondering, they saw that the head of the barrel
was newly closed. They opened the cask, and found
therein a woman at the point of death, for air had failed
her. Her body was gross, her visage swollen, and the
eyes started horribly from her head. When she breathed
the fresh air and felt the wind blow upon her, she sighed
a little, so that the merchants standing by, spoke com-
fortably to her, but she might not answer them a word.
In the end, heart and speech came again to her. She
spoke to the chapmen and the sailors who pressed about
her, and much she marvelled how she found herself
amongst them. When she perceived that she was with
merchants and Christian men she was the more easy,
and fervently she praised Jesus Christ in her heart,
thanking Him for the lovingkindness which had kept
her from death. For this lady was altogether contrite
in heart, and earnestly desired to amend her life towards
God, repenting the trespass she had done to others,
and fearing the judgment that was rightly her due.
The merchants inquired of the lady whence she came,
and she told them the truth, saying that she was a
miserable wretch and a poor sinner, as they could see
for themselves. She related the cruel adventure which
had chanced to her, and prayed them to take pity on
a most unhappy lady, and they answered that mercy
they would show. So with meat and drink her former
beauty came to her again.

Now this merchant ship fared so far that she came to
the land of the Paynims, and cast anchor in the port
of Aumarie. Galleys of these Saracens came to know
their business, and they answered that they were
traffickers in divers merchandise in many a realm.
They showed them also the safe conduct they carried

of princes and mighty lords that they might pass in
safety through their countries to buy and sell their
goods. The merchants got them to land in this port,
taking the lady with them. They sought counsel one
of the other to know what it were best to do with her.
One was for selling her as a slave, but his companion
proposed to give her as a sop to the rich Soudan of
Aumarie, that their business should be the less hindered.
To this they all agreed. They arrayed the lady freshly
in broidered raiment, and carried her before the Soudan,
who was a lusty young man. He accepted their gift,
receiving the lady with a right glad heart, for she was
passing fair. The Soudan inquired of them as to who
she was.

" Sire," answered the merchants, " we know no more
than you, but marvellous was the fashion in which she
came to our hands."

The gift was so greatly to the Soudan's mind that he
served the chapmen to the utmost of his power. He
loved the lady very tenderly, and entreated her in all
honour. He held and tended her so well, that her sweet
colour came again to her, and her beauty increased
beyond measure. The Soudan sought to know by those
who had the gift of tongues as to the lady's home and
race, but these she would not reveal to any. He was
the more thoughtful therefore, because he might see
that she was a dame of birth and lineage. He inquired
of her as to whether she were a Christian woman, promising that if she would deny her faith, he would take her
as his wife, since he was yet unwed. The lady saw
clearly that it were better to be converted by love than
perforce ; so she answered that her religion was to do
her master's pleasure. When she had renounced her
faith, and rejected the Christian law, the Soudan made
her his dame according to the use and wont of this

country of the Paynim. He held her very dear, cherishing her in all honour, for his love waxed deeper as the days wore on.

In due time it was with this lady after the manner of women, and she came to bed of a son. The Soudan rejoiced greatly, being altogether merry and content. The lady, for her part, lived in fair fellowship with the folk of her husband's realm. Very courteous was she, and very serviceable, so that presently she was instructed in the Saracen tongue. In no long while after the birth of her son she conceived of a maid, who in the years that befell grew passing sweet and fair, and richly was she nurtured as became the daughter of so high a prince. Thus for two years and a half the lady dwelt with the Paynim in much softness and delight.

Now the story keeps silence as to the lady and the Soudan, her husband, till later, as you may hear, and returns to the Count of Ponthieu, the son of the Count, and to my lord Thibault of Dommare, who were left grieving for the dame who was flung into the sea, as you have heard, nor knew aught of her tidings, but deemed that she were rather dead than alive. Now tells the story—and the truth bears witness to itself and is its own confirmation—that the Count was in Ponthieu, together with his son, and Messire Thibault. Very heavy was the Count, for in no wise could he get his daughter from his mind, and grievously he lamented the wrong that he had done her. Messire Thibault dared not take to himself another wife, because of the anguish of his friend. The son of the Count might not wed also; neither durst he to become knight, though he was come to an age when such things are greatly to a young man's mind.

On a day the Count considered deeply the sin that he had committed against his own flesh. He sought the

Archbishop of Rheims in confession, and opened out
his grief, telling in his ear the crime that he had wrought.
He determined to seek those holy fields beyond the sea,
and sewed the Cross upon his mantle. When Messire
Thibault knew that his lord, the Count, had taken the
Cross, he confessed him, and did likewise. And when
the Count's son was assured of the purpose of his sire
and of Messire Thibault, whom he loved dearly, he took
the Cross with them. Passing heavy was the Count to
mark the Sign upon his son's raiment.

" Fair son, what is this you have done ; for now the
land remains without a lord ! "

The son answered, and said,

" Father, I wear the Sign first and foremost for the
love of God ; afterwards for the saving of my soul, and
by reason that I would serve and honour Him to the
utmost of my power, so long as I have life in my body."

The Count put his realm in ward full wisely. He
used diligence in making all things ready, and bade
farewell to his friends. Messire Thibault and the son
of the Count ordered their business, and the three set
forth together, with a fair company. They came to
that holy land beyond the sea, safe of person and of
gear. There they made devout pilgrimage to every
place where they were persuaded it was meet to go,
and God might be served. When the Count had done
all that he was able, he deemed that there was yet one
thing to do. He gave himself and his fellowship to the
service of the Temple for one year ; and at the end of
this term he purposed to seek his country and his home.
He sent to Acre, and made ready a ship against his
voyage. He took his leave of the Knights Templar,
and other lords of that land, and greatly they praised
him for the worship that he had brought them. When
the Count and his company were come to Acre they

entered in the ship, and departed from the haven with
a fair wind. But little was their solace. For when they
drew to the open sea a strong and horrible tempest
sprang suddenly upon them, so that the sailors knew
not where they went, and feared each hour that all
would be drowned. So piteous was their plight that,
with ropes, they bound themselves one to another, the
son to the father, the uncle to the nephew, according
as they stood. The Count, his son, and Messire Thibault
for their part, fastened themselves together, so that the
same end should chance to all. In no long time after
this was done they saw land, and inquired of the shipmen whither they were come. The mariners answered
that this realm belonged to the Paynim, and was called
the Land of Aumarie. They asked of the Count,

"Sire, what is your will that we do? If we seek the
shore, doubtless we shall be made captives, and fall
into the hands of the Saracen."

The Count made answer,

"Not my will, but the will of Jesus Christ be done.
Let the ship go as He thinks best. We will commit our
bodies and our lives to His good keeping, for a fouler
and an uglier death we cannot die, than to perish in
this sea."

They drove with the wind along the coast of Aumarie,
and the galleys and warships of the Saracens put out
to meet them. Be assured that this was no fair meeting,
for the Paynims took them and led them before the
Soudan, who was lord of that realm. There they gave
him the goods and the bodies of these Christians as a
gift. The Soudan sundered this fair fellowship, setting
them in many places and in divers prisons; but since
the Count, his son, and Messire Thibault were so securely
bound together, he commanded that they should be
cast into a dungeon by themselves, and fed upon the

bread of affliction and the water of affliction. So it was done, even as he commanded. In this prison they lay for a space, till such time as the Count's son fell sick. His sickness was so grievous that the Count and Messire Thibault feared greatly that this sorrow was to death.

Now it came to pass that the Soudan held high Court because of the day of his birth, for such was the custom of the Saracens. After they had well eaten, the Saracens stood before the Soudan, and said,

" Sire, we require of you our right."

He inquired of what right they were speaking, and they answered,

" Sire, a Christian captive to set as a mark for our arrows."

When the Soudan heard this he gave no thought to such a trifle, but made reply,

" Get you to the prison, and take out that captive who has the least of life in him."

The Paynim hastened to the dungeon, and brought forth the Count, bearded, unkempt and foredone. The Soudan marked his melancholy case, so he said to them,

" This man has not long to live; take him hence, and do your will on him."

The wife of the Soudan, of whom you have heard, the daughter of this very Count, was in the hall, when they brought forth her father to slay him. Immediately that her eyes fell upon him the blood in her veins turned to water; not so much that she knew him as her sire, but rather that Nature tugged at her heart strings. Then spake the dame to the Soudan,

" Husband, I, too, am French, and would gladly speak with this poor wretch ere he die, if so I may."

" Wife," answered the Soudan, " truly, yes; it pleases me well."

The lady came to the Count. She took him apart, and bidding the Saracens fall back, she inquired of him whence he was.

"Lady, I am from the kingdom of France, of a county that men call Ponthieu."

When the lady heard this her bowels were moved. Earnestly she demanded his name and race.

"Of a truth, lady, I have long forgotten my father's house, for I have suffered such pain and anguish since I departed, that I would rather die than live. But this you may know, that I—even the man who speaks to you—was once the Count of Ponthieu."

The lady hearkened to this, but yet she made no sign. She went from the Count, and coming to the Soudan, said,

"Husband, give me this captive as a gift, if such be your pleasure. He knows chess and draughts and many fair tales to bring solace to the hearer. He shall play before you, and we will make our pastime of his skill."

"Wife," answered the Soudan, "I grant him to you very willingly; do with him as you wish."

The lady took the captive, and bestowed him in her chamber. The gaolers sought another in his stead, and brought forth my lord Thibault, the husband to the dame. He came out in tatters, for he was clothed rather in his long hair and great beard, than in raiment. His body was lean and bony, and he seemed as one who had endured pain and sorrow enough, and to spare. When the lady saw him she said to the Soudan,

"Husband, with this one also would I gladly speak, if so I may."

"Wife," answered the Soudan, "it pleases me well."

The lady came to my lord Thibault, and inquired of him whence he was.

" Lady, I am of the realm of that ancient gentleman who was taken from prison before me. I had his daughter to wife, and am his knight."

The lady knew well her lord, so she returned to the Soudan, and said to him,

" Husband, great kindness will you show me, if you give me this captive also."

" Wife," said the Soudan, " I grant him to you very willingly."

She thanked him sweetly, and bestowed the gift in her chamber, with the other.

The archers hastened together, and drawing before the Soudan said,

" Sire, you do us wrong, for the day is far spent."

They went straight to the prison, and brought forth the son of the Count, shagged and filthy, as one who had not known of water for many a day. He was a young man, so young that his beard had not come on him, but for all his youth he was so thin and sick and weak, that he scarce could stand upon his feet. When the lady saw him she had compassion upon him. She came to him asking whose son he was and of his home, and he replied that he was son to that gentleman, who was first brought out of the dungeon. She knew well that this was her brother, but she made herself strange unto him.

" Husband," said she to the Soudan, " verily you will shew kindness to your wife beyond measure if you grant me this captive. He knows chess and draughts and other delights passing fair to see and hear."

And the Soudan made answer,

" Wife, by our holy law if they were a hundred I would give them all to you gladly."

The lady thanked him tenderly, and bestowed the captive swiftly in her chamber. The Saracens went again to the prison and fetched out another, but the lady left him to his fate, when she looked upon his face. So he won a martyr's crown, and our Lord Jesus Christ received his soul. As for the dame, she hid herself from the sight, for it gave her little joy, this slaying of the Christian by the Paynims.

The lady came to her chamber, and at her coming the captives would have got them to their feet, but she made signs that they should remain seated. Drawing close she made gestures of friendship. The Count, who was very shrewd, asked at this,

" Lady, when will they slay us ? "

She answered that their time had not yet come.

" Lady," said he, " the sorer grief is ours, for we are so anhungered, that for a little our souls would leave our bodies."

The lady went out, and bade meat to be made ready. This she carried in, giving to each a little, and to each a little drink. When they had eaten, they had yet greater hunger than before. In this manner she fed them, little by little, ten times a day, for she deemed that should they eat to their desire, they would die of repletion. For this reason she caused them to break their fast temperately. Thus the good lady dealt with them for the first seven days, and at nights, by her grace, they lay softly at their ease. She did away with their rags, and clad them in seemly apparel. When the week was done she set before them meat and drink to their heart's desire, so that their strength returned to them again. They had chess and draughts, and played these games to their great content. The Soudan was often with them. He watched the play, and took pleasure in their gladness. But the lady refrained, so that none might conceive, either by speech or fashion, that he had known her before.

Now a short while after this matter of the captives, the story tells that the Soudan had business enough of his own, for a mighty Sultan laid waste his realm, and sought to do him much mischief. To avenge his wrong the Soudan commanded his vassals from every place, and assembled a great host. When the lady knew this, she entered the chamber where the captives lay, and sitting amidst them lifted her hand, and said,

"Sirs, you have told me somewhat of your business; now will I be assured whether you are true men or not. You told me that in your own land you were once the Count of Ponthieu, that this man was wedded to your daughter, and that this other was your son. Know that I am a Saracen, having the science of astrology; so I tell you plainly that you were never so near to a shameful death, as you are now, if you hide from me the truth. What chanced to your daughter, the wife of this knight?"

"Lady," replied the Count, "I deem her to be dead."

"How came she to her death?"

"Certes, lady," said the Count, "because for once she received her deserts."

"Tell me of these deservings," said the dame.

Then the Count began to tell, with tears, of how she was wedded, but was yet a barren wife; how the good knight vowed pilgrimage to my lord St. James in Galicia, and how the lady prayed that she might go with him, which prayer he granted willingly. He told how they went their way with joy, till alone, in the deep wood, they met with sturdy felons who set upon them. The good knight might do nothing against so many, for he was a naked man; but despite of all, he slew three, and five were left, who killed his palfrey, and spoiling him to the very shirt, bound him hands and feet, and flung him into a thorn bush. They spoiled the lady also and stole her palfrey from her. When they looked upon her, and saw that she was fair, each would have taken her. Afterwards they accorded that she should be to all, and having had their will in her despite, they departed and left her weeping bitterly. This the good knight saw, so he besought her courteously to unloose his hands, that they might get them from the wood. But the lady marked a sword belonging to one of these felons that were slain. She handselled it, and hastening where he lay, cried in furious fashion, " You are unbound already." Then she raised the naked sword, and struck at his body. But by the loving kindness of God, and the vigour of the knight, she but sundered the bonds that bound him, so that he sprang forth, and wounded as he was, cried,

" Dame, by the grace of God it is not to-day that you shall kill me with the sword."

At this word that fair lady, the wife of the Soudan, spoke suddenly, and said,

" Ah, sir, you have told the tale honestly, and very clear it is why she would have slain him."

" For what reason, lady ? "

" Certes," answered she, " for reason of the great shame which had befallen her."

When Messire Thibault heard this he wept right tenderly, and said,

" Alas, what part had she in this wickedness ! May God keep shut the doors of my prison if I had shown her the sourer face therefore, seeing that her will was not in the deed."

" Sir," said the lady, " she feared your reproach. But tell me which is the more likely, that she be alive or dead ? "

" Lady," said Thibault, " we know not what to think."

" Well I know," cried the Count, " of the great

anguish we have suffered, by reason of the sin I sinned against her."

"If it pleased God that she were yet living," inquired the lady, "and tidings were brought which you could not doubt, what would you have to say?"

"Lady," said the Count, "I should be happier than if I were taken from this prison, or were granted more wealth than ever I have had in my life."

"Lady," said Messire Thibault, "so God give me no joy of my heart's dearest wish, if I had not more solace than if men crowned me King of France."

"Certes, lady," said the dansellon, who was her brother, "none could give or promise me aught so sweet, as the life of that sister, who was so fair and good."

When the lady hearkened to these words her heart yearned with tenderness. She praised God, rendering Him thanks, and said to them,

"Be sure that you speak with unfeigned lips."

And they answered and said that they spoke with unfeigned lips. Then the lady began to weep with happy tears, and said to them,

"Sir, now may you truly say that you are my father, for I am that daughter on whom you wrought such bitter justice. And you, Messire Thibault, are my lord and husband; and you, sir dansellon, are my brother."

Then she rehearsed to them in what manner she was found of the chapmen, and how they bestowed her as a gift on the Soudan. They were very glad, and rejoiced mightily, humbling themselves before her, but she forbade them to show their mirth, saying,

"I am a Saracen, and have renounced the faith; otherwise I should not be here, but were dead already. Therefore I pray and beseech you as you love your lives and would prolong your days, whatever you may see or hear, not to show me any affection, but keep yourselves strange to me, and leave me to unravel the coil. Now I will tell why I have revealed myself to you. My husband, the Soudan, rides presently to battle. I know well, Messire Thibault, that you are a hardy knight, and I will pray the Soudan to take you with him. If ever you were brave, now is the time to make it plain. See to it that you do him such service that he have no grievance against you."

The lady departed forthwith, and coming before the Soudan, said,

" Husband, one of my captives desires greatly to go with you, if such be your pleasure."

" Wife," answered he, " I dare not put myself in his hand, for fear that he may do me a mischief."

" Husband, he will not dare to be false, since I hold his companions as hostages."

" Wife," said he, " I will take him with me, because of your counsel, and I will deliver him a good horse and harness, and all that warrior may require."

The lady returned straightway to the chamber. She said to Messire Thibault,

" I have persuaded the Soudan to bring you to the battle. Act therefore manfully."

At this her brother knelt at her knee, praying her to plead with the Soudan that he might go also.

" That I may not do," said she, " or the thing will be too clear."

The Soudan ordered his business, and went forth, Messire Thibault being with him, and came upon the enemy. According to his word, the Soudan had given to the knight both horse and harness. By the will of Jesus Christ, who faileth never such as have faith and affiance in Him, Messire Thibault did such things in arms that in a short space the enemies of the Soudan

were put under his feet. The Soudan rejoiced greatly
at his knight's deeds and his victory, and returned
bringing many captives with him. He went straight
to the dame, and said,

"Wife, by my law I have naught but good to tell
of your prisoner, for he has done me faithful service.
So he deny his faith, and receive our holy religion, I
will grant him broad lands, and find him a rich heiress
in marriage."

"Husband, I know not, but I doubt if he will do this
thing."

No more was spoken of the matter; but the lady set
her house in order, as best she was able, and coming
to her captives said,

"Sirs, go warily, so that the Saracens see nothing
of what is in our mind; for, please God, we shall yet
win to France and the county of Ponthieu."

On a day the lady came before the Soudan. She
went in torment, and lamented very grievously.

"Husband, it is with me as it was before. Well I
know it, for I have fallen into sore sickness, and my food
has no relish in my mouth, no, not since you went to
the battle."

"Wife, I am right glad to hear that you are with
child, although your infirmity is very grievous unto
me. Consider and tell me those things that you deem will
be to your healing, and I will seek and procure them
whatever the cost."

When the lady heard this, her heart beat lightly in
her breast. She showed no semblance of joy, save this
only, that she said,

"Husband, my old captive tells me that unless I
breathe for awhile such air as that of my native land,
and that quickly, I am but dead, for in nowise have I
long to live."

"Wife," said the Soudan, "your death shall not be on my conscience. Consider and show me where you would go, and there I will cause you to be taken."

"Husband, it is all one to me, so I be out of this city."

Then the Soudan made ready a ship, both fair and strong, and garnished her plenteously with wines and meats.

"Husband," said the lady to the Soudan, "I will take of my captives the agèd and the young, that they may play chess and draughts at my bidding, and I will carry with me my son for my delight."

"Wife," answered he, "your will is my pleasure. But what shall be done with the third captive?"

"Husband, deal with him after your desire."

"Wife, I desire that you take him on the ship; for he is a brave man, and will keep you well, both on land and sea, if you have need of his sword."

The lady took leave of the Soudan, bidding him farewell, and urgently he prayed her to return so soon as she was healed of her sickness. The stores being put upon the ship and all things made ready, they entered therein and set sail from the haven. With a fair wind they went very swiftly, so that the shipmen sought the lady, saying,

"Madam, this wind is driving the boat to Brindisi. Is it your pleasure to take refuge there, or to go elsewhere?"

"Let the ship keep boldly on her course," answered the lady to them, "for I speak French featly and other tongues also, so I will bring you to a good end."

They made such swift passage by day and by night, that according to the will of Our Lord they came quickly to Brindisi. The ship cast anchor safely in the harbour, and they lighted on the shore, being welcomed gladly by the folk of that country. The lady, who was very shrewd, drew her captives apart, and said,

"Sirs, I desire you to call to mind the pledge and the covenant you have made. I must now be certain that you are true men, remembering your oaths and plighted words. I pray you to let me know, by all that you deem of God, whether you will abide or not by our covenant together; for it is yet not too late to return to my home."

They answered,

"Lady, know beyond question that the bargain we have made we will carry out loyally. By our faith in God and as christened men we will abide by this covenant; so be in no doubt of our assurance."

"I trust you wholly," replied the lady; "but, sirs, see here my son, whom I had of the Soudan, what shall we do with him?"

"Lady, the boy is right welcome, and to great honour shall he come in our own land."

"Sirs," said the dame, "I have dealt mischievously with the Soudan, for I have stolen my person from him, and the son who was so dear to his heart."

The lady went again to the shipmen, and lifting her hand, said to them,

"Sirs, return to the Soudan whence you came, and greet him with this message. Tell him that I have taken from him my body and the son he loved so well, that I might deliver my father, my lord, and my brother from the prison where they were captive."

When the sailors heard this they were very dolent, but there was naught that they might do. They set sail for their own country, sad and very heavy by reason of the lady, of the young lad, whom they loved greatly, and of the captives who were escaped altogether from their hand.

For his part the Count arrayed himself meetly by grace of merchants and Templars, who lent him gladly of their wealth. He abode in the town, together with his fellowship, for their solace, till they made them ready for the journey, and took the road to Rome. The Count sought the Pontiff, and his company with him. Each confessed him of the secrets of his heart, and when the Bishop heard thereof, he accepted their devotion, and comforted them right tenderly. He baptised the child, who was named William. He reconciled the lady with Holy Church, and confirmed the lady and Messire Thibault her lord, in their marriage bond, reknitting them together, giving penance to each, and absolution for their sins. After this they made no long sojourn in Rome, but took their leave of the Apostle who had honoured them so greatly. He granted them his benison, and commended them to God. So they went their way in great solace and delight, praising God and His Mother, and all the calendar of saints, and rendering thanks for the mercies which had been vouchsafed to them. Journeying thus they came at last to the country of their birth, and were met by a fair procession of bishops and abbots, monks and priests, who had desired them fervently. But of all these welcomes they welcomed most gladly her who was recovered from death, and had delivered her sire, her lord, and her brother from the hands of the Paynim, even as you have heard. There we leave them for awhile, and will tell you of the shipmen and Saracens who had fared with them across the sea.

The sailors and Saracens who had carried them to Brindisi, returned as quickly as they were able, and with a fair wind cast anchor before Aumarie. They got them to land, very sad and heavy, and told their tidings to the Soudan.

Right sorrowful was the Soudan, and neither for time nor reason could he forget his grief. Because of this mischief he loved that daughter the less who tarried with him, and showed her the less courtesy. Nevertheless the maiden increased in virtue and in wisdom, so that the Paynim held her in love and honour, praising her for the good that was known of her. But now the story is silent as to that Soudan who was so tormented by reason of the flight of his dame and captives; and comes again to the Count of Ponthieu, who was welcomed to his realm with such pomp and worship, as became a lord of his degree.

In no long while after his return the son of the Count was dubbed knight, and rich was the feast. He became a knight both chivalrous and brave. Greatly he loved all honourable men, and gladly he bestowed fair gifts on the poor knights and poor gentlewomen of the country. Much was he esteemed of lord and hind, for he was a worthy knight, generous, valiant and debonair, proud only to his foes. Yet his days on earth were but a span, which was the sorer pity, for he died lamented of all.

Now it befell that the Count held high Court, and many a knight and lord sat with him at the feast. Amongst these came a very noble man and knight, of great place in Normandy, named my lord Raoul des Preaux. This Raoul had a daughter, passing sweet and fair. The Count spoke so urgently to Raoul and to the maiden's kin that a marriage was accorded between William, his grandson, the son of the Soudan of Aumarie, and the daughter of my lord Raoul, the heiress to all his wealth. William wedded the damsel with every rich observance, and in right of his wife this William became Lord of Preaux.

For a long while the realm had peace from its foes.

Messire Thibault dwelt with the lady, and had of her two sons, who in later days were worthy gentlemen of great worship. The son of the Count of Ponthieu, of whom we have spoken much and naught but good, died shortly after, to the grief of all the land. The Count of St. Pol was yet alive; therefore the two sons of my lord Thibault were heirs to both these realms, and attained thereto in the end. That devout lady, their mother, because of her contrite heart, gave largely to the poor; and Messire Thibault, like the honourable gentleman he was, abounded in good works so long as he was quick.

Now it chanced that the daughter of the lady, who abode with the Soudan her father, increased greatly in favour and in virtue. She was called The Fair Captive, by reason that her mother had left her in the Soudan's keeping, as you have heard. A certain brave Turk in the service of the Soudan—Malakin of Baudas by name—saw this damsel, so fair and gracious, and desired her dearly in his heart, because of the good men told of her. He came before his master, and said to him,

"Sire, in return for his labour your servant craves a gift."

"Malakin," returned the Soudan, "what gift would you have?"

"Sire, I would dare to tell it to your face, if only she were not so high above my reach."

The Sultan who was both shrewd and quick witted made reply,

"Say out boldly what is in your mind, for I hold you dear, and remember what you have done. If there is aught it beseems me to grant—saving only my honour—be assured that it is yours."

"Sire, well I know that your honour is without spot, nor would I seek anything against it. I pray you to bestow on your servant—if so it be your pleasure—my lady your daughter, for she is the gift I covet most in all the world."

The Soudan kept silence, and considered for a space. He knew well that Malakin was both valiant and wise, and might easily come to great honour and degree. Since the servant was worthy of his high desire, the Soudan said,

"By my law you have required of me a great thing, for I love my daughter dearly, and have no other heir. You know well, and it is the simple truth, that she comes of the best and bravest blood in France, for her mother is the child of the Count of Ponthieu. But since you too are valiant, and have done me loyal service, for my part I will give her to you willingly, save only that it be to the maiden's mind."

"Sire," said Malakin, "I would not take her against her wish."

The Soudan bade the girl be summoned. When she came, he said,

"Fair daughter, I have granted you in marriage, if it pleases you."

"Sir," answered the maiden, "my pleasure is in your will."

The Soudan took her by the hand, saying,

"Take her, Malakin, the maid is yours."

Malakin received her with a glad heart, and wedded her according to the Paynim rite, bringing her to his house right joyously, with the countenance of all his friends. Afterwards he returned with her to his own land. The Soudan escorted them upon their way, with such a fair company of his household as seemed good to him. Then he bade farewell to his child and her lord, and returned to his home. But a great part of his fellowship he commanded to go with her for their service.

Malakin came back to his own land, where he was welcomed right gladly of his friends, and served and honoured by all the folk of his realm. He lived long and tenderly with his wife, neither were they childless, as this story testifies. For of this lady, who was called the Fair Captive, was born the mother of that courteous Turk, the Sultan Saladin, an honourable, a wise, and a conquering lord.

XVII

THE CHATELAINE OF VERGI

THERE are divers men who make a great show of loyalty, and pretend to such discretion in the hidden things they hear, that at the end folk come to put faith in them. When by their false seeming they have persuaded the simple to open out to them their love and their deeds, then they noise the matter about the country, and make it their song and their mirth. Thus it chances that the lesser joy is his who has bared to them his heart. For the sweeter the love, the more bitter is the pang that lovers know, when each deems the other to have bruited abroad the secret he should conceal. Oftentimes these blabbers do such mischief with their tongue, that the love they spoil comes to its close in sorrow and in care. This indeed happened in Burgundy to a brave and worthy knight, and to the Lady of Vergi. This knight loved his lady so dearly that she granted him her tenderness, on such covenant as this—that the day he showed her favour to any, that very hour he would lose the love and the grace she bestowed on him. To seal this bond they devised together that the knight should come a days to an orchard, at such hour as seemed good to his friend. He must remain coy in his nook within the wall till he might see the lady's lapdog run across the orchard. Then without further tarrying he should enter her chamber, knowing full well she was alone, whom so fondly he desired to greet. This he did, and in this fashion they met together for a great while, none being privy to their sweet and stolen love, save themselves alone.

The knight was courteous and fair, and by reason of his courage was right welcome to that Duke who was lord of Burgundy. He came and went about the Court, and that so often that the Duchess set her mind upon him. She cared so little to hide her thought, that had his heart not been in another's keeping, he must surely have perceived in her eyes that she loved him. But however tender her semblance the knight showed no kindness in return, for he marked nothing of her inclination. Passing troubled was the dame that he should treat her thus; so that on a day she took him apart, and sought to make him of her counsel.

" Sir, as men report, you are a brave and worthy knight, for the which give God thanks. It would not be more than your deserts, if you had for friend a lady in so high a place that her love would bring to you both honour and profit. How richly could such a lady serve you ! "

" Lady," said he, " I have never yet had this in my thought."

" By my faith," she answered, " it seems to me that the longer you wait, the less is your hope. Perchance the lady will stoop very readily from her throne, if you but kneel at her knee."

The knight replied,

" Lady, by my faith, I know little why you speak such words, and I understand their meaning not at all. I am neither duke nor count to dare to set my love in so high a seat. There is nought in me to gain the love of so sovereign a dame, pain me how I may."

" Such things have been," said she, " and so may chance again. Many more marvellous works have been wrought than this, and the day of miracles is not yet past. Tell me, know you not yet that you have gained the love of some high princess, even mine ? "

The knight made answer forthwith,

" Lady, I know it not. I would desire to have your love in a fair and honourable fashion ; but may God keep me from such love between us, as would put shame upon my lord. In no manner, nor for any reason, will I enter on such a business as would lead me to deal my true and lawful lord so shrewd and foul a wrong."

Bitter at heart was the dame to see her love so scorned.

" Fie upon you," she cried, " and who required of you any such thing ? "

" Ah, lady, to God be the praise ; you have said enough to make your meaning passing plain."

The lady strove no more to show herself kind to him. Great was the wrath and sharp the malice that she hid within her heart, and well she purposed that, if she might, she would avenge herself speedily. All the day she considered her anger. That night as she lay beside the Duke she began to sigh, and afterwards to weep. Presently the Duke inquired of her grief, bidding her show it him forthwith.

" Certes," said the dame, " I make this great sorrow because no prince can tell who is his faithful servant, and who is not. Often he gives the more honour and wealth to those who are traitors rather than friends, and sees nothing of their wrong."

" In faith, wife," answered the Duke, " I know not why you speak these words. At least I am free of such blame as this, for in nowise would I nourish a traitor, if only a traitor I knew him to be."

" Hate then this traitor," cried she,—and she named a name—" who gives me no peace, praying and requiring me the livelong day that I should grant him my love.

For a great while he had been in this mind—as he says—but did not dare to speak his thoughts. I considered the whole matter, fair lord, and resolved to show it you at once. It is likely enough to be true that he cherished this hope, for we have never heard that he loves elsewhere. I entreat you in guerdon, to look well to your own honour, since this, as you know, is your duty and right."

Passing grievous was this business to the Duke. He answered to the lady,

" I will bring it to a head, and very quickly, as I deem."

That night the Duke lay upon a bed of little ease. He could neither sleep nor rest, by reason of that lord, his friend, who, he was persuaded, had done him such bitter wrong as justly to have forfeited his love. Because of this he kept vigil the whole night through. He rose very early on the morrow, and bade him come whom his wife had put to blame, although he had done nothing blameworthy. Then he took him to task, man to man, when there were but these two together.

" Certes," he said, " it is a heavy grief that you who are so comely and brave, should yet have no honour in you. You have deceived me the more, for I have long believed you to be a man of good faith, giving loyalty, at least, to me, in return for the love I have given to you. I know not how you can have harboured such a felon's wish, as to pray and require the Duchess to grant you her grace. You are guilty of such treachery that conduct more vile it would be far to seek. Get you hence from my realm. You have my leave to part, and it is denied to you for ever. If you return here it will be at your utmost peril, for I warn you beforehand that if I lay hands upon you, you will die a shameful death."

When the knight heard this judgment, such wrath and mortification were his that his members trembled beneath him. He called to mind his friend, of whom he would have no joy, if he might not come and go and sojourn in that realm from which the Duke had banished him. Moreover he was sick at heart that his lord should deem him a disloyal traitor, without just cause. He knew such sore discomfort that he held himself as dead and betrayed.

" Sire," said he, " for the love of God believe this never, neither think that I have been so bold. To do that of which you wrongfully charge me, has never entered my mind, not one day, nor for one single hour. Who has told you this lie has wrought a great ill."

" You gain nothing by such denials," answered the Duke, " for of a surety the thing is true. I have heard from her own lips the very guise and fashion in which you prayed and required her love, like the envious traitor that you are. Many another word it may well be that you spoke, as to which the lady of her courtesy keeps silence."

" My lady says what it pleases her to say," replied the dolorous knight, " and my denials are lighter than her word. Naught is there for me to say ; nothing is left for me to do, so that I may be believed that this adventure never happened."

" Happen it did, by my soul," said the Duke, remembering certain words of his wife. Well he deemed that he might be assured of the truth, if but the lady's testimony were true that this lord had never loved otherwhere. Therefore the Duke said to the knight,

" If you will pledge your faith to answer truly what I may ask, I shall be certified by your words whether or not you have done this deed of which I misdoubt you."

The knight had but one desire—to turn aside his lord's wrath, which had so wrongfully fallen upon him. He feared only lest he should be driven from the land where lodged the dame who was the closest to his mind. Knowing nothing of what was in the Duke's thought, he considered that his question could only concern the one matter ; so he replied that without fraud or concealment he would do as his lord had said. Thus he pledged his faith, and the Duke accepted his affiance.

When this was done the Duke made question,

" I have loved you so dearly that at the bottom of my heart I cannot believe you guilty of such shameless misdoing as the Duchess tells me. I would not credit it a moment, if you yourself were not the cause of my doubtfulness. From your face, the care you bestow upon your person, and a score of trifles, any who would know, can readily see that you are in love with some lady. Since none about the Court perceives damsel or dame on whom you have set your heart, I ask myself whether indeed it may not be my wife, who tells me that you have entreated her for love. Nothing that any one may do can take this suspicion from my mind, except you tell me yourself that you love elsewhere, making it so plain that I am left without doubt that I know the naked truth. If you refuse her name you will have broken your oath, and forth from my realm you go as an outlawed man."

The knight had none to give him counsel. To himself he seemed to stand at the parting of two ways, both one and the other leading to death. If he spoke the simple truth (and tell he must if he would not be a perjurer) then was he as good as dead ; for if he did such wrong as to sin against the covenant with his lady and his friend, certainly he would lose her love, so it came to her knowledge. But if he concealed the truth from the Duke, then he was false to his oath, and had lost both country and friend. But little he recked of country, so only he might keep his Love, since of all his riches she was the most dear. The knight called to heart and remembrance the fair joy and the solace that were his when he had this lady between his arms. He considered within himself that if by reason of his misdoing she came to harm, or were lost to him, since he might not take her where he went, how could he live without her. It would be with him also, as erst with the Castellan of Couci, who having his Love fast only in his heart, told over in his song,

Ah, God, strong Love, I sit and weep alone,
  Remembering the solace that was given ;
The tender guise, the semblance that was shown
  By her, my friend, my comrade, and my Heaven.
When grief brings back the joy that was mine own,
  I would the heart from out my breast were riven.
Ah, Lord, the sweet words hushed, the beauty flown ;
  Would God that I were dead, and low, and shriven.

The knight was in anguish such as this, for he knew not whether to make clear the truth, or to lie and be banished from the country.

Whilst he was deep in thought, turning over in his mind what it were best to do, tears rose in his heart and flowed from his eyes, so that his face was wet, by reason of the sorrow that he suffered. The Duke had no more mirth than the knight, deeming that his secret was so heavy that he dared not make it plain. The Duke spoke swiftly to his friend,

" I see clearly that you fear to trust me wholly, as a knight should trust his lord. If you confess your counsel privily to me, you cannot think that I shall show the matter to any man. I would rather have my teeth drawn one by one, than speak a word."

"Ah," cried the knight, "for God's love, have pity, Sire. I know not what I ought to say, nor what will become of me ; but I would rather die than lose what lose I shall if she only hears that you have the truth, and that you heard it from my lips, whilst I am a living man."

The Duke made answer,

"I swear to you by my body and my soul, and on the faith and love I owe you again by reason of your homage, that never in my life will I tell the tale to any creature born, or even breathe a word or make a sign about the business."

With the tears yet running down his face the knight said to him,

"Sire, right or wrong, now will I show my secret. I love your niece of Vergi, and she loves me, so that no friends can love more fondly."

"If you wish to be believed," replied the Duke, "tell me now, if any, save you two alone, knows anything of this joy ? "

And the knight made answer to him,

"Nay, not a creature in the world."

Then said the Duke,

"No love is so privy as that. If none has heard thereof, how do you meet together, and how devise time and place ? "

"By my faith, Sire, I will tell you all, and keep back nothing, since you know so much of our counsel."

So he related the whole story of his goings to and fro within the pleasaunce ; of that first covenant with his friend, and of the office of the little dog.

Then said the Duke,

"I require of you that I may be your comrade at such fair meeting. When you go again to the orchard, I too, would enter therein, and mark for myself the success of your device. As for my niece she shall perceive naught."

" Sire, if it be your will it is my pleasure also; save, only, that you find it not heavy or burdensome. Know well that I go this very night."

The Duke said that he would go with him, for the vigil would in no wise be burdensome, but rather a frolic and a game. They accorded between them a place of meeting, where they would draw together on foot, and alone. When nightfall was come they fared to the hostel of the Duke's niece, for her dwelling was near at hand. They had not tarried long in the garden, when the Duke saw his niece's lapdog run straight to that end of the orchard where the knight was hidden. Wondrous kindness showed the knight to his lady's dog. Immediately he took his way to her lodging, and left his master in his nook by the wall. The Duke followed after till he drew near the chamber, and held himself coy, concealing him as best he might. It was easy enough to do this, for a great tree stood there, high and leafy, so that he was covered close as by a shield. From this place he marked the little dog enter the chamber, and presently saw his niece issue therefrom, and hurry forth to meet her lover in the pleasaunce. He was so close that he could see and hear the solace of that greeting, the salutation of her mouth and of her hands. She embraced him closely in her fair white arms, kissing him more than a hundred times, whilst she spoke many comforting words. The knight for his part kissed her again, and held her fast, praising her with many tender names.

" My lady, my friend, my love," said he, " heart and mistress and hope, and the sum of all that I hold dear, know well that I have yearned to be with you as we are now, every day and all day long since we met."

" Sweet lord, sweet friend, sweet love," replied the lady, " never has a day nor an hour gone by but I was awearied of its length. But I grieve no longer over the past, for I have my heart's desire when you are with me, joyous and well. Right welcome are you to your friend."

And the knight made answer,

"Love, you are welcome and wellmet."

From his place of hiding, near the entrance to the chamber, the Duke hearkened to every word. His niece's voice and face were so familiar to him, that he could not doubt that the Duchess had lied. Greatly was he content, for he was now assured that his friend had not done amiss in that of which he had misdoubted him. All through the night he kept watch and ward. But during his vigil the dame and the knight, close and sleepless in the chamber, knew such joy and tenderness as it is not seemly should be told or heard, save of those who hope themselves to attain such solace, when Love grants them recompense for all their pains. For he who desires nothing of this joy and quittance, even if it were told him, would but listen to a tongue he could not understand, since his heart is not turned to Love, and none can know the wealth of such riches, except Love whisper it in his ear. Of such kingdom not all are worthy : for there joy goes without anger, and solace is crowned with fruition. But so fleet are things sweet, that to the lover his joy seems to find but a brief content. So pleasant is the life he passes that he wishes his night a week, his week to stretch to a month, the month become a year, and one year three, and three years twenty, and the twenty attain to a hundred. Yea, when the term and end were reached, he would that the dusk were closing, rather than the dawn had come.

This was the case with the lover whom the Duke awaited in the orchard. When day was breaking, and he durst remain no longer, he came with his lady to the door. The Duke marked the fashion of their leave-taking, the kisses given and granted, the sighs and the weeping as they bade farewell. When they had wept many tears, and devised an hour for their next meeting, the knight departed in this fashion, and the lady shut the door. But so long as she might see him, she followed his going with her pretty eyes, since there was nothing better she could do.

When the Duke knew the postern was made fast, he hastened on his road until he overtook the knight, who to himself was making his complaint of the season, that all too short was his hour. The same thought and the self same words were hers from whom he had parted, for the briefness of the time had betrayed her delight, and she had no praises for the dawn. The knight was deep in his thought and speech, when he was over-taken by the Duke. The Duke embraced his friend, greeting him very tenderly. Then he said to him,

" I pledge my faith that I will love you all the days of my life, never on any day seeking to do you a mischief, for you have told me the very truth, and have not lied to me by a single word."

" Sire," he made answer, " thanks and gramercy. But for the love of God I require and pray of you that it be your pleasure to hide this counsel ; for I should lose my love, and the peace and comfort of my life—yea, and should die without sin of my own, if I deemed that any other in this realm than yourself knew aught of the business."

" Now speak of it never," replied the Duke. " Know that the counsel shall be kept so hidden, that by me shall not a syllable be spoken."

On this covenant they came again whence they had set forth together. That day, when men sat at meat, the Duke showed to his knight a friendlier semblance and a

fairer courtesy than ever he had done before. The
Duchess felt such wrath and despitefulness at this,
that—without any leasing—she rose from the table,
and making pretence of sudden sickness, went to lie
upon her bed, where she found little softness. When
the Duke had eaten and washed and made merry, he
afterwards sought his wife's chamber, and causing her
to be seated on her bed, commanded that none should
remain, save himself. So all men went forth at his
word, even as he had bidden. Thereupon the Duke
inquired of the lady how this evil had come to her, and
of what she was sick. She made answer,

"As God hears me, never till I ate at table did I deem
that you had so little sense or decency, as when I saw
you making much of him, who, I have told you already,
strove to bring shame and disgrace on me. When I
watched you entreat him with more favour than even
was your wont, such great sorrow and such great anger
took hold on me, that I could not contain myself in the
hall."

"Sweet friend," replied the Duke, "know that I shall
never believe—either from your lips or from those of
any creature in the world—that the story ever happened
as you rehearsed it. I am so deep in his counsel that he
has my quittance, for I have full assurance that he never
dreamed of such a deed. But as to this you must ask
of me no more."

The Duke went straightway from the chamber, leaving
the lady sunk in thought. However long she had to live,
never might she know an hour's comfort, till she had
learnt something of that secret of which the Duke
forbade her to seek further. No denial could now stand
in her way, for in her heart swiftly she devised a means
to unriddle this counsel, so only she might endure
until the evening, and the Duke was in her arms. She

was persuaded that, beyond doubt, such solace would win her wish more surely than wrath or tears. For this purpose she held herself coy, and when the Duke came to lie at her side she betook herself to the further side of the bed, making semblance that his company gave her no pleasure. Well she knew that such show of anger was the device to put her lord beneath her feet. Therefore she turned her back upon him, that the Duke might the more easily be drawn by the cords of her wrath. For this same reason when he had no more than kissed her, she burst out,

"Right false and treacherous and disloyal are you to make such a pretence of affection, who yet have never loved me truly one single day. All these years of our wedded life I have been foolish enough to believe, what you took such pains in the telling, that you loved me with a loyal heart. To-day I see plainly that I was the more deceived."

"In what are you deceived?" inquired the Duke.

"By my faith," cried she, who was sick of her desire, "you warn me that I be not so bold as to ask aught of that of which you know the secret."

"In God's name, sweet wife, of what would you know?"

"Of all that he has told you, the lies and the follies he has put in your mind, and led you to believe. But it matters little now whether I hear it or not, for I remember how small is my gain in being your true and loving wife. For good or for ill I have shown you all my counsel. There was nothing that was known and seen of my heart that you were not told at once; and of your courtesy you repay me by concealing your mind. Know, now, without doubt, that never again shall I have in you such affiance, nor grant you my love with such sweetness, as I have bestowed them in the past."

Thereat the Duchess began to weep and sigh, making the most tender sorrow that she was able. The Duke felt such pity for her grief that he said to her,

" Fairest and dearest, your wrath and anger are more heavy than I can bear; but learn that I cannot tell what you wish me to say without sinning against my honour too grievously."

Then she replied forthwith,

" Husband, if you do not tell me, the reason can only be that you do not trust me to keep silence in the business. I wonder the more sorely at this, because there is no matter, either great or small, that you have told me, which has been published by me. I tell you honestly that never in my life could I be so indiscreet."

When she had said this, she betook her again to her tears. The Duke kissed and embraced her, and was so sick of heart that strength failed him to keep his purpose.

" Fair wife," he said to her, " by my soul I am at my wits' end. I have such trust and faith in you that I deem I should hide nothing, but show you all that I know. Yet I dread that you will let fall some word. Know, wife—and I tell it you again—that if ever you betray this counsel you will get death for your payment."

The Duchess made answer,

" I agree to the bargain, for it is not possible that I should deal you so shrewd a wrong."

Then he who loved her, because of his faith and his credence in her word, told all this story of his niece, even as he had learned it from the knight. He told how those two were alone together in the shadow of the wall, when the little dog ran to them. He showed plainly of that coming forth from the chamber, and of the entering in; nothing was hid, he concealed naught of that he had heard and seen. When the Duchess understood that the love of a mighty dame was despised for the sake of a lowly gentlewoman, her humiliation was bitter in her mouth as death. She showed no semblance of despitefulness, but made covenant and promise with the Duke to keep the matter close, saying that should she repeat his tale he might hang her from a tree.

Time went very heavily with the lady, till she could get speech with her, whom she hated from the hour she knew her to be the friend of him who had caused her such shame and grief. She was persuaded that for this reason he would not give her love, in return for that she set on him. She confirmed herself in her purpose, that at such time and place she saw the Duke speaking with his niece, she would go swiftly to the lady, and tell out all her mind, hiding nothing because it was evil. Neither time nor place was met, till Pentecost was come, and the Duke held high Court, commanding to the feast all the ladies of his realm, amongst the first that lady, his niece, who was the Chatelaine of Vergi. When the Duchess looked on her, the blood pricked in her veins, for reason that she hated her more than aught else in the world. She had the courage to hide her malice, and greeted the lady more gladly than ever she had done before. But she yearned to show openly the anger that burned in her heart, and the delay was much against her mind. On Pentecost, whilst the tables were removed, the Duchess brought the ladies to her chamber with her, that, apart from the throng, they might the more graciously attire them for the dance. She deemed her hour had come, and having no longer the power to refrain her lips, she said gaily, as if in jest,

" Chatelaine, array yourself very sweetly, since there is a fair and worthy lord you have to please."

The lady answered right simply,

" In truth, madam, I know not what you are thinking of ; but for my part I wish for no such friendship as may not be altogether according to my honour and to that of my lord."

" I grant that readily," replied the Duchess, " you are a good mistress, and have an apt pupil in your little dog."

The ladies returned with the Duchess to the hall, where the dances were already set. They had listened to the tale, but could not mark the jest. The chatelaine remained in the chamber. Her colour came and went, and because of her wrath and trouble the heart throbbed thickly in her breast. She passed within a tiring chamber, where a little maiden was lying at the foot of the bed ; but for grief she might not perceive her. The chatelaine flung herself upon the bed, bewailing her evil plight, for she was exceedingly sorrowful. She said,

" Ah, Lord God, take pity on me ! What may this mean, that I have listened to my lady's reproaches because of the training of my little dog ! This she can have learned from none—as well I know—save from him whom I have loved, and who has betrayed me. He would never have shown her this thing, except that he was her familiar friend, and doubtless loves her more dearly than me, whom he has betrayed. I see now the value of his oaths, since he finds it so easy to fail in his covenant. Sweet God, and I loved him so fondly, more fondly than any woman has loved before ; who never had him from my thoughts one single hour, whether it were night or day. For he was my mirth and my carol ; in him were my joy and my pleasure ; he alone was my solace and comfort. Ah, my friend, how can this have come ; you who were always with me, even when I

might not see you with my eyes! What ill has befallen
you, that you durst prove false to me? I deemed you
more faithful—God take me in His keeping—than ever
was Tristan to Isoude. May God pity a poor fool, I
loved you half as much again than I had love for myself.
From the first to the last of our friendship, never by
thought, or by word, or by deed, have I done amiss;
there is no wrong doing, trifling or great, to make plain
your hatred, or to excuse so vile a betrayal as this
scorning of our love for a fresher face, this desertion
of me, this proclaiming of our secret. Alas, my friend,
I marvel greatly; for as God is my witness my heart
was not thus towards you. If God had offered me all
the kingdoms of the world, yea, and His Heaven and its
Paradise besides, I would have refused them gladly, had
my gain meant the losing of you. For you were my
wealth and my song and my health, and nothing can
hurt me any more, since my heart has learnt that yours
no longer loves me. Ah, lasting, precious love! Who
could have guessed that he would deal this blow, to
whom I gave the grace of my tenderness—who said
that I was his lady both in body and in soul, and
he the slave at my bidding. Yea, he told it over so
sweetly, that I believed him faithfully, nor thought in
any wise that his heart would bear wrath and malice
against me, whether for Duchess or for Queen. How
good was this love, since the heart in my breast must
always cleave to his! I counted him to be my friend,
in age as in youth, our lives together; for well I knew
that if he died first I should not dare to endure long
without him, because of the greatness of my love. The
grave, with him, would be fairer, than life in a world
where I might never see him with my eyes. Ah, lasting,
precious love! Is it then seemly that he should publish
our counsel, and destroy her who had done him no

wrong ? When I gave him my love without grudging, I warned him plainly, and made covenant with him, that he would lose me the self same hour that he made our tenderness a song. Since part we must, I may not live after so bitter a sorrow ; nor would I choose to live, even if I were able. Fie upon life, it has no savour in it. Since it pleases me naught, I pray to God to grant me death, and—so truly as I have loved him who requites me thus—to have mercy on my soul. I forgive him his wrong, and may God give honour and life to him who has betrayed and delivered me to death. Since it comes from his hand, death, meseems, is no bitter potion ; and when I remember his love, to die for his sake is no grievous thing."

When the chatelaine had thus spoken she kept silence, save only that she said in sighing,

" Sweet friend, I commend you to God."

With these words she strained her arms tightly across her breast, the heart failed her, and her face lost its fair colour. She swooned in her anguish, and lay back, pale and discoloured in the middle of the bed, without life or breath.

Of this her friend knew nothing, for he sought his delight in the hall, at carol and dance and play. But amongst all those ladies he had no pleasure in any that he saw, since he might not perceive her to whom his heart was given, and much he marvelled thereat. He took the Duke apart, and said in his ear,

" Sire, whence is this that your niece tarries so long, and comes not to the dancing ? Have you put her in prison ? "

The Duke looked upon the dancers, for he had not concerned himself with the revels. He took his friend by the hand, and led him directly to his wife's chamber. When he might not find her there he bade the knight seek her boldly in the tiring chamber ; and this he did

of his courtesy that these two lovers might solace
themselves with clasp and kiss. The knight thanked his
lord sweetly, and entered softly in the chamber, where
his friend lay dark and discoloured upon the bed. Time
and place being met together, he took her in his arms
and touched her lips. But when he found how cold was
her mouth, how pale and rigid her person, he knew by
the semblance of all her body that she was quite dead.
In his amazement he cried out swiftly,

"What is this ? Alas, is my dear one dead ? "

The maiden started from the foot of the bed where
she still lay, making answer,

"Sir, I deem truly that she be dead. Since she came
to this room she has done nothing but call upon death,
by reason of her friend's falsehood, whereof my lady
assured her, and because of a little dog, whereof my
lady made her jest. This sorrow brought her to her
death."

When the knight understood from this that the words
he had spoken to the Duke had slain his friend, he was
discomforted beyond measure.

"Alas," said he, "sweet love, the most gracious and
the best that ever knight had, loyal and true, how have
I slain you, like the faithless traitor that I am ! It
were only just that I should receive the wages for my
deed, so that you could have gone free of blame. But
you were so faithful of heart that you took it on yourself
to pay the price. Then I will do justice on myself for
the treason I have wrought."

The knight drew from its sheath a sword that was
hanging from the wall, and thrust it throught his heart.
He pained himself to fall upon his lady's body ; and
because of the mightiness of his hurt, bled swiftly to
death. The maiden fled forth from the chamber, when
she marked these lifeless lovers, for she was all adread

at what she saw. She lighted on the Duke, and told him all that she had heard and seen, keeping back nothing. She showed him the beginning of the matter, and also of the little dog, whereof the Duchess had spoken.

Hearken all to what befell. The Duke went straightway to the tiring chamber, and drew from out the wound that sword by which the knight lay slain. He said no word, but hastened forthwith to the hall where the guests were yet at their dancing. Entering there he acquitted himself of his promise, for he smote the Duchess on the head with the naked sword he carried in his hand. He struck the blow without one word, since his wrath was too deep for speech. The Duchess fell at his feet, in the sight of the barons of his realm, whereat the feast was sorely troubled, for in place of mirth and carol, now were blood and death. Then the Duke told loudly and swiftly, before all who cared to hear, this pitiful story, in the midst of his Court. There was not one but wept, and his tears were the more piteous when he beheld those two lovers who lay dead in the chamber, and the Duchess in her hall. So the Court broke up in dole and anger, for of this deed came mighty mischief. On the morrow the Duke caused the lovers to be laid in one tomb, and the Duchess in a place apart. But of this adventure the Duke had such bitterness that never was he known to laugh again. He took the Cross, and went beyond the sea, where joining himself to the Knights Templar, he never returned to his own realm.

Ah, God! all this mischief and encumbrance chanced to the knight by reason of his making plain that he should have hid, and of publishing what his friend forbade him to speak, if he would keep her love. From this ensample we may learn that it is not seemly to love, and tell. He who blabs and blazons his friendship gets not one kiss the more; but he who goes discreetly preserves life and love and fame. For the friendship of the discreet lover falls not before the mine of such false and felon pryers as burrow privily into their neighbour's secret love.

A CATALOG OF SELECTED
DOVER BOOKS
IN ALL FIELDS OF INTEREST

A CATALOG OF SELECTED DOVER
BOOKS IN ALL FIELDS OF INTEREST

CONCERNING THE SPIRITUAL IN ART, Wassily Kandinsky. Pioneering work by father of abstract art. Thoughts on color theory, nature of art. Analysis of earlier masters. 12 illustrations. 80pp. of text. 5⅜ x 8½. 23411-8

ANIMALS: 1,419 Copyright-Free Illustrations of Mammals, Birds, Fish, Insects, etc., Jim Harter (ed.). Clear wood engravings present, in extremely lifelike poses, over 1,000 species of animals. One of the most extensive pictorial sourcebooks of its kind. Captions. Index. 284pp. 9 x 12. 23766-4

CELTIC ART: The Methods of Construction, George Bain. Simple geometric techniques for making Celtic interlacements, spirals, Kells-type initials, animals, humans, etc. Over 500 illustrations. 160pp. 9 x 12. (Available in U.S. only.) 22923-8

AN ATLAS OF ANATOMY FOR ARTISTS, Fritz Schider. Most thorough reference work on art anatomy in the world. Hundreds of illustrations, including selections from works by Vesalius, Leonardo, Goya, Ingres, Michelangelo, others. 593 illustrations. 192pp. 7⅛ x 10¼. 20241-0

CELTIC HAND STROKE-BY-STROKE (Irish Half-Uncial from "The Book of Kells"): An Arthur Baker Calligraphy Manual, Arthur Baker. Complete guide to creating each letter of the alphabet in distinctive Celtic manner. Covers hand position, strokes, pens, inks, paper, more. Illustrated. 48pp. 8¼ x 11. 24336-2

EASY ORIGAMI, John Montroll. Charming collection of 32 projects (hat, cup, pelican, piano, swan, many more) specially designed for the novice origami hobbyist. Clearly illustrated easy-to-follow instructions insure that even beginning papercrafters will achieve successful results. 48pp. 8¼ x 11. 27298-2

THE COMPLETE BOOK OF BIRDHOUSE CONSTRUCTION FOR WOODWORKERS, Scott D. Campbell. Detailed instructions, illustrations, tables. Also data on bird habitat and instinct patterns. Bibliography. 3 tables. 63 illustrations in 15 figures. 48pp. 5¼ x 8½. 24407-5

BLOOMINGDALE'S ILLUSTRATED 1886 CATALOG: Fashions, Dry Goods and Housewares, Bloomingdale Brothers. Famed merchants' extremely rare catalog depicting about 1,700 products: clothing, housewares, firearms, dry goods, jewelry, more. Invaluable for dating, identifying vintage items. Also, copyright-free graphics for artists, designers. Co-published with Henry Ford Museum & Greenfield Village. 160pp. 8¼ x 11. 25780-0

HISTORIC COSTUME IN PICTURES, Braun & Schneider. Over 1,450 costumed figures in clearly detailed engravings–from dawn of civilization to end of 19th century. Captions. Many folk costumes. 256pp. 8⅜ x 11¾. 23150-X

CATALOG OF DOVER BOOKS

STICKLEY CRAFTSMAN FURNITURE CATALOGS, Gustav Stickley and L. & J. G. Stickley. Beautiful, functional furniture in two authentic catalogs from 1910. 594 illustrations, including 277 photos, show settles, rockers, armchairs, reclining chairs, bookcases, desks, tables. 183pp. 6½ x 9¼. 23838-5

AMERICAN LOCOMOTIVES IN HISTORIC PHOTOGRAPHS: 1858 to 1949, Ron Ziel (ed.). A rare collection of 126 meticulously detailed official photographs, called "builder portraits," of American locomotives that majestically chronicle the rise of steam locomotive power in America. Introduction. Detailed captions. xi+ 129pp. 9 x 12. 27393-8

AMERICA'S LIGHTHOUSES: An Illustrated History, Francis Ross Holland, Jr. Delightfully written, profusely illustrated fact-filled survey of over 200 American lighthouses since 1716. History, anecdotes, technological advances, more. 240pp. 8 x 10¾. 25576-X

TOWARDS A NEW ARCHITECTURE, Le Corbusier. Pioneering manifesto by founder of "International School." Technical and aesthetic theories, views of industry, economics, relation of form to function, "mass-production split" and much more. Profusely illustrated. 320pp. 6⅛ x 9¼. (Available in U.S. only.) 25023-7

HOW THE OTHER HALF LIVES, Jacob Riis. Famous journalistic record, exposing poverty and degradation of New York slums around 1900, by major social reformer. 100 striking and influential photographs. 233pp. 10 x 7⅞. 22012-5

FRUIT KEY AND TWIG KEY TO TREES AND SHRUBS, William M. Harlow. One of the handiest and most widely used identification aids. Fruit key covers 120 deciduous and evergreen species; twig key 160 deciduous species. Easily used. Over 300 photographs. 126pp. 5⅜ x 8½. 20511-8

COMMON BIRD SONGS, Dr. Donald J. Borror. Songs of 60 most common U.S. birds: robins, sparrows, cardinals, bluejays, finches, more—arranged in order of increasing complexity. Up to 9 variations of songs of each species.
Cassette and manual 99911-4

ORCHIDS AS HOUSE PLANTS, Rebecca Tyson Northen. Grow cattleyas and many other kinds of orchids—in a window, in a case, or under artificial light. 63 illustrations. 148pp. 5⅜ x 8½. 23261-1

MONSTER MAZES, Dave Phillips. Masterful mazes at four levels of difficulty. Avoid deadly perils and evil creatures to find magical treasures. Solutions for all 32 exciting illustrated puzzles. 48pp. 8¼ x 11. 26005-4

MOZART'S DON GIOVANNI (DOVER OPERA LIBRETTO SERIES), Wolfgang Amadeus Mozart. Introduced and translated by Ellen H. Bleiler. Standard Italian libretto, with complete English translation. Convenient and thoroughly portable—an ideal companion for reading along with a recording or the performance itself. Introduction. List of characters. Plot summary. 121pp. 5¼ x 8½. 24944-1

TECHNICAL MANUAL AND DICTIONARY OF CLASSICAL BALLET, Gail Grant. Defines, explains, comments on steps, movements, poses and concepts. 15-page pictorial section. Basic book for student, viewer. 127pp. 5⅜ x 8½. 21843-0

THE CLARINET AND CLARINET PLAYING, David Pino. Lively, comprehensive work features suggestions about technique, musicianship, and musical interpretation, as well as guidelines for teaching, making your own reeds, and preparing for public performance. Includes an intriguing look at clarinet history. "A godsend," *The Clarinet,* Journal of the International Clarinet Society. Appendixes. 7 illus. 320pp. 5⅜ x 8½. 40270-3

HOLLYWOOD GLAMOR PORTRAITS, John Kobal (ed.). 145 photos from 1926-49. Harlow, Gable, Bogart, Bacall; 94 stars in all. Full background on photographers, technical aspects. 160pp. 8⅜ x 11¼. 23352-9

THE ANNOTATED CASEY AT THE BAT: A Collection of Ballads about the Mighty Casey/Third, Revised Edition, Martin Gardner (ed.). Amusing sequels and parodies of one of America's best-loved poems: Casey's Revenge, Why Casey Whiffed, Casey's Sister at the Bat, others. 256pp. 5⅜ x 8½. 28598-7

THE RAVEN AND OTHER FAVORITE POEMS, Edgar Allan Poe. Over 40 of the author's most memorable poems: "The Bells," "Ulalume," "Israfel," "To Helen," "The Conqueror Worm," "Eldorado," "Annabel Lee," many more. Alphabetic lists of titles and first lines. 64pp. 5$\frac{3}{16}$ x 8¼. 26685-0

PERSONAL MEMOIRS OF U. S. GRANT, Ulysses Simpson Grant. Intelligent, deeply moving firsthand account of Civil War campaigns, considered by many the finest military memoirs ever written. Includes letters, historic photographs, maps and more. 528pp. 6⅛ x 9¼. 28587-1

ANCIENT EGYPTIAN MATERIALS AND INDUSTRIES, A. Lucas and J. Harris. Fascinating, comprehensive, thoroughly documented text describes this ancient civilization's vast resources and the processes that incorporated them in daily life, including the use of animal products, building materials, cosmetics, perfumes and incense, fibers, glazed ware, glass and its manufacture, materials used in the mummification process, and much more. 544pp. 6⅛ x 9¼. (Available in U.S. only.) 40446-3

RUSSIAN STORIES/RUSSKIE RASSKAZY: A Dual-Language Book, edited by Gleb Struve. Twelve tales by such masters as Chekhov, Tolstoy, Dostoevsky, Pushkin, others. Excellent word-for-word English translations on facing pages, plus teaching and study aids, Russian/English vocabulary, biographical/critical introductions, more. 416pp. 5⅜ x 8½. 26244-8

PHILADELPHIA THEN AND NOW: 60 Sites Photographed in the Past and Present, Kenneth Finkel and Susan Oyama. Rare photographs of City Hall, Logan Square, Independence Hall, Betsy Ross House, other landmarks juxtaposed with contemporary views. Captures changing face of historic city. Introduction. Captions. 128pp. 8¼ x 11. 25790-8

AIA ARCHITECTURAL GUIDE TO NASSAU AND SUFFOLK COUNTIES, LONG ISLAND, The American Institute of Architects, Long Island Chapter, and the Society for the Preservation of Long Island Antiquities. Comprehensive, well-researched and generously illustrated volume brings to life over three centuries of Long Island's great architectural heritage. More than 240 photographs with authoritative, extensively detailed captions. 176pp. 8¼ x 11. 26946-9

NORTH AMERICAN INDIAN LIFE: Customs and Traditions of 23 Tribes, Elsie Clews Parsons (ed.). 27 fictionalized essays by noted anthropologists examine religion, customs, government, additional facets of life among the Winnebago, Crow, Zuni, Eskimo, other tribes. 480pp. 6⅛ x 9¼. 27377-6

FRANK LLOYD WRIGHT'S DANA HOUSE, Donald Hoffmann. Pictorial essay of residential masterpiece with over 160 interior and exterior photos, plans, elevations, sketches and studies. 128pp. 9¼ x 10¾.   29120-0

THE MALE AND FEMALE FIGURE IN MOTION: 60 Classic Photographic Sequences, Eadweard Muybridge. 60 true-action photographs of men and women walking, running, climbing, bending, turning, etc., reproduced from rare 19th-century masterpiece. vi + 121pp. 9 x 12.   24745-7

1001 QUESTIONS ANSWERED ABOUT THE SEASHORE, N. J. Berrill and Jacquelyn Berrill. Queries answered about dolphins, sea snails, sponges, starfish, fishes, shore birds, many others. Covers appearance, breeding, growth, feeding, much more. 305pp. 5¼ x 8¼.   23366-9

ATTRACTING BIRDS TO YOUR YARD, William J. Weber. Easy-to-follow guide offers advice on how to attract the greatest diversity of birds: birdhouses, feeders, water and waterers, much more. 96pp. 5³⁄₁₆ x 8¼.   28927-3

MEDICINAL AND OTHER USES OF NORTH AMERICAN PLANTS: A Historical Survey with Special Reference to the Eastern Indian Tribes, Charlotte Erichsen-Brown. Chronological historical citations document 500 years of usage of plants, trees, shrubs native to eastern Canada, northeastern U.S. Also complete identifying information. 343 illustrations. 544pp. 6½ x 9¼.   25951-X

STORYBOOK MAZES, Dave Phillips. 23 stories and mazes on two-page spreads: Wizard of Oz, Treasure Island, Robin Hood, etc. Solutions. 64pp. 8¼ x 11.   23628-5

AMERICAN NEGRO SONGS: 230 Folk Songs and Spirituals, Religious and Secular, John W. Work. This authoritative study traces the African influences of songs sung and played by black Americans at work, in church, and as entertainment. The author discusses the lyric significance of such songs as "Swing Low, Sweet Chariot," "John Henry," and others and offers the words and music for 230 songs. Bibliography. Index of Song Titles. 272pp. 6½ x 9¼.   40271-1

MOVIE-STAR PORTRAITS OF THE FORTIES, John Kobal (ed.). 163 glamor, studio photos of 106 stars of the 1940s: Rita Hayworth, Ava Gardner, Marlon Brando, Clark Gable, many more. 176pp. 8⅜ x 11¼.   23546-7

BENCHLEY LOST AND FOUND, Robert Benchley. Finest humor from early 30s, about pet peeves, child psychologists, post office and others. Mostly unavailable elsewhere. 73 illustrations by Peter Arno and others. 183pp. 5⅜ x 8½.   22410-4

YEKL and THE IMPORTED BRIDEGROOM AND OTHER STORIES OF YIDDISH NEW YORK, Abraham Cahan. Film Hester Street based on *Yekl* (1896). Novel, other stories among first about Jewish immigrants on N.Y.'s East Side. 240pp. 5⅜ x 8½.   22427-9

SELECTED POEMS, Walt Whitman. Generous sampling from *Leaves of Grass*. Twenty-four poems include "I Hear America Singing," "Song of the Open Road," "I Sing the Body Electric," "When Lilacs Last in the Dooryard Bloom'd," "O Captain! My Captain!"–all reprinted from an authoritative edition. Lists of titles and first lines. 128pp. 5³⁄₁₆ x 8¼.   26878-0

THE BEST TALES OF HOFFMANN, E. T. A. Hoffmann. 10 of Hoffmann's most important stories: "Nutcracker and the King of Mice," "The Golden Flowerpot," etc. 458pp. 5⅜ x 8½. 21793-0

FROM FETISH TO GOD IN ANCIENT EGYPT, E. A. Wallis Budge. Rich detailed survey of Egyptian conception of "God" and gods, magic, cult of animals, Osiris, more. Also, superb English translations of hymns and legends. 240 illustrations. 545pp. 5⅜ x 8½. 25803-3

FRENCH STORIES/CONTES FRANÇAIS: A Dual-Language Book, Wallace Fowlie. Ten stories by French masters, Voltaire to Camus: "Micromegas" by Voltaire; "The Atheist's Mass" by Balzac; "Minuet" by de Maupassant; "The Guest" by Camus, six more. Excellent English translations on facing pages. Also French-English vocabulary list, exercises, more. 352pp. 5⅜ x 8½. 26443-2

CHICAGO AT THE TURN OF THE CENTURY IN PHOTOGRAPHS: 122 Historic Views from the Collections of the Chicago Historical Society, Larry A. Viskochil. Rare large-format prints offer detailed views of City Hall, State Street, the Loop, Hull House, Union Station, many other landmarks, circa 1904-1913. Introduction. Captions. Maps. 144pp. 9⅜ x 12¼. 24656-6

OLD BROOKLYN IN EARLY PHOTOGRAPHS, 1865-1929, William Lee Younger. Luna Park, Gravesend race track, construction of Grand Army Plaza, moving of Hotel Brighton, etc. 157 previously unpublished photographs. 165pp. 8⅞ x 11¾. 23587-4

THE MYTHS OF THE NORTH AMERICAN INDIANS, Lewis Spence. Rich anthology of the myths and legends of the Algonquins, Iroquois, Pawnees and Sioux, prefaced by an extensive historical and ethnological commentary. 36 illustrations. 480pp. 5⅜ x 8½. 25967-6

AN ENCYCLOPEDIA OF BATTLES: Accounts of Over 1,560 Battles from 1479 B.C. to the Present, David Eggenberger. Essential details of every major battle in recorded history from the first battle of Megiddo in 1479 B.C. to Grenada in 1984. List of Battle Maps. New Appendix covering the years 1967-1984. Index. 99 illustrations. 544pp. 6½ x 9¼. 24913-1

SAILING ALONE AROUND THE WORLD, Captain Joshua Slocum. First man to sail around the world, alone, in small boat. One of great feats of seamanship told in delightful manner. 67 illustrations. 294pp. 5⅜ x 8½. 20326-3

ANARCHISM AND OTHER ESSAYS, Emma Goldman. Powerful, penetrating, prophetic essays on direct action, role of minorities, prison reform, puritan hypocrisy, violence, etc. 271pp. 5⅜ x 8½. 22484-8

MYTHS OF THE HINDUS AND BUDDHISTS, Ananda K. Coomaraswamy and Sister Nivedita. Great stories of the epics; deeds of Krishna, Shiva, taken from puranas, Vedas, folk tales; etc. 32 illustrations. 400pp. 5⅜ x 8½. 21759-0

THE TRAUMA OF BIRTH, Otto Rank. Rank's controversial thesis that anxiety neurosis is caused by profound psychological trauma which occurs at birth. 256pp. 5⅜ x 8½. 27974-X

A THEOLOGICO-POLITICAL TREATISE, Benedict Spinoza. Also contains unfinished Political Treatise. Great classic on religious liberty, theory of government on common consent. R. Elwes translation. Total of 421pp. 5⅜ x 8½. 20249-6

MY BONDAGE AND MY FREEDOM, Frederick Douglass. Born a slave, Douglass became outspoken force in antislavery movement. The best of Douglass' autobiographies. Graphic description of slave life. 464pp. 5⅜ x 8½.   22457-0

FOLLOWING THE EQUATOR: A Journey Around the World, Mark Twain. Fascinating humorous account of 1897 voyage to Hawaii, Australia, India, New Zealand, etc. Ironic, bemused reports on peoples, customs, climate, flora and fauna, politics, much more. 197 illustrations. 720pp. 5⅜ x 8½.   26113-1

THE PEOPLE CALLED SHAKERS, Edward D. Andrews. Definitive study of Shakers: origins, beliefs, practices, dances, social organization, furniture and crafts, etc. 33 illustrations. 351pp. 5⅜ x 8½.   21081-2

THE MYTHS OF GREECE AND ROME, H. A. Guerber. A classic of mythology, generously illustrated, long prized for its simple, graphic, accurate retelling of the principal myths of Greece and Rome, and for its commentary on their origins and significance. With 64 illustrations by Michelangelo, Raphael, Titian, Rubens, Canova, Bernini and others. 480pp. 5⅜ x 8½.   27584-1

PSYCHOLOGY OF MUSIC, Carl E. Seashore. Classic work discusses music as a medium from psychological viewpoint. Clear treatment of physical acoustics, auditory apparatus, sound perception, development of musical skills, nature of musical feeling, host of other topics. 88 figures. 408pp. 5⅜ x 8½.   21851-1

THE PHILOSOPHY OF HISTORY, Georg W. Hegel. Great classic of Western thought develops concept that history is not chance but rational process, the evolution of freedom. 457pp. 5⅜ x 8½.   20112-0

THE BOOK OF TEA, Kakuzo Okakura. Minor classic of the Orient: entertaining, charming explanation, interpretation of traditional Japanese culture in terms of tea ceremony. 94pp. 5⅜ x 8½.   20070-1

LIFE IN ANCIENT EGYPT, Adolf Erman. Fullest, most thorough, detailed older account with much not in more recent books, domestic life, religion, magic, medicine, commerce, much more. Many illustrations reproduce tomb paintings, carvings, hieroglyphs, etc. 597pp. 5⅜ x 8½.   22632-8

SUNDIALS, Their Theory and Construction, Albert Waugh. Far and away the best, most thorough coverage of ideas, mathematics concerned, types, construction, adjusting anywhere. Simple, nontechnical treatment allows even children to build several of these dials. Over 100 illustrations. 230pp. 5⅜ x 8½.   22947-5

THEORETICAL HYDRODYNAMICS, L. M. Milne-Thomson. Classic exposition of the mathematical theory of fluid motion, applicable to both hydrodynamics and aerodynamics. Over 600 exercises. 768pp. 6⅛ x 9¼.   68970-0

SONGS OF EXPERIENCE: Facsimile Reproduction with 26 Plates in Full Color, William Blake. 26 full-color plates from a rare 1826 edition. Includes "The Tyger," "London," "Holy Thursday," and other poems. Printed text of poems. 48pp. 5¼ x 7.
     24636-1

OLD-TIME VIGNETTES IN FULL COLOR, Carol Belanger Grafton (ed.). Over 390 charming, often sentimental illustrations, selected from archives of Victorian graphics—pretty women posing, children playing, food, flowers, kittens and puppies, smiling cherubs, birds and butterflies, much more. All copyright-free. 48pp. 9¼ x 12¼.
     27269-9

PERSPECTIVE FOR ARTISTS, Rex Vicat Cole. Depth, perspective of sky and sea, shadows, much more, not usually covered. 391 diagrams, 81 reproductions of drawings and paintings. 279pp. 5⅜ x 8½. 22487-2

DRAWING THE LIVING FIGURE, Joseph Sheppard. Innovative approach to artistic anatomy focuses on specifics of surface anatomy, rather than muscles and bones. Over 170 drawings of live models in front, back and side views, and in widely varying poses. Accompanying diagrams. 177 illustrations. Introduction. Index. 144pp. 8⅜ x11¼. 26723-7

GOTHIC AND OLD ENGLISH ALPHABETS: 100 Complete Fonts, Dan X. Solo. Add power, elegance to posters, signs, other graphics with 100 stunning copyright-free alphabets: Blackstone, Dolbey, Germania, 97 more–including many lower-case, numerals, punctuation marks. 104pp. 8⅛ x 11. 24695-7

HOW TO DO BEADWORK, Mary White. Fundamental book on craft from simple projects to five-bead chains and woven works. 106 illustrations. 142pp. 5⅜ x 8.
20697-1

THE BOOK OF WOOD CARVING, Charles Marshall Sayers. Finest book for beginners discusses fundamentals and offers 34 designs. "Absolutely first rate . . . well thought out and well executed."–E. J. Tangerman. 118pp. 7¾ x 10⅝. 23654-4

ILLUSTRATED CATALOG OF CIVIL WAR MILITARY GOODS: Union Army Weapons, Insignia, Uniform Accessories, and Other Equipment, Schuyler, Hartley, and Graham. Rare, profusely illustrated 1846 catalog includes Union Army uniform and dress regulations, arms and ammunition, coats, insignia, flags, swords, rifles, etc. 226 illustrations. 160pp. 9 x 12. 24939-5

WOMEN'S FASHIONS OF THE EARLY 1900s: An Unabridged Republication of "New York Fashions, 1909," National Cloak & Suit Co. Rare catalog of mail-order fashions documents women's and children's clothing styles shortly after the turn of the century. Captions offer full descriptions, prices. Invaluable resource for fashion, costume historians. Approximately 725 illustrations. 128pp. 8⅜ x 11¼. 27276-1

THE 1912 AND 1915 GUSTAV STICKLEY FURNITURE CATALOGS, Gustav Stickley. With over 200 detailed illustrations and descriptions, these two catalogs are essential reading and reference materials and identification guides for Stickley furniture. Captions cite materials, dimensions and prices. 112pp. 6½ x 9¼. 26676-1

EARLY AMERICAN LOCOMOTIVES, John H. White, Jr. Finest locomotive engravings from early 19th century: historical (1804–74), main-line (after 1870), special, foreign, etc. 147 plates. 142pp. 11⅜ x 8¼. 22772-3

THE TALL SHIPS OF TODAY IN PHOTOGRAPHS, Frank O. Braynard. Lavishly illustrated tribute to nearly 100 majestic contemporary sailing vessels: Amerigo Vespucci, Clearwater, Constitution, Eagle, Mayflower, Sea Cloud, Victory, many more. Authoritative captions provide statistics, background on each ship. 190 black-and-white photographs and illustrations. Introduction. 128pp. 8⅞ x 11¾.
27163-3

LITTLE BOOK OF EARLY AMERICAN CRAFTS AND TRADES, Peter Stockham (ed.). 1807 children's book explains crafts and trades: baker, hatter, cooper, potter, and many others. 23 copperplate illustrations. 140pp. 4⅝ x 6. 23336-7

VICTORIAN FASHIONS AND COSTUMES FROM HARPER'S BAZAR, 1867–1898, Stella Blum (ed.). Day costumes, evening wear, sports clothes, shoes, hats, other accessories in over 1,000 detailed engravings. 320pp. 9⅜ x 12¼. 22990-4

GUSTAV STICKLEY, THE CRAFTSMAN, Mary Ann Smith. Superb study surveys broad scope of Stickley's achievement, especially in architecture. Design philosophy, rise and fall of the Craftsman empire, descriptions and floor plans for many Craftsman houses, more. 86 black-and-white halftones. 31 line illustrations. Introduction 208pp. 6½ x 9¼. 27210-9

THE LONG ISLAND RAIL ROAD IN EARLY PHOTOGRAPHS, Ron Ziel. Over 220 rare photos, informative text document origin (1844) and development of rail service on Long Island. Vintage views of early trains, locomotives, stations, passengers, crews, much more. Captions. 8⅞ x 11¾. 26301-0

VOYAGE OF THE LIBERDADE, Joshua Slocum. Great 19th-century mariner's thrilling, first-hand account of the wreck of his ship off South America, the 35-foot boat he built from the wreckage, and its remarkable voyage home. 128pp. 5⅜ x 8½. 40022-0

TEN BOOKS ON ARCHITECTURE, Vitruvius. The most important book ever written on architecture. Early Roman aesthetics, technology, classical orders, site selection, all other aspects. Morgan translation. 331pp. 5⅜ x 8½. 20645-9

THE HUMAN FIGURE IN MOTION, Eadweard Muybridge. More than 4,500 stopped-action photos, in action series, showing undraped men, women, children jumping, lying down, throwing, sitting, wrestling, carrying, etc. 390pp. 7⅞ x 10⅝. 20204-6 Clothbd.

TREES OF THE EASTERN AND CENTRAL UNITED STATES AND CANADA, William M. Harlow. Best one-volume guide to 140 trees. Full descriptions, woodlore, range, etc. Over 600 illustrations. Handy size. 288pp. 4½ x 6⅜. 20395-6

SONGS OF WESTERN BIRDS, Dr. Donald J. Borror. Complete song and call repertoire of 60 western species, including flycatchers, juncoes, cactus wrens, many more–includes fully illustrated booklet. Cassette and manual 99913-0

GROWING AND USING HERBS AND SPICES, Milo Miloradovich. Versatile handbook provides all the information needed for cultivation and use of all the herbs and spices available in North America. 4 illustrations. Index. Glossary. 236pp. 5⅜ x 8½. 25058-X

BIG BOOK OF MAZES AND LABYRINTHS, Walter Shepherd. 50 mazes and labyrinths in all–classical, solid, ripple, and more–in one great volume. Perfect inexpensive puzzler for clever youngsters. Full solutions. 112pp. 8⅛ x 11. 22951-3

PIANO TUNING, J. Cree Fischer. Clearest, best book for beginner, amateur. Simple repairs, raising dropped notes, tuning by easy method of flattened fifths. No previous skills needed. 4 illustrations. 201pp. 5⅜ x 8½. 23267-0

HINTS TO SINGERS, Lillian Nordica. Selecting the right teacher, developing confidence, overcoming stage fright, and many other important skills receive thoughtful discussion in this indispensible guide, written by a world-famous diva of four decades' experience. 96pp. 5⅜ x 8½. 40094-8

THE COMPLETE NONSENSE OF EDWARD LEAR, Edward Lear. All nonsense limericks, zany alphabets, Owl and Pussycat, songs, nonsense botany, etc., illustrated by Lear. Total of 320pp. 5⅜ x 8½. (Available in U.S. only.) 20167-8

VICTORIAN PARLOUR POETRY: An Annotated Anthology, Michael R. Turner. 117 gems by Longfellow, Tennyson, Browning, many lesser-known poets. "The Village Blacksmith," "Curfew Must Not Ring Tonight," "Only a Baby Small," dozens more, often difficult to find elsewhere. Index of poets, titles, first lines. xxiii + 325pp. 5⅜ x 8¼. 27044-0

DUBLINERS, James Joyce. Fifteen stories offer vivid, tightly focused observations of the lives of Dublin's poorer classes. At least one, "The Dead," is considered a masterpiece. Reprinted complete and unabridged from standard edition. 160pp. 5$\frac{3}{16}$ x 8¼. 26870-5

GREAT WEIRD TALES: 14 Stories by Lovecraft, Blackwood, Machen and Others, S. T. Joshi (ed.). 14 spellbinding tales, including "The Sin Eater," by Fiona McLeod, "The Eye Above the Mantel," by Frank Belknap Long, as well as renowned works by R. H. Barlow, Lord Dunsany, Arthur Machen, W. C. Morrow and eight other masters of the genre. 256pp. 5⅜ x 8½. (Available in U.S. only.) 40436-6

THE BOOK OF THE SACRED MAGIC OF ABRAMELIN THE MAGE, translated by S. MacGregor Mathers. Medieval manuscript of ceremonial magic. Basic document in Aleister Crowley, Golden Dawn groups. 268pp. 5⅜ x 8½. 23211-5

NEW RUSSIAN-ENGLISH AND ENGLISH-RUSSIAN DICTIONARY, M. A. O'Brien. This is a remarkably handy Russian dictionary, containing a surprising amount of information, including over 70,000 entries. 366pp. 4½ x 6⅛. 20208-9

HISTORIC HOMES OF THE AMERICAN PRESIDENTS, Second, Revised Edition, Irvin Haas. A traveler's guide to American Presidential homes, most open to the public, depicting and describing homes occupied by every American President from George Washington to George Bush. With visiting hours, admission charges, travel routes. 175 photographs. Index. 160pp. 8¼ x 11. 26751-2

NEW YORK IN THE FORTIES, Andreas Feininger. 162 brilliant photographs by the well-known photographer, formerly with *Life* magazine. Commuters, shoppers, Times Square at night, much else from city at its peak. Captions by John von Hartz. 181pp. 9¼ x 10¾. 23585-8

INDIAN SIGN LANGUAGE, William Tomkins. Over 525 signs developed by Sioux and other tribes. Written instructions and diagrams. Also 290 pictographs. 111pp. 6⅛ x 9¼. 22029-X

ANATOMY: A Complete Guide for Artists, Joseph Sheppard. A master of figure drawing shows artists how to render human anatomy convincingly. Over 460 illustrations. 224pp. 8⅜ x 11¼. 27279-6

MEDIEVAL CALLIGRAPHY: Its History and Technique, Marc Drogin. Spirited history, comprehensive instruction manual covers 13 styles (ca. 4th century through 15th). Excellent photographs; directions for duplicating medieval techniques with modern tools. 224pp. 8⅜ x 11¼. 26142-5

DRIED FLOWERS: How to Prepare Them, Sarah Whitlock and Martha Rankin. Complete instructions on how to use silica gel, meal and borax, perlite aggregate, sand and borax, glycerine and water to create attractive permanent flower arrangements. 12 illustrations. 32pp. 5⅜ x 8½. 21802-3

EASY-TO-MAKE BIRD FEEDERS FOR WOODWORKERS, Scott D. Campbell. Detailed, simple-to-use guide for designing, constructing, caring for and using feeders. Text, illustrations for 12 classic and contemporary designs. 96pp. 5⅜ x 8½. 25847-5

SCOTTISH WONDER TALES FROM MYTH AND LEGEND, Donald A. Mackenzie. 16 lively tales tell of giants rumbling down mountainsides, of a magic wand that turns stone pillars into warriors, of gods and goddesses, evil hags, powerful forces and more. 240pp. 5⅜ x 8½. 29677-6

THE HISTORY OF UNDERCLOTHES, C. Willett Cunnington and Phyllis Cunnington. Fascinating, well-documented survey covering six centuries of English undergarments, enhanced with over 100 illustrations: 12th-century laced-up bodice, footed long drawers (1795), 19th-century bustles, 19th-century corsets for men, Victorian "bust improvers," much more. 272pp. 5⅜ x 8¼. 27124-2

ARTS AND CRAFTS FURNITURE: The Complete Brooks Catalog of 1912, Brooks Manufacturing Co. Photos and detailed descriptions of more than 150 now very collectible furniture designs from the Arts and Crafts movement depict davenports, settees, buffets, desks, tables, chairs, bedsteads, dressers and more, all built of solid, quarter-sawed oak. Invaluable for students and enthusiasts of antiques, Americana and the decorative arts. 80pp. 6½ x 9¼. 27471-3

WILBUR AND ORVILLE: A Biography of the Wright Brothers, Fred Howard. Definitive, crisply written study tells the full story of the brothers' lives and work. A vividly written biography, unparalleled in scope and color, that also captures the spirit of an extraordinary era. 560pp. 6⅛ x 9¼. 40297-5

THE ARTS OF THE SAILOR: Knotting, Splicing and Ropework, Hervey Garrett Smith. Indispensable shipboard reference covers tools, basic knots and useful hitches; handsewing and canvas work, more. Over 100 illustrations. Delightful reading for sea lovers. 256pp. 5⅜ x 8½. 26440-8

FRANK LLOYD WRIGHT'S FALLINGWATER: The House and Its History, Second, Revised Edition, Donald Hoffmann. A total revision–both in text and illustrations–of the standard document on Fallingwater, the boldest, most personal architectural statement of Wright's mature years, updated with valuable new material from the recently opened Frank Lloyd Wright Archives. "Fascinating"–*The New York Times*. 116 illustrations. 128pp. 9¼ x 10¾. 27430-6

PHOTOGRAPHIC SKETCHBOOK OF THE CIVIL WAR, Alexander Gardner. 100 photos taken on field during the Civil War. Famous shots of Manassas Harper's Ferry, Lincoln, Richmond, slave pens, etc. 244pp. 10⅝ x 8¼.   22731-6

FIVE ACRES AND INDEPENDENCE, Maurice G. Kains. Great back-to-the-land classic explains basics of self-sufficient farming. The one book to get. 95 illustrations. 397pp. 5⅜ x 8½.   20974-1

SONGS OF EASTERN BIRDS, Dr. Donald J. Borror. Songs and calls of 60 species most common to eastern U.S.: warblers, woodpeckers, flycatchers, thrushes, larks, many more in high-quality recording.   Cassette and manual 99912-2

A MODERN HERBAL, Margaret Grieve. Much the fullest, most exact, most useful compilation of herbal material. Gigantic alphabetical encyclopedia, from aconite to zedoary, gives botanical information, medical properties, folklore, economic uses, much else. Indispensable to serious reader. 161 illustrations. 888pp. 6½ x 9¼. 2-vol. set. (Available in U.S. only.)   Vol. I: 22798-7
Vol. II: 22799-5

HIDDEN TREASURE MAZE BOOK, Dave Phillips. Solve 34 challenging mazes accompanied by heroic tales of adventure. Evil dragons, people-eating plants, blood-thirsty giants, many more dangerous adversaries lurk at every twist and turn. 34 mazes, stories, solutions. 48pp. 8¼ x 11.   24566-7

LETTERS OF W. A. MOZART, Wolfgang A. Mozart. Remarkable letters show bawdy wit, humor, imagination, musical insights, contemporary musical world; includes some letters from Leopold Mozart. 276pp. 5⅜ x 8½.   22859-2

BASIC PRINCIPLES OF CLASSICAL BALLET, Agrippina Vaganova. Great Russian theoretician, teacher explains methods for teaching classical ballet. 118 illustrations. 175pp. 5⅜ x 8½.   22036-2

THE JUMPING FROG, Mark Twain. Revenge edition. The original story of The Celebrated Jumping Frog of Calaveras County, a hapless French translation, and Twain's hilarious "retranslation" from the French. 12 illustrations. 66pp. 5⅜ x 8½.
22686-7

BEST REMEMBERED POEMS, Martin Gardner (ed.). The 126 poems in this superb collection of 19th- and 20th-century British and American verse range from Shelley's "To a Skylark" to the impassioned "Renascence" of Edna St. Vincent Millay and to Edward Lear's whimsical "The Owl and the Pussycat." 224pp. 5⅜ x 8½.
27165-X

COMPLETE SONNETS, William Shakespeare. Over 150 exquisite poems deal with love, friendship, the tyranny of time, beauty's evanescence, death and other themes in language of remarkable power, precision and beauty. Glossary of archaic terms. 80pp. 5³⁄₁₆ x 8¼.   26686-9

THE BATTLES THAT CHANGED HISTORY, Fletcher Pratt. Eminent historian profiles 16 crucial conflicts, ancient to modern, that changed the course of civilization. 352pp. 5⅜ x 8½.   41129-X

THE WIT AND HUMOR OF OSCAR WILDE, Alvin Redman (ed.). More than 1,000 ripostes, paradoxes, wisecracks: Work is the curse of the drinking classes; I can resist everything except temptation; etc. 258pp. 5⅜ x 8½. 20602-5

SHAKESPEARE LEXICON AND QUOTATION DICTIONARY, Alexander Schmidt. Full definitions, locations, shades of meaning in every word in plays and poems. More than 50,000 exact quotations. 1,485pp. 6½ x 9¼. 2-vol. set.
Vol. 1: 22726-X
Vol. 2: 22727-8

SELECTED POEMS, Emily Dickinson. Over 100 best-known, best-loved poems by one of America's foremost poets, reprinted from authoritative early editions. No comparable edition at this price. Index of first lines. 64pp. 5$\frac{3}{16}$ x 8¼. 26466-1

THE INSIDIOUS DR. FU-MANCHU, Sax Rohmer. The first of the popular mystery series introduces a pair of English detectives to their archnemesis, the diabolical Dr. Fu-Manchu. Flavorful atmosphere, fast-paced action, and colorful characters enliven this classic of the genre. 208pp. 5$\frac{3}{16}$ x 8¼. 29898-1

THE MALLEUS MALEFICARUM OF KRAMER AND SPRENGER, translated by Montague Summers. Full text of most important witchhunter's "bible," used by both Catholics and Protestants. 278pp. 6⅝ x 10. 22802-9

SPANISH STORIES/CUENTOS ESPAÑOLES: A Dual-Language Book, Angel Flores (ed.). Unique format offers 13 great stories in Spanish by Cervantes, Borges, others. Faithful English translations on facing pages. 352pp. 5⅜ x 8½. 25399-6

GARDEN CITY, LONG ISLAND, IN EARLY PHOTOGRAPHS, 1869–1919, Mildred H. Smith. Handsome treasury of 118 vintage pictures, accompanied by carefully researched captions, document the Garden City Hotel fire (1899), the Vanderbilt Cup Race (1908), the first airmail flight departing from the Nassau Boulevard Aerodrome (1911), and much more. 96pp. 8⅞ x 11¾. 40669-5

OLD QUEENS, N.Y., IN EARLY PHOTOGRAPHS, Vincent F. Seyfried and William Asadorian. Over 160 rare photographs of Maspeth, Jamaica, Jackson Heights, and other areas. Vintage views of DeWitt Clinton mansion, 1939 World's Fair and more. Captions. 192pp. 8⅞ x 11. 26358-4

CAPTURED BY THE INDIANS: 15 Firsthand Accounts, 1750-1870, Frederick Drimmer. Astounding true historical accounts of grisly torture, bloody conflicts, relentless pursuits, miraculous escapes and more, by people who lived to tell the tale. 384pp. 5⅜ x 8½. 24901-8

THE WORLD'S GREAT SPEECHES (Fourth Enlarged Edition), Lewis Copeland, Lawrence W. Lamm, and Stephen J. McKenna. Nearly 300 speeches provide public speakers with a wealth of updated quotes and inspiration–from Pericles' funeral oration and William Jennings Bryan's "Cross of Gold Speech" to Malcolm X's powerful words on the Black Revolution and Earl of Spenser's tribute to his sister, Diana, Princess of Wales. 944pp. 5⅜ x 8⅜. 40903-1

THE BOOK OF THE SWORD, Sir Richard F. Burton. Great Victorian scholar/adventurer's eloquent, erudite history of the "queen of weapons"–from prehistory to early Roman Empire. Evolution and development of early swords, variations (sabre, broadsword, cutlass, scimitar, etc.), much more. 336pp. 6⅛ x 9¼. 25434-8

AUTOBIOGRAPHY: The Story of My Experiments with Truth, Mohandas K. Gandhi. Boyhood, legal studies, purification, the growth of the Satyagraha (nonviolent protest) movement. Critical, inspiring work of the man responsible for the freedom of India. 480pp. 5⅜ x 8½. (Available in U.S. only.) 24593-4

CELTIC MYTHS AND LEGENDS, T. W. Rolleston. Masterful retelling of Irish and Welsh stories and tales. Cuchulain, King Arthur, Deirdre, the Grail, many more. First paperback edition. 58 full-page illustrations. 512pp. 5⅜ x 8½. 26507-2

THE PRINCIPLES OF PSYCHOLOGY, William James. Famous long course complete, unabridged. Stream of thought, time perception, memory, experimental methods; great work decades ahead of its time. 94 figures. 1,391pp. 5⅜ x 8½. 2-vol. set. Vol. I: 20381-6 Vol. II: 20382-4

THE WORLD AS WILL AND REPRESENTATION, Arthur Schopenhauer. Definitive English translation of Schopenhauer's life work, correcting more than 1,000 errors, omissions in earlier translations. Translated by E. F. J. Payne. Total of 1,269pp. 5⅜ x 8½. 2-vol. set. Vol. 1: 21761-2 Vol. 2: 21762-0

MAGIC AND MYSTERY IN TIBET, Madame Alexandra David-Neel. Experiences among lamas, magicians, sages, sorcerers, Bonpa wizards. A true psychic discovery. 32 illustrations. 321pp. 5⅜ x 8½. (Available in U.S. only.) 22682-4

THE EGYPTIAN BOOK OF THE DEAD, E. A. Wallis Budge. Complete reproduction of Ani's papyrus, finest ever found. Full hieroglyphic text, interlinear transliteration, word-for-word translation, smooth translation. 533pp. 6½ x 9¼. 21866-X

MATHEMATICS FOR THE NONMATHEMATICIAN, Morris Kline. Detailed, college-level treatment of mathematics in cultural and historical context, with numerous exercises. Recommended Reading Lists. Tables. Numerous figures. 641pp. 5⅜ x 8½. 24823-2

PROBABILISTIC METHODS IN THE THEORY OF STRUCTURES, Isaac Elishakoff. Well-written introduction covers the elements of the theory of probability from two or more random variables, the reliability of such multivariable structures, the theory of random function, Monte Carlo methods of treating problems incapable of exact solution, and more. Examples. 502pp. 5⅜ x 8½. 40691-1

THE RIME OF THE ANCIENT MARINER, Gustave Doré, S. T. Coleridge. Doré's finest work; 34 plates capture moods, subtleties of poem. Flawless full-size reproductions printed on facing pages with authoritative text of poem. "Beautiful. Simply beautiful."–*Publisher's Weekly*. 77pp. 9¼ x 12. 22305-1

NORTH AMERICAN INDIAN DESIGNS FOR ARTISTS AND CRAFTSPEOPLE, Eva Wilson. Over 360 authentic copyright-free designs adapted from Navajo blankets, Hopi pottery, Sioux buffalo hides, more. Geometrics, symbolic figures, plant and animal motifs, etc. 128pp. 8⅜ x 11. (Not for sale in the United Kingdom.) 25341-4

SCULPTURE: Principles and Practice, Louis Slobodkin. Step-by-step approach to clay, plaster, metals, stone; classical and modern. 253 drawings, photos. 255pp. 8⅛ x 11. 22960-2

THE INFLUENCE OF SEA POWER UPON HISTORY, 1660–1783, A. T. Mahan. Influential classic of naval history and tactics still used as text in war colleges. First paperback edition. 4 maps. 24 battle plans. 640pp. 5⅜ x 8½. 25509-3

CATALOG OF DOVER BOOKS

THE STORY OF THE TITANIC AS TOLD BY ITS SURVIVORS, Jack Winocour (ed.). What it was really like. Panic, despair, shocking inefficiency, and a little heroism. More thrilling than any fictional account. 26 illustrations. 320pp. 5⅜ x 8½. 20610-6

FAIRY AND FOLK TALES OF THE IRISH PEASANTRY, William Butler Yeats (ed.). Treasury of 64 tales from the twilight world of Celtic myth and legend: "The Soul Cages," "The Kildare Pooka," "King O'Toole and his Goose," many more. Introduction and Notes by W. B. Yeats. 352pp. 5⅜ x 8½. 26941-8

BUDDHIST MAHAYANA TEXTS, E. B. Cowell and others (eds.). Superb, accurate translations of basic documents in Mahayana Buddhism, highly important in history of religions. The Buddha-karita of Asvaghosha, Larger Sukhavativyuha, more. 448pp. 5⅜ x 8½. 25552-2

ONE TWO THREE . . . INFINITY: Facts and Speculations of Science, George Gamow. Great physicist's fascinating, readable overview of contemporary science: number theory, relativity, fourth dimension, entropy, genes, atomic structure, much more. 128 illustrations. Index. 352pp. 5⅜ x 8½. 25664-2

EXPERIMENTATION AND MEASUREMENT, W. J. Youden. Introductory manual explains laws of measurement in simple terms and offers tips for achieving accuracy and minimizing errors. Mathematics of measurement, use of instruments, experimenting with machines. 1994 edition. Foreword. Preface. Introduction. Epilogue. Selected Readings. Glossary. Index. Tables and figures. 128pp. 5⅜ x 8½. 40451-X

DALÍ ON MODERN ART: The Cuckolds of Antiquated Modern Art, Salvador Dalí. Influential painter skewers modern art and its practitioners. Outrageous evaluations of Picasso, Cézanne, Turner, more. 15 renderings of paintings discussed. 44 calligraphic decorations by Dalí. 96pp. 5⅜ x 8½. (Available in U.S. only.) 29220-7

ANTIQUE PLAYING CARDS: A Pictorial History, Henry René D'Allemagne. Over 900 elaborate, decorative images from rare playing cards (14th–20th centuries): Bacchus, death, dancing dogs, hunting scenes, royal coats of arms, players cheating, much more. 96pp. 9¼ x 12¼. 29265-7

MAKING FURNITURE MASTERPIECES: 30 Projects with Measured Drawings, Franklin H. Gottshall. Step-by-step instructions, illustrations for constructing handsome, useful pieces, among them a Sheraton desk, Chippendale chair, Spanish desk, Queen Anne table and a William and Mary dressing mirror. 224pp. 8⅛ x 11¼. 29338-6

THE FOSSIL BOOK: A Record of Prehistoric Life, Patricia V. Rich et al. Profusely illustrated definitive guide covers everything from single-celled organisms and dinosaurs to birds and mammals and the interplay between climate and man. Over 1,500 illustrations. 760pp. 7½ x 10⅞. 29371-8

Paperbound unless otherwise indicated. Available at your book dealer, online at **www.doverpublications.com**, or by writing to Dept. GI, Dover Publications, Inc., 31 East 2nd Street, Mineola, NY 11501. For current price information or for free catalogues (please indicate field of interest), write to Dover Publications or log on to **www.doverpublications.com** and see every Dover book in print. Dover publishes more than 500 books each year on science, elementary and advanced mathematics, biology, music, art, literary history, social sciences, and other areas.